# PUBLIC HEALTH

*Career Choices That Make a Difference*

## BERNARD J. TURNOCK, MD, MPH

CLINICAL PROFESSOR OF COMMUNITY HEALTH SCIENCES
DIRECTOR, CENTER FOR PUBLIC HEALTH PRACTICE
SCHOOL OF PUBLIC HEALTH
UNIVERSITY OF ILLINOIS AT CHICAGO
CHICAGO, IL

## JONES AND BARTLETT PUBLISHERS

*Sudbury, Massachusetts*

BOSTON    TORONTO    LONDON    SINGAPORE

*World Headquarters*

| | | |
|---|---|---|
| Jones and Bartlett Publishers | Jones and Bartlett Publishers | Jones and Bartlett Publishers |
| 40 Tall Pine Drive | Canada | International |
| Sudbury, MA 01776 | 6339 Ormindale Way | Barb House, Barb Mews |
| 978-443-5000 | Mississauga, ON L5V 1J2 | London W6 7PA |
| info@jbpub.com | CANADA | UK |
| www.jbpub.com | | |

Jones and Bartlett's books and products are available through most bookstores and online booksellers. To contact Jones and Bartlett Publishers directly, call 800-832-0034, fax 978-443-8000, or visit our website, www.jbpub.com.

Substantial discounts on bulk quantities of Jones and Bartlett's publications are available to corporations, professional associations, and other qualified organizations. For details and specific discount information, contact the special sales department at Jones and Bartlett via the above contact information or send an email to specialsales@jbpub.com.

Copyright © 2006 by Jones and Bartlett Publishers, Inc.
ISBN-13: 978-0-7637-3790-0
ISBN-10: 0-7637-3790-9

All rights reserved. No part of the material protected by this copyright may be reproduced or utilized in any form, electronic or mechanical, including photocopying, recording, or by any information storage and retrieval system, without written permission from the copyright owner.

**Library of Congress Cataloging-in-Publication Data**

Turnock, Bernard J.
   Public health : career choices that make a difference / Bernard J. Turnock.
      p. ; cm.
   Includes bibliographical references and index.
   ISBN-13: 978-0-7637-3790-0 (pbk.)
   1. Public health—Vocational guidance.
   [DNLM: 1. Career Choice. 2. Public Health. 3. Health Occupations. WA 21 T956p 2006]
I. Title.
   RA440.9.T87 2006
   362.1071—dc22
                                                                                    2005028351
   6048

**Production Credits**
Acquisitions Editor: Michael Brown
Production Director: Amy Rose
Associate Editor: Kylah McNeill
Production Assistant: Alison Meier
Manufacturing Buyer: Therese Connell
Cover Design: Timothy Dziewit
Cover Image: Courtesy of Petty Officer 2nd Class Kyle Niemi/U.S. Coast Guard; Photo Courtesy of the U.S. Army; Courtesy of Photographer's Mate 1st Class William R. Goodwin/U.S. Navy; © Photos.com
Composition: Auburn Associates, Inc.
Printing and Binding: Malloy, Inc.
Cover Printing: Malloy, Inc.

Printed in the United States of America
10 09 08 07 06   10 9 8 7 6 5 4 3 2

# Dedication

To the thousands of public health workers and students who have shaped my understanding of and appreciation for the field, and most especially to Charles Catania who exemplified its aspirations and values in his professional career and personal life.

# Contents

Preface . . . . . . . . . . . . . . . . . . . . . . . . . . . . . . .ix

**Chapter 1**  **The Public Health Workforce**  . . . . . . . . . . . . . . . . .1
Brief History of Public Health Practice  . . . . . . . . . . . .2
Definitions of Public Health  . . . . . . . . . . . . . . . . . .7
Public Health Work and Public Health Workers  . . . .11
Size and Distribution of the Public Health
Workforce  . . . . . . . . . . . . . . . . . . . . . . . . . . . .13
Composition of the Public Health Workforce  . . . . . .19
Public Health Worker Ethics, Skills, and
Competencies  . . . . . . . . . . . . . . . . . . . . . . . . . .21
Conclusion  . . . . . . . . . . . . . . . . . . . . . . . . . . .24

**Chapter 2**  **Public Health Occupations and Organizations**  . . .27
Characteristics of Public Health Occupations  . . . . . .27
Occupational Classifications  . . . . . . . . . . . . . . . . . .30
Public Health Practice Profile  . . . . . . . . . . . . . . . .36
Important and Essential Duties  . . . . . . . . . . . . . . . .38
Minimum Qualifications . . . . . . . . . . . . . . . . . . . . .38
Workplace Considerations . . . . . . . . . . . . . . . . . . . .39
Salary Estimates . . . . . . . . . . . . . . . . . . . . . . . . . .39
Career Prospects  . . . . . . . . . . . . . . . . . . . . . . . . .40
Additional Information  . . . . . . . . . . . . . . . . . . . . .41
Public Health Organizations and Agencies . . . . . . . .42
Conclusion  . . . . . . . . . . . . . . . . . . . . . . . . . . .55

**Chapter 3**  **Public Health Administration**  . . . . . . . . . . . . . . .57
Occupational Classification  . . . . . . . . . . . . . . . . . .57
Public Health Practice Profile  . . . . . . . . . . . . . . . .59
Important and Essential Duties  . . . . . . . . . . . . . . . .60

|                | Minimum Qualifications | 66 |
| --- | --- | --- |
|                | Workplace Considerations | 71 |
|                | Salary Estimates | 73 |
|                | Career Prospects | 73 |
|                | Additional Information | 74 |
|                | Conclusion | 76 |
| **Chapter 4** | **Environmental and Occupational Health** | **77** |
|                | Occupational Classification | 78 |
|                | Public Health Practice Profile | 81 |
|                | Important and Essential Duties | 81 |
|                | Minimum Qualifications | 90 |
|                | Workplace Considerations | 96 |
|                | Salary Estimates | 97 |
|                | Career Prospects | 99 |
|                | Additional Information | 100 |
|                | Conclusion | 103 |
| **Chapter 5** | **Public Health Nursing** | **105** |
|                | Occupational Classification | 107 |
|                | Public Health Practice Profile | 107 |
|                | Important and Essential Duties | 108 |
|                | Minimum Qualifications | 113 |
|                | Workplace Considerations | 117 |
|                | Salary Estimates | 118 |
|                | Career Prospects | 119 |
|                | Additional Information | 120 |
|                | Conclusion | 123 |
| **Chapter 6** | **Epidemiology and Disease Control** | **125** |
|                | Occupational Classification | 125 |
|                | Public Health Practice Profile | 128 |
|                | Important and Essential Duties | 129 |
|                | Minimum Qualifications | 135 |
|                | Workplace Considerations | 140 |
|                | Salary Estimates | 141 |
|                | Career Prospects | 142 |
|                | Additional Information | 143 |
|                | Conclusion | 143 |
| **Chapter 7** | **Public Health Education and Information** | **147** |
|                | Occupational Classification | 147 |

Public Health Practice Profile . . . . . . . . . . . . . . . .149
Important and Essential Duties . . . . . . . . . . . . . . .149
Minimum Qualifications . . . . . . . . . . . . . . . . . . . . .154
Workplace Considerations . . . . . . . . . . . . . . . . . . .159
Salary Estimates . . . . . . . . . . . . . . . . . . . . . . . . . .159
Career Prospects . . . . . . . . . . . . . . . . . . . . . . . . . .160
Additional Information . . . . . . . . . . . . . . . . . . . . .161
Conclusion . . . . . . . . . . . . . . . . . . . . . . . . . . . . . .167

**Chapter 8**    **Other Public Health Professional Occupations . .169**
Nutritionists and Dieticians . . . . . . . . . . . . . . . . . .170
Public Health Social, Behavioral, and
    Mental Health Workers . . . . . . . . . . . . . . . . . . .174
Public Health Laboratory Workers . . . . . . . . . . . . .179
Public Health Physicians, Veterinarians, and
    Pharmacists . . . . . . . . . . . . . . . . . . . . . . . . . . .185
Public Health Dental Workers . . . . . . . . . . . . . . . .186
Administrative Judges and Hearing Officers . . . . . . .187
Additional Information . . . . . . . . . . . . . . . . . . . . .187
Conclusion . . . . . . . . . . . . . . . . . . . . . . . . . . . . . .188

**Chapter 9**    **Public Health Program Occupations . . . . . . . . .191**
Public Health Program Specialists and
    Coordinators . . . . . . . . . . . . . . . . . . . . . . . . . .192
Public Health Emergency Preparedness and
    Response Coordinators . . . . . . . . . . . . . . . . . . .198
Public Health Policy Analysts . . . . . . . . . . . . . . . . .201
Public Health Information Specialists and
    Analysts . . . . . . . . . . . . . . . . . . . . . . . . . . . . . .203
Community Outreach and Other Technical
    Occupations . . . . . . . . . . . . . . . . . . . . . . . . . . .204
Additional Information . . . . . . . . . . . . . . . . . . . . .205
Conclusion . . . . . . . . . . . . . . . . . . . . . . . . . . . . . .206

**Chapter 10**    **Looking to the Future . . . . . . . . . . . . . . . . . . . .207**
Public Health Workforce Growth . . . . . . . . . . . . . .208
Public Health Workforce Distribution and
    Composition . . . . . . . . . . . . . . . . . . . . . . . . . . .212
Public Health Workforce Skills and Competencies . .217
Public Health Workforce Development . . . . . . . . . .223
Conclusion . . . . . . . . . . . . . . . . . . . . . . . . . . . . . .225

Appendices ..............................229
Appendix A—Council on Linkages Between
    Academia and Practice Core Competencies
    with Skill Levels ........................231
Appendix B—Core Public Health Worker
    Competencies for Emergency Preparedness
    and Response .........................241
Appendix C—Association of Schools of
    Public Health (ASPH) Core Competency
    Development Project Version 1.2 ..........245
Appendix D—Accredited Schools of Public
    Health and Public Health Programs ........253
Appendix E—Public Health Training,
    Continuing Education, and Employment
    Resources for Public Health Workers .......265
Index ..................................267

# Preface

My appreciation for the field of public health stems from two sources: the work and the workers. In the initial stages of developing this book, I taped a post-it note onto my computer monitor with the words, "It's the workers, stupid!" I adapted this guidance from the sign above James Carville's desk when he served as national campaign director for Bill Clinton's bid for the presidency in 1992. Carville's sign, "It's the economy, stupid!" served as a constant reminder that focusing on the state of the economy was the key to winning the presidential election. Whenever the focus shifted to some other topic such as health care, foreign relations, or even the character of the presidential nominees, Carville sought to return the focus to the economy. This strategy was successful, and the rest of that story is history.

In a similar fashion, this book is about public health workers, both current and future, and what they do, offering basic information for those considering a career in or career change into public health. Admittedly, this is neither the only nor the best way to approach this subject. There are many fascinating and inspiring stories of modern public health heroes and role models that are not told in these pages. The focus of this book, however, is on the nuts and bolts of public health jobs and careers in terms of what they do and how they do it. Job duties, qualifications, skills, salary expectations, career ladders, and professional networks take center stage—although these can be dry and mundane topics.

Those looking for the inspiring personal success stories of modern day public health heroes can find them in other publications. For example, the global pharmaceutical company Pfizer publishes two wonderful compilations of professional profiles of public health notables. Pfizer's *Guide to Public Health Careers*[1] examines the career paths, aspirations, and insights of more than 30 different public health professionals. *The Faces of Public Health* [2] takes this personal story approach to an even higher level in highlighting another 25 respected public health figures. The Pfizer books greatly enrich our understanding of public health workers and public health practice, coloring these topics with personal tones. The stories are indeed interesting and inspiring, but, in some respects, the focus on public health heroes and successful careers tells the story of only that part of the public health workforce with advanced degrees and lofty positions. Alongside these leaders and field generals of the public health movement are the foot soldiers carrying on the battle from the trenches. For example, only 2 of the 30 plus public health workers highlighted in Pfizer's career guide did not have a master's or doctoral degree. Those two were a health reporter and a registered nurse who was working on her master's degree in public health at the time. Similarly, only one-fourth of careers highlighted in *The Faces of Public Health* were workers with less than a graduate degree.

This book seeks to complement and supplement those that tell the personal stories of successful and respected public health professionals. In this book, the emphasis is on key aspects of the work of different public health occupations and titles in order to provide an understanding of the basic underpinnings of public health jobs and careers.

Despite an increasing recognition of its importance, there is little information available on the public health workforce in terms of its size, distribution, composition, skills, and impact on health goals. Only a few public health leaders and researchers have been active in these topics. Nonetheless, Kristine Gebbie and Hugh Tilson have modeled the way. Kristine Gebbie spearheaded the only attempt in two decades to gather comprehensive information on the public health workforce,[3] and Hugh Tilson influenced the involvement of Pfizer in the two publications already cited and described. Prior to their work in this area, only a few works on public health careers were published in the 1980s and 1990s.[4,5]

This book builds on the foundation established by Gebbie, Tilson, Maureen Lichtveld, Joan Cioffi, Kathy Miner, Maggie Potter, Virginia Kennedy, Jack Thompson, Chris Atchison, Mike Reid, Deb Olson, George Pickett, Ed Baker, the National Association of County and City Health Officials, and others to bring together existing information on the major occupational categories and careers in the field of public health. The introductory chapter examines overall trends affecting the public health workforce. Key characteristics for occupations and careers in public health practice are defined and explained in the second chapter. This framework of career characteristics becomes the lens to examine many of the major occupational categories and career pathways available to public health workers in subsequent chapters of the book. The concluding chapter focuses on future implications for public health workers and those considering a career in public health.

A book on public health careers serves several needs. First, it complements texts and courses on public health in graduate and undergraduate degree programs. Current texts provide only minimal information on public health occupations and careers. Secondly, it provides a stand-alone introduction to career possibilities for individuals looking for a career in the health sector. There are many sources of information on medicine, nursing, dentistry, and pharmacy as careers but only a few on career opportunities in the field of public health. Finally, this book advances the notion that public health workers are the most important asset and most critical component of the public health infrastructure. There have been only a few champions of this cause in recent years, but they have been staunch and consistent in serving this cause. Their efforts and work provide a foundation for this book.

Several other acknowledgments are also necessary. Mike Brown and Kylah McNeill at Jones and Bartlett Publishers were instrumental in advancing the need for this book. Alison Meier, also at Jones and Bartlett, and copyeditor Mark Goodin helped make it a reality. Kevin Hutchison, Mike Bacon, Laura Landrum, Jack Thompson, Suzet McKinney, Patrick Lenihan, Michele Issel, Leslie Nickels, Mike Vernon, Elaine Ricketts, Vikki Wiebel, and Guddi Kapadia have all provided thoughtful comments and suggestions. Their contributions are gratefully acknowledged.

## REFERENCES

1. Pfizer Pharmaceutical Group, Pfizer, Inc. *Advancing Healthy Populations: The Pfizer Guide to Careers in Public Health.* New York, NY: Pfizer, 2002. Available at http://www.pfizercareerguides.com/publichealth.html. Accessed August 2005.
2. Pfizer Pharmaceutical Group, Pfizer, Inc. *The Faces of Public Health.* New York, NY: Pfizer, 2004.
3. Health Resources and Services Administration (HRSA), Bureau of Health Professions, National Center for Health Workforce Information and Analysis and Center for Health Policy, Columbia School of Nursing. *The Public Health*

*Workforce Enumeration 2000.* Washington, DC: HRSA, 2000. Available at http://www.phppo.cdc.gov/owpp/docs/library/2000/Public%20Health%20 Workforce%20Enumeration%202000.pdf. Accessed August 2005.

4. Pickett G, Pickett TW. *Opportunities in Public Health Careers.* New York, NY: McGraw-Hill; 1988.

5. National Association of County and City Health Officials (NACCHO). *Exploring Public Health Career Paths: An Overview of Public Health and Career Opportunities.* Washington, DC: NACCHO; 1996.

# CHAPTER 1

# The Public Health Workforce

Public health is important work and the people who carry out that work contribute substantially to the health status and quality of life of the individuals, families, and communities they serve. Yet public health is not among the best known or most highly respected careers, in part because when public health efforts are successful, nothing happens. Events that don't occur don't attract attention. For example, the remarkable record of declining mortality rates and ever-increasing spans of healthy life, due in large part to public health efforts, draws little public attention. Indeed the vast majority of those who will ultimately benefit from the efforts of past and present public health workers are yet to be born. With public health workers not recognized and valued for their accomplishments and contributions, it should not be surprising that careers in public health are among the least understood and appreciated in the health sector.

But even if the public views public health as poorly defined and abstract, public health workers are real and tangible. These workers make up a public health workforce that can be defined and described in several important dimensions, including its size, distribution, composition, skills, and career pathways. Unfortunately, there is less information on these vital statistics of the public health workforce than for many other professional and occupational categories working in the health sector today.

This book aims to bring together the information that is available on public health occupations and careers in order to assist individuals seeking to make career decisions. In this chapter, a brief history of public health, followed by an examination of what public health has become, sets the stage for an appreciation of what public health workers do and how they contribute to societal well-being in the 21st century.

# BRIEF HISTORY OF
# PUBLIC HEALTH PRACTICE[1]

Although the complete history of public health is an amazing saga in its own right, this section presents only selected highlights. Suffice it to say that when ancient cultures perceived disease and illness as manifestations of supernatural forces, they also felt that little was possible in the way of either personal or collective action. For many centuries, the health status of populations was synonymous with the presence or absence of epidemics. Diseases, including horrific epidemics of infectious diseases such as the Black Death (plague), leprosy, and cholera, appeared in wave after wave as phenomena to be accepted. Avoidance was another strategy, although often not a very effective one as little was known at that time about how diseases spread. It was not until the so-called Age of Reason and the Age of Enlightenment that scholarly inquiry began to challenge the "givens" or accepted realities of society. The subsequent expansion of the science and knowledge base for these diseases and their causative factors would eventually reap substantial rewards.

With the advent of industrialism and imperialism, the stage was set for epidemic diseases to increase their terrible toll. As populations shifted to urban centers for the purpose of commerce and industry, public health conditions worsened. The mixing of dense populations living in unsanitary conditions and working long hours in unsafe and exploitative industries was a formula for disaster: wave after wave of cholera, smallpox, typhoid, tuberculosis, yellow fever, and other diseases struck again and again across the globe, but most seriously and most often at the industrialized seaport cities. These city ports provided the portal of entry for diseases transported as stowaways alongside commercial cargo. The life experiences, and subsequent susceptibility, of different cultures to these diseases partly explains how relatively small groups of Europeans were able to overcome and subjugate vast Native American cultures. Perceiving the Europeans as unaffected by scourges such as smallpox reinforced beliefs among Native Americans that these light-skinned visitors were supernatural figures, apparently beyond the control of natural forces.

The British colonies in North America and the fledgling United States certainly bore their share of the burden. American diaries of the 1600s and 1700s chronicle the onslaught of one infectious disease after another. These epidemics left their mark on families, communities, and even history. For example, the national capital had to be moved out of Philadelphia, due to a devastating yellow fever epidemic in 1793. This epidemic also prompted the city to develop its first board of health in that same year.

The formulation of local boards of distinguished citizens, the first boards of health, was one of the earliest organized responses to epidemics. This response was revealing, in that it represented an attempt to confront disease collectively. Because science had not yet determined that specific microorganisms were the causes of epidemics, acceptance and avoidance had long been the primary tactics used. Avoidance meant evacuating the general location of the epidemic until it subsided or isolating diseased individuals or those recently exposed to diseases on the basis of a mix of fear, tradition, and scientific speculation. Several developments, however, were swinging the pendulum ever closer to more effective counteractions.

The work of public health pioneers such as Edward Jenner, John Snow, and Edwin Chadwick illustrates the value of public health, even when its methods are applied amidst scientific uncertainty. Well before Koch's postulates established scientific methods for linking bacteria with specific diseases and before Pasteur's experiments helped to establish the germ theory, both Jenner and Snow used deductive logic and common sense to do battle with smallpox and cholera, respectively. In 1796, Jenner successfully used vaccination for a disease that ran rampant through communities across the globe. This was the first shot fired in a long and arduous campaign that, by the year 1977, had totally eradicated smallpox from all of its human hiding places in every country in the world.

Snow's accomplishments even further advanced the art and science of public health practice. In 1854, Snow traced an outbreak of cholera to the water of a well drawn from the pump at Broad Street in London and helped to prevent hundreds, perhaps thousands, of cholera cases. In that same year he demonstrated that another large outbreak could be traced to one particular water company that drew its water from the Thames River, downstream from London, while a second company that drew its water upstream from London was not linked with cholera cases. In both efforts, Snow's ability to collect and analyze data allowed him to determine causation, which, in turn, allowed him to implement corrective actions that prevented additional cases. All of this occurred without benefit of the knowledge that there was an odd-shaped little bacterium that was carried in water and spread from person to person by hand-to-mouth contact!

Chadwick was a leader of what has become known as the sanitary movement of the latter half of the 1800s. In a variety of official capacities, he played a major part in structuring government's role and responsibilities for protecting the public's health. Due to the growing concern over the social and sanitary conditions in England, a National Vaccination Board was established in 1837. Shortly thereafter, Chadwick's *Report on an Inquiry into the Sanitary Conditions of the Laboring Population of Great Britain* articulated a framework for broad public actions that served as a blueprint for the growing sanitary movement.

In the latter half of the 1800s, as sanitation and environmental engineering methods evolved, more effective interventions became available against epidemic diseases. Further, the scientific advances of this period paved the way for modern disease control efforts targeting specific microorganisms.

In the United States, Lemuel Shattuck's *Report of the Sanitary Commission of Massachusetts* in 1850 outlined existing and future public health needs for that state and became America's blueprint for development of a public health system. Shattuck called for the establishment of state and local health departments to organize public efforts aimed at sanitary inspections, communicable disease control, food sanitation, vital statistics, and services for infants and children. Although Shattuck's report closely paralleled Chadwick's efforts in Great Britain, acceptance of his recommendations did not occur for several decades. Eventually, in the latter part of the century, his farsighted and far-reaching recommendations came to be widely implemented. With greater understanding of the value of environmental controls for water and sewage and of the role of specific control measures for specific diseases (including quarantine, isolation, and vaccination), the creation of local health agencies to carry out these activities supplemented—and, in some cases, supplanted—local boards of health.

These local health departments developed rapidly in the seaport and other industrial urban centers, beginning with a health department in Baltimore in 1798, because these were the settings where the problems were reaching unacceptable levels. Because infectious and environmental hazards are no respecters of local jurisdictional boundaries, states began to develop their own boards and agencies after 1870. These agencies often had very broad powers to protect the health and lives of state residents, although the clear intent at the time was that these powers be used to battle epidemics of infectious diseases.

Several factors influenced the organization and delegation of public health responsibilities in the United States. For example, the powers and authority of the federal government for public health appear quite limited based on a strict interpretation of the U.S. Constitution. Public health was not one of those powers (as was international diplomacy, defense, printing currency, and regulating commerce) explicitly bestowed upon the federal government in the Constitution. Consequently, the federal government had to gradually acquire power and influence through less direct means, including the power to regulate commerce, promote the general welfare, and raise vast sums of money through a national tax on income. This power and influence steadily expanded during the 1900s through the federal government's role in directly protecting the public through efforts that promoted food and drug safety, environmental protection, and occupational health and safety. After 1965, this power was even further bolstered as the federal government became a major purchaser of personal health care services through the Medicare and Medicaid titles of the Social Security Act.

One hundred fifty years of minimal federal involvement in public health ended with the economic and social chaos of the Great Depression in the 1930s. First, to meet this national challenge, government at all levels was encouraged and indeed expected to play a more direct role in meeting the health and welfare needs of the population. In addition, the shift from an agrarian to an industrial society changed the nature of the revenue basis for governmental resources. Property-based taxation gave way to income-based taxes, and the federal government's share of total tax resources increased while that of state and local governments declined. Money is power, and sharing federal tax revenue resources became both possible and necessary despite the limited authorities granted to the federal government in matters related to health.

Distrust of state and local governments based on fears of misuse and lack of accountability led to the earmarking of resources for specific purposes through conditions attached to the sharing of these resources. The categorical approach to problem solving evolved to a new level and became the federal government's primary strategy for influencing state and local public health efforts. Indeed, for some health priorities the federal agencies not only provided financial resources but also detailed federal employees to work in and often manage programs that handled such problems as sexually transmitted diseases, tuberculosis, immunization, and childhood lead poisoning.

Few aspects of operational federalism had greater impact on state and local governments than attaching conditions to the receipt of federal funds. The result contributed to the institutionalization of isolated silos, as opposed to integrated systems, of public health services through the creation of categorical programs developed to operationalize federal priorities. Few resources were provided for discretionary or generalized public health practice concerns, and such programs often obscured if not ignored the federal responsibilities of state and local governments. Attempts occurred in the 1970s and 1990s to create block grants by consolidating categorical grants and providing greater flexibility to state and local governments. In the 1970s the total amounts awarded under the block grants were reduced by 25% and reporting requirements were largely eliminated. Although states had greater discretion over how these grants were used, categorical programs continued to dominate the federal health landscape and were extensively replicated at the state level.

Through the 1980s the overall scenario described here was one in which the potential for federal influence grew rapidly at a time when federal authority remained limited, state responsibility was still paramount, and local needs increasingly drove state and local governments to respond. These shifts paralleled changes in the public health world. As the focus of public health threats moved from infectious diseases and environmental hazards to chronic diseases with behavioral antecedents and then to social issues with social roots, the substance of public health efforts began to place greater emphasis on state and local solutions. Influences on health are more often shaped by communities than some distant government. Modern public health practice has emerged around these more local concerns.

But it is not easy for every community to have its own local public health agency. In smaller and more rural communities, public health agencies are often quite small with only a handful of staff to provide basic public health services. The range of duties expands for staff, including those with specializations in particular aspects of public health practice, within small agencies. It is important to keep this in mind in understanding the wide range of roles and duties for the public health occupations described in later chapters.

To explain more easily the broad trends of public health in the United States, it is useful to delineate distinct eras in its history. One simple scheme uses the years 1850, 1950, and 2000 as approximate dividers. The era prior to 1850 was characterized by recurrent epidemics of infectious diseases, with little in the way of collective response possible. During the sanitary movement in the second half of the 1800s and first half of the 1900s, science-based control measures were organized and deployed through a public health infrastructure that developed in the form of local and state health departments. After 1950, gaps in the medical care system and federal grant dollars acted together to increase public provision of a wide range of health services. That increase set the stage for the current reexamination of the links between medical and public health practice. Some retrenchment from the direct service provision role has occurred since 1990. The modern era for public health seeks to balance community-driven public health practice with preparedness and response for public health emergencies.

As the various eras of public health practice evolved, so did the need for workers with new and different skills. Prior to 1850, public health workers could not be distinguished from the other health professionals of the time. With scientific and laboratory advancements in the second half of the 1800s, public health workers often came from the ranks of physicians, microbiologists, environmental engineers, and nurses. Between 1900 and 1950, a variety of new public health jobs emerged, including food, milk, and water inspectors; environmental health specialists; maternal and child health workers; and laboratory professionals. After 1950, health educators, dentists, planners, epidemiologists, and others were more widely employed in public health efforts. And now after 2000, emergency response coordinators and information and communication specialists are now considered key components of the public health workforce.

## DEFINITIONS OF PUBLIC HEALTH[1]

The historical development of public health responses in the United States provides a basis for understanding what public health is today. Nonetheless, the term *public health* evokes several different images among the general public and those dedicated to its improvement.

To some, the term describes the professionals and workforce whose job it is to address certain important health problems. Still another image of public health is that of a body of knowledge and techniques that can be applied to health-related problems. Here, public health is seen as what public health does. Snow's investigations exemplify this perspective.

Similarly, many people perceive public health primarily as the activities ascribed to governmental public health agencies. For the majority of the public, this latter image represents public health in modern America and has resulted in the common view that public health primarily involves the provision of medical care to indigent populations. Since 2001, however, public health has also emerged as a frontline defense against bioterrorism and other threats to personal security and safety. Public health responses have also increasingly involved nongovernmental organizations and agencies at the community, state, and national levels.

Another image of public health is that of the intended results of these endeavors. In this image, public health is literally the health of the public, as measured in terms of health and illness in a population. In sum, the public views public health sometimes as a profession, occasionally as a set of methods, oftentimes as governmental services, and infrequently as the ultimate outcomes of its efforts. Together, these facets of public health form a composite image of public health as a broad social enterprise in which many entities and workers contribute to its efforts and success.

With varying images of what public health is, we would expect no shortage of definitions. There have been many, and it serves little purpose to catalog them here. Three definitions from the 1900s, each separated by a generation, provide important insights into what public health is; these are summarized in Table 1–1.

In 1988, the prestigious Institute of Medicine (IOM) provided an insightful definition in its landmark study of public health in the United States, *The Future of Public Health*. The IOM report characterized public health's mission as "fulfilling society's interest in assuring conditions in which people can be healthy."[2(p7)] This definition directs our attention to the many conditions that influence health and wellness, underscoring the broad scope of public health and legitimizing its interest in social, economic, political, and medical care factors that affect health and illness. The definition's premise that society has an interest in the health of its members implies that improving conditions and health status for others is acting in our own self-interest. The assertion that improving the

**Table 1-1** Selected Definitions of Public Health

- "The science and art of preventing disease, prolonging life, and promoting health and efficiency through organized community effort" (Winslow, 1920)
- "Successive redefinings of the unacceptable" (Vickers, 1958)
- "Fulfilling society's interest in assuring conditions in which people can be healthy" (IOM report, 1988)

*Source:* Turnock BJ. *Public Health: What It Is and How It Works.* 3rd ed. Sudbury, MA: Jones and Bartlett; 2004:9.

health status of others provides benefits to all is a core value of public health.

Another core value of public health is reflected in the IOM definition's use of the term *assuring*. Assuring conditions in which people can be healthy means vigilantly promoting and protecting everyone's interests in health and well-being. This value echoes the wisdom in the often-quoted African aphorism that "It takes a village to raise a child." Former Surgeon General David Satcher, the first African-American to head this country's most respected federal public health agency, the Centers for Disease Control and Prevention (CDC), once described a visit to Africa in which he met with African teenagers to learn firsthand of their personal health attitudes and behaviors. Satcher was struck by their concerns over the rapid urbanization of the various African nations and the changes that were affecting their culture and sense of community. These young people felt lost and abandoned; they questioned Satcher as to what the CDC, the U.S. government, and the world community would do to help them survive these changes. As one young man put it, "Where will we find our village?" Public health's role is one of serving us all as our village, whether we are teens in Africa or adults in the United States. The IOM report's characterization of public health advocated for just such a social enterprise and stands as a bold philosophical statement of mission and purpose.

The IOM report also sought to define the boundaries of public health by identifying three core functions of public health: assessment, policy development, and assurance. In one sense, these functions are comparable to those generally ascribed to the medical care system involving diagnosis and treatment. Assessment is the analogue of diagnosis, except that the diagnosis, or problem identification, is made for a group or population of individuals. Similarly, assurance is analogous to treatment and implies that the necessary remedies or interventions are put into place. Finally, policy development is an intermediate role of collectively deciding which remedies or interventions are most appropriate for the problems identified (the formulation of a treatment plan is the medical system's analogue). These core functions broadly describe what public health does (as opposed to what it is) and are especially relevant to the various public health careers described in later chapters.

The concepts embedded in the IOM definition are also reflected in Winslow's definition, developed more than 80 years ago. His definition describes both what public health does and how this gets done. It is a comprehensive definition that has stood the test of time in characterizing public health:

> The science and art of preventing disease, prolonging life, and promoting health and efficiency through organized community effort for the sanitation of the environment, the control of communicable infections, the education of the individual in personal hygiene, the organization of medical and nursing services for the early diagnosis and preventive treatment of disease, and for the development of the social machinery to ensure everyone a standard of living adequate for the maintenance of health, so organizing these benefits as to enable every citizen to realize his birthright of health and longevity.[3(p183)]

There is much to consider in Winslow's definition. The phrases "science and art," "organized community effort," and "birthright of health and longevity" capture much of the substance and aims of public health. Winslow's catalog of methods illuminates the scope of the endeavor, embracing public health's initial targeting of infectious and environmental risks, as well as current activities related to the organization, financing, and accountability of medical care services. His allusion to the "social machinery necessary to ensure everyone a standard of living adequate for the maintenance of health" speaks to the relationship between social conditions and health in all cultures.

There have been many other attempts to define public health, although these have received less attention than either the Winslow or IOM definitions. Several build on the observation that, over time, public health activities reflect the interaction of disease with two other phenomena that can be roughly characterized as science and social values. What do we know, and what do we choose to do with that knowledge?

A prominent British industrialist, Geoffrey Vickers, provided an interesting addition to this mix more than a half century ago while serving as

Secretary of the Medical Research Council. In identifying the forces that set the agenda for public health, Vickers noted, "The landmarks of political, economic, and social history are the moments when some condition passed from the category of the given into the category of the intolerable. I believe that the history of public health might well be written as a record of successive redefinings of the unacceptable."[4(p600)]

The usefulness of Vickers' formulation lies in its focus on the delicate and shifting interface between science and social values. Through this lens, we can view a tracing of public health over history, facilitating an understanding of why and how different societies have reacted to health risks differently at various times. In this light, the history of public health is one of blending knowledge with social values to shape responses to problems that require collective action after they have crossed the boundary from the acceptable to the unacceptable.

## PUBLIC HEALTH WORK AND PUBLIC HEALTH WORKERS

From a functional perspective it is the individuals involved in carrying out the core functions and essential services of public health who constitute the public health workforce. Critical to an understanding of this characterization of the public health workforce are the terms *core functions* and *essential public health services*. While a full explanation of these terms is better left to public health texts, a useful summary of these concepts is provided in the "Public Health in America" statement (Table 1–2). In it, the practice of public health is described in terms of both its ends (vision, mission, and six broad responsibilities) and how it accomplishes those ends (10 essential public health services). These constitute an aggregate job description for the entire public health workforce with the workload divided among the many different professional and occupational categories composing the total public health workforce.

This functional perspective clearly links public health workers to public health practice. Unfortunately, this does not simplify the practical task of determining who is, and who is not, part of the public health workforce. There has never been any specific academic degree, even the Master's of Public Health (MPH) degree, or unique set of experiences that distinguish public health's workers from those in other fields. Many public health workers have a primary professional discipline in addition to their attachment to

---

**Table 1–2** Public Health in the United States

---

Vision:

*Healthy People in Healthy Communities*

Mission:

*Promote physical and mental health and prevent disease, injury, and disability*

Public Health

- Prevents epidemics and the spread of disease
- Protects against environmental hazards
- Prevents injuries
- Promotes and encourages healthy behaviors
- Responds to disasters and assists communities in recovery
- Assures the quality and accessibility of health services

Essential Public Health Services

- Monitor health status to identify community health problems.
- Diagnose and investigate health problems and health hazards in the community.
- Inform, educate, and empower people about health issues.
- Mobilize community partnerships to identify and solve health problems.
- Develop policies and plans that support individual and community health efforts.
- Enforce laws and regulations that protect health and ensure safety.
- Link people with needed personal health services, and assure the provision of health care when otherwise unavailable.
- Assure a competent public health and personal health care workforce.
- Evaluate effectiveness, accessibility, and quality of personal and population-based health services.
- Research new insights and innovative solutions to health problems.

---

*Source:* Essential Public Health Services Working Group of the Core Public Health Functions Steering Committee; 1994. Available at http://www.health.gov/phfunctions/public.htm. Accessed August 2005.

public health. Physicians, nurses, dentists, social workers, nutritionists, health educators, anthropologists, psychologists, architects, sanitarians, economists, political scientists, engineers, epidemiologists, biostatisticians, managers, lawyers, and dozens of other professions and disciplines carry out the work of public health. This multidisciplinary workforce, with somewhat divided loyalties to multiple professions, blurs the distinctiveness of public health as a unified profession. At the same time, however, it facilitates the interdisciplinary approaches to community problem identification and problem solving, which are hallmarks of public health practice.

The history of public health and how it has been defined over time offers important insights into what public health is and what its workers do. Individually and collectively, public health workers contribute to a social enterprise that is both important and unique.

## SIZE AND DISTRIBUTION OF THE PUBLIC HEALTH WORKFORCE

There is little agreement as to the size of the public health workforce in the United States today except that it is only a small subset of the 13 million persons employed in the health sector of the American economy. Enumerations and estimates of public health workers in general and public health professionals in particular suffer from several limitations: the definition of a public health worker is unclear; public health workers employed outside governmental public health agencies are difficult to identify; and not all employees of governmental public health agencies have public health responsibilities associated with their jobs. Enumerating specific types of public health workers is also difficult because many have other professional affiliations.

Due to these limitations, a clear picture of the public health workforce is not available. But it is clear that efforts to identify and categorize public health workers must take into account three important aspects of public health practice:

- Work setting: Public health workers work for organizations actively engaged in promoting, protecting, and preserving the health of a defined population group. The organization may be public or private, and its public health objectives may be secondary or subsidiary to its principal objectives. In addition to governmental public health agencies, other public and private organizations employ public health workers. For example, school health nurses working for the local school district and health educators employed by the local Red Cross chapter are part of the public health workforce.
- Work content: Public health workers perform work addressing one or more of the essential public health services. Many job descriptions for public health workers are tailored from the essential public health services, and the scope of tasks can be very broad. A focus on populations as opposed to individuals is often a distinguishing characteristic of these job descriptions. For example, an individual trained as a

health educator who works for a community-based teen pregnancy prevention program is clearly a public health worker. But the same can't be said of a health educator working for a commercial advertising firm promoting cosmetics.

- Worker: The individual must occupy a position that conventionally requires at least one year of postsecondary specialized public health training and that is (or can be) assigned a professional, administrative, or technical occupational title (to be defined in Chapter 2). This distinction may seem artificial, but rests on the notion that public health practice relies on a foundation of knowledge, skills, and attitudes that, in most circumstances, cannot be imparted through work experiences alone.

If public health workers cannot be counted from the ground up, maybe they can be approximated from the top down. Various sources estimate that public health activities, including both clinical and population-based services, make up 3–4% of all health expenditures.[1] If public health workers composed a similar percentage of the 13 million health workers in the United States, the number of public health workers would be between 400,000 and 525,000. Because expenditures for some public health activities, such as those for many environmental and occupational health services, are not captured in the total for health expenditures, the actual number of public health workers may range as high as 450,000 to 600,000.

That range is consistent with a crude enumeration of the public health workforce conducted in the year 2000, which identified 450,000 public health workers.[5] The year 2000 enumeration missed most public health workers employed by nongovernmental agencies as well as many public health workers employed by government agencies other than official public health agencies. As a result, the actual total exceeds the 450,000 workers identified in the enumeration.

Data from another source, the ongoing employment census of federal, state, and local health agencies, indicated that there were 552,000 full-time equivalent (FTE) governmental public health workers in 2004.[6] There were slightly more than 424,000 worked in state and local governments, and another 128,000 were employed by federal agencies (see Table 1–3). Adding in even the admittedly low estimate of 64,000 nongovernmental public health workers from the year 2000 enumeration study, the size of the public health workforce in 2004, using these figures, was nearly 620,000 FTE positions.

The overall workforce in the health sector of the American economy has more than doubled in size since 1975 and has increased by more than 30% since 1990.[7] Table 1–3 indicates that the number of public health workers employed by federal, state, and local health agencies has also been steadily increasing, largely among workers of local public health agencies. Unquestionably, the number of public health workers employed by nongovernmental agencies also grew during this period. The increase in the number of FTE workers in state and local health agencies contrasts sharply with the relatively unchanged number of federal health workers.[6] The number of FTE employees working for governmental health agencies was 487,000 FTEs in 1994 (126,000 federal, 158,000 state, 203,000 local). By 2004, the total was 552,000 (128,000 federal, 174,000 state, 250,000 local). Figure 1–1 demonstrates that the ratio of public health workers to population has also increased during this period, although there is evidence that it may be declining somewhat since reaching its highest level (15.1 per 10,000) in 2001. This is surprising in view of a

**Table 1–3** FTE Health Workers for Federal, State, and Local Governmental Health Agencies, 1994–2004, United States

| Year | Federal Health FTE | State Health FTE | Local Health FTE | State + Local FTE | Total (F+S+L) FTE |
|---|---|---|---|---|---|
| 1994 | 126,292 | 157,962 | 202,732 | 360,694 | 486,986 |
| 1995 | 125,048 | 160,031 | 208,588 | 368,619 | 493,667 |
| 1997 | 119,921 | 162,605 | 214,824 | 377,429 | 497,350 |
| 1998 | 119,846 | 166,930 | 219,655 | 386,585 | 506,431 |
| 1999 | 121,033 | 169,213 | 223,999 | 393,212 | 514,245 |
| 2000 | 120,362 | 172,678 | 236,496 | 409,174 | 529,536 |
| 2001 | 122,999 | 172,414 | 251,399 | 423,813 | 546,812 |
| 2002 | 124,979 | 176,345 | 252,326 | 428,671 | 553,650 |
| 2003 | 124,828 | 176,868 | 253,888 | 430,756 | 555,584 |
| 2004 | 127,933 | 174,301 | 249,857 | 424,128 | 552,061 |

Due to changes in the data collection process, comparable data for 1996 are not available.
*Source:* U.S. Bureau of the Census. Federal, State, and Local Governments, Public Employment and Payroll Data. Available at http://www.census.gov/govs/www/aps.html. Accessed August 2005.

substantial influx of federal funding for state and local public health agencies since 2002. These trends are further discussed in Chapter 10.

Like most health sector workers, public health workers are more likely to be found in urban and suburban settings rather than rural communities. The public health worker to population ratio, however, is often higher in rural areas than in urban areas. States show significant variation as well with higher ratios in many of the smaller and less urban states in the east and west and lower ratios in the central states (see Table 1–4).

In 1980, Health Resources and Services Administration estimated the size of the public health workforce at 500,000 workers including a primary public health workforce of 250,000 professional workers, most working in governmental public health agencies.[8] More than 50,000 occupational health physicians, nurses and specialists working in the private sector, as well as 20,000 health educators working in schools and 45,000 administrators working in nursing homes, hospitals, and medical group practices were included in the 250,000 professionals characterized by HRSA as the primary public health workforce at the time. If only those working for

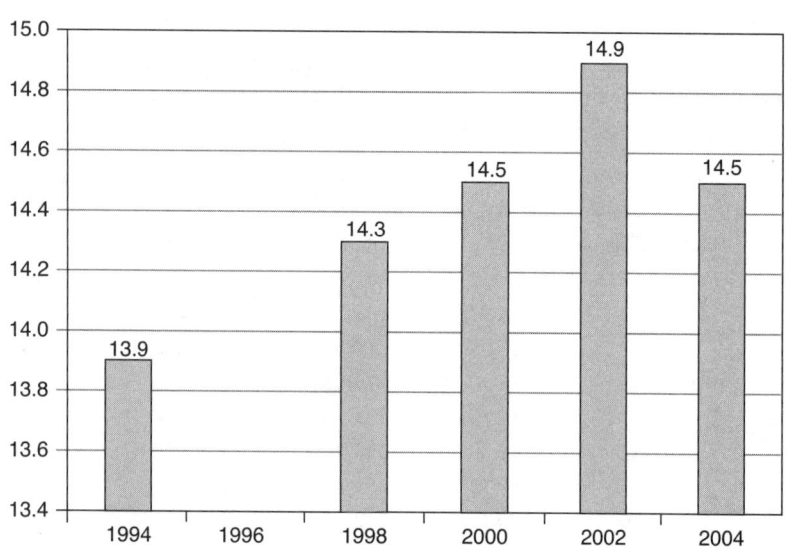

Due to changes in the data collection process, comparable data for 1996 are not available.
Source: U.S. Bureau of the Census. Federal, State, and Local Governments, Public Employment and Payroll Data. Available at http://www.census.gov/govs/www/aps.html. Accessed August 2005.

**FIGURE 1–1** FTE Workers for State and Local Health Agencies per 10,000 Population, Selected Years 1994–2004, United States

**Table 1–4** FTE Workers for State and Local Health Agencies by State, 2004

| State | State + Local FTE | State+ Local FTE per 10,000 pop. |
| --- | --- | --- |
| AL | 10,090 | 22.3 |
| AK | 1,056 | 16.1 |
| AZ | 4,932 | 8.6 |
| AR | 4,932 | 17.9 |
| CA | 54,533 | 15.2 |
| CO | 4,558 | 9.9 |
| CN | 3,425 | 9.8 |
| DE | 2,169 | 26.1 |
| DC | 1,977 | 34.6 |
| FL | 25,501 | 14.7 |
| GA | 16,077 | 18.2 |
| HI | 2,710 | 21.5 |
| ID | 2,095 | 15.0 |
| IL | 9,930 | 7.8 |
| IN | 5,346 | 8.6 |
| IA | 3,171 | 10.7 |
| KS | 3,893 | 14.2 |
| KY | 7,939 | 19.2 |
| LA | 5,621 | 12.5 |
| ME | 1,587 | 12.1 |
| MD | 11,192 | 20.1 |
| MA | 10,035 | 15.6 |
| MI | 13,395 | 13.3 |
| MN | 5,866 | 11.5 |
| MS | 3,214 | 11.1 |
| MO | 7,543 | 13.1 |
| MT | 1,667 | 18.0 |
| NE | 1,455 | 8.3 |
| NV | 2,033 | 8.7 |
| NH | 1,045 | 8.0 |
| NJ | 7,695 | 8.9 |
| NM | 2,617 | 13.8 |
| NY | 27,022 | 14.1 |
| NC | 23,709 | 27.8 |
| ND | 1,829 | 28.8 |

*continues*

**Table 1–4** *continued*

| State | State + Local FTE | State+ Local FTE per 10,000 pop. |
| --- | --- | --- |
| OH | 21,818 | 19.0 |
| OK | 7,151 | 20.3 |
| OR | 7,081 | 19.7 |
| PA | 7,216 | 5.8 |
| RI | 1,385 | 12.8 |
| SC | 9,214 | 22.0 |
| SD | 893 | 11.6 |
| TN | 7,060 | 12.0 |
| TX | 32,249 | 15.2 |
| UT | 3,326 | 13.9 |
| VT | 776 | 12.5 |
| VA | 11,614 | 15.6 |
| WA | 9,476 | 15.3 |
| WV | 2,445 | 13.5 |
| WI | 7,541 | 13.7 |
| WY | 1,054 | 20.8 |
| U.S. Total | 424,158 | 14.5 |

*Source:* U.S. Bureau of the Census. Federal, State, and Local Governments, Public Employment and Payroll Data. Available at http://www.census.gov/govs/www/aps.html. Accessed August 2005.

governmental public health agencies had been included, the number would have been closer to 140,000. The year 2000 public health enumeration identified 40,000 fewer occupational health professionals and did not seek to include health educators working in schools or administrators in nongovernmental clinical settings.

Comparing the overall 1980 estimate (500,000 workers) with the year 2000 public health workforce enumeration suggests that the public health workforce is shrinking. Comparing the 1980 HRSA estimate with current employment census data, on the other hand, suggests that the public health workforce is growing. As the methods used for the 1980 estimation were considerably different from those in the more recent studies, direct comparison of the results is of questionable value.

The public health workforce enumeration completed in 2000 found one third of public health workers employed by state agencies and another one third employed by agencies of local government with less than 20% working at the federal level and 14% outside government entirely.[5] Chapter 2 examines key characteristics of the governmental public health agencies that employ these workers. Government employment census data, which excludes nongovernmental workers, also classify one third as state workers but 45% as employees of local government and 22% as working for federal agencies. Some of these differences can be attributed to state public health systems in which state employees work at the local level and may be counted as state employees in the employment census data and as local health department employees in the public health enumeration study. These differences may also be partly attributed to the inclusion of workers in state and local governmental agencies other than the local public health agency in the government employment census data but not in the year 2000 public health enumeration study. For example, substance abuse and mental health prevention services, school health services, or restaurant inspections may operate from local mental health agencies, school districts, or consumer affairs agencies rather than from the local health department.

Although recent decades have witnessed an increase in the number of public health workers employed by nongovernmental agencies due to expanded partnerships for public health priorities, governmental public health workers are often considered the primary public health workforce. Their number, composition, distribution, and competence are issues of public concern. The government employment census data provide useful insights into overall trends at the national level and among the various levels of government. The year 2000 public health enumeration study, however, provides richer information on the composition of the public health workforce, such as the proportion and types of professional occupational categories within that workforce. Both sources enrich understanding of the size and composition of the public health workforce today.

## COMPOSITION OF THE PUBLIC HEALTH WORKFORCE

Public health is multidisciplinary with many different professions and occupations involved in its work. In recent years there has been an effort to identify standard occupational classifications for public health workers (see Chapter 2), resulting in nearly 30 different job categories. Since the total number of public health workers is not clear, the precise proportion of the various subgroups cannot be determined. It is clear that nurses and environmental health practitioners constitute the largest subgroups of public health workers. Managers, epidemiologists, health educators, and laboratory workers are also significant subgroups. Professionals comprise more than one half of the overall public health workforce, as will be further described in Chapter 2. It is the administrative, professional, and technical positions in the public health workforce that are the focus of this book.

Despite the lack of precise information, it appears that professional occupational categories comprise more than 300,000 or one half of the estimated 620,000 workers in the public health workforce. For comparison purposes, there are approximately 2.3 million nurses, 800,000 physicians, 200,000 pharmacists, 170,000 dentists, and 90,000 dieticians/nutritionists working in the United States at the turn of the 21st century.[7]

Studies of local public health agencies indicate that three positions are found in more than two thirds of all local public health agencies (LPHAs)—public health nurse, administrator, and sanitarian/environmental health specialist.[9,10] These positions are present in large and small agencies alike. The next most frequent positions (registered nurse, dietitian/nutritionist, licensed practical nurse, nurse practitioner, health educator, and social worker) are found in only 20–33% of LPHAs. There is considerable variation in the proportion of LPHAs with these positions, associated with agency size. For example, health educators are employed in only 10% of LPHAs serving populations under 50,000 persons but in 85% of agencies serving 500,000 or more.

Two general patterns of LPHA staffing exist around a core set of employees. One pattern focuses on clinical services, the other on more population-based programs.[11] The core employees consist of dietitian/nutritionists, sanitarians/environmental specialists, administrators, lab specialists, and health educators. The clinical pattern adds physicians, nurses, and dental health workers. The population-based pattern includes epidemiologists, public health nurses, social workers, and program specialists.

The availability of information on public health workers at the state and local level varies from state to state, and is often inconsistent and incomplete. Detailed information from the official state health departments has not been available since the late 1980s and even then did not include public health workers employed by state agencies other than the official state health department. The periodic profiles of LPHAs completed by the National Association of County and City Health Officials (NACCHO) provide only general data on the proportion of responding agencies that employ specific public health job titles, either directly or through contracted services. This information does not allow for aggregation into an actual enumeration of public health workers in the various job categories.

The lack of information on the public health workforce extends to some of the most basic and important characteristics of that workforce. For example, there is very little information available on the racial and ethnic characteristics of the overall public health workforce. Data on cultural competency is also lacking.

## PUBLIC HEALTH WORKER ETHICS, SKILLS, AND COMPETENCIES

Public health workers may come from different academic, professional, and experiential backgrounds, but they share a common bond. All are committed to a common mission and share common ethical principles, as exemplified by the following list advanced by the American Public Health Association:[12]

- Public health should address principally the fundamental causes of disease and requirements for health, aiming to prevent adverse health outcomes.
- Public health should achieve community health in a way that respects the rights of individuals in the community.
- Public health policies, programs, and priorities should be developed and evaluated through processes that ensure an opportunity for input from community members.
- Public health should advocate and work for the empowerment of disenfranchised community members, aiming to ensure that the basic resources and conditions necessary for health are accessible to all.
- Public health should seek the information needed to implement effective policies and programs that protect and promote health.
- Public health institutions should provide communities with the information they have that is needed for decisions on policies or

programs and should obtain the community's consent for their implementation.

- Public health institutions should act in a timely manner on the information they have within the resources and the mandate given to them by the public.
- Public health programs and policies should incorporate a variety of approaches that anticipate and respect diverse values, beliefs, and cultures in the community.
- Public health programs and policies should be implemented in a manner that most enhances the physical and social environment.
- Public health institutions should protect the confidentiality of information that can bring harm to an individual or community if made public. Exceptions must be justified on the basis of the high likelihood of significant harm to the individual or others.
- Public health institutions should ensure the professional competence of their employees.
- Public health institutions and their employees should engage in collaborations and affiliations in ways that build the public's trust and the institution's effectiveness.

Information from public health agencies indicates that the majority of public health workers lack formal education and training in public health. In 1980, HRSA determined that only 20% of the 250,000 professionals in the primary public health workforce had formal training in public health.[8] Two decades later, there is little evidence that this situation has improved. While the proportion of those who have formal training varies by category of worker, the lack of formal training is striking in even some of the most critical categories. For example, a NACCHO survey in 1997 found that 78% of local health department leaders have had no formal public health education or training.[13] A survey of Illinois local health jurisdictions in the year 2000 yielded similar results with 79% of local health agency administrators lacking formal preparation in public health.[14]

For many public health workers, formal training focuses only on a specific aspect of public health practice such as environmental health or community or school health nursing. Environmental health practitioners, nurses, administrators, and health educators account for the majority of public health workers with formal training in public health. Even among those with formal training in public health, public health workers with graduate degrees from schools of public health or other graduate public health programs represent only a small fraction of the total. In view of the number of master's-level graduates of schools of public health and other graduate-level public health degree programs—about 7000 in 2005—this is not surprising.

Evidence of the lack of formal training within this workforce, however, doesn't necessarily lead to the conclusion that public health workers are unprepared.[15] On the contrary, public health workers enter the field having earned a wide variety of degrees and professional training credentials from academic programs and institutions unrelated to public health. Often overlooked, these institutions produce the bulk of the public health workforce and represent major assets for addressing unmet needs. On-the-job training and work experience contribute substantially to the overall competency and preparedness of the public health workforce. For example, public health workers are frequently involved in responses to earthquakes, floods, and other disasters and have increasingly acquired and demonstrated skills in assessing community health needs and devising community health improvement plans. These are skills that most public health workers acquired through real-world work experience rather than through their formal training.

Continuing education and career development for public health workers has long been a cottage industry involving many different parties. Academic institutions certainly are contributors, but public health agencies at the state and local level, public health associations (national, state, and local), and other voluntary-sector health organizations participate as well. Many different entities offer credits for continuing education, including professional organizations, academic institutions, and hospitals, among others. Public health workers value continuing education credits as a means to satisfy requirements of their core disciplines in order to maintain some level of credentialing status (such as licensed physicians and nurses, certified health education specialists, and so on) A few states, such as New Jersey, enforce continuing education requirements for the public health disciplines licensed by that state. There is no formal system of public health-specific continuing education units (CEUs) and only fledgling efforts toward credentialing public health workers. The final chapter will crystallize current challenges, strategies, and initiatives for public health workforce development.

## CONCLUSION

Recent decades have witnessed an increase in the number of public health workers employed by both governmental and nongovernmental agencies caused by expanded public health priorities and partnerships. This expansion of the workforce, however, leaves many questions unanswered as to the number, distribution, training, and preparedness of the public health workforce, making these issues of public concern.[16] Some of these concerns have persisted since the late 1800s as suggested by an editorial appearing in the *Journal of the American Medical Association* more than 110 years ago:

> It is unfortunate that in the absence of epidemics or pestilence, too little attention is paid to the protection of the public health, and as a necessary consequence, to the selection of those whose duties require them to guard the public health.[17(p189)]

Subsequent chapters will examine these issues for various categories of public health workers.

## REFERENCES

1. Turnock BJ. *Public Health: What It Is and How It Works.* 3rd ed. Sudbury, MA: Jones and Bartlett; 2004. (Note: The sections titled "Brief History of Public Health Practice" and "Definitions of Public Health" are adapted from this text.)
2. Institute of Medicine, National Academy of Sciences. *The Future of Public Health.* Washington, DC: National Academy Press; 1988.
3. Winslow CEA. The untilled field of public health. *Mod Med.* 1920;2:183–191.
4. Vickers G. What sets the goals of public health? *Lancet.* 1958;1:599–604.
5. Health Resources and Services Administration (HRSA), Bureau of Health Professions, National Center for Health Workforce Information and Analysis and Center for Health Policy, Columbia School of Nursing. *The Public Health Workforce Enumeration 2000.* Washington, DC: HRSA; 2000. Available at http://www.phppo.cdc.gov/owpp/docs/library/2000/Public%20Health%20 Workforce%20Enumeration%202000.pdf. Accessed August 2005.
6. U.S. Bureau of the Census. Federal, State, and Local Governments, Public Employment and Payroll Data. Available at http://www.census.gov/govs/www/ apes.html. Accessed August 2005.

7. U.S. Department of Health and Human Services (DHHS). *Health United States 2004.* Washington, DC: National Center for Health Statistics; 2004.

8. Health Resources and Services Administration (HRSA), U.S. Department of Health and Human Services. *Public Health Personnel in the United States, 1980: Second Report to Congress.* Washington, DC: U.S. Public Health Service (PHS); 1982.

9. National Association of County and City Health Officials (NACCHO). *Profile of Local Health Departments, 1996–1997 Dataset.* Washington, DC: NACCHO; 1997.

10. National Association of County and City Health Officials. *Public Health Infrastructure Chartbook.* Washington, DC: NACCHO; 2001.

11. Gerzoff RB, Baker EL. The use of scaling techniques to analyze U.S. local health department staffing structures, 1992–1993. *1998 Proceedings of the Section on Government Statistics and Section on Social Statistics of the American Statistical Association.* 209–213.

12. American Public Health Association. Public health code of ethics. Available at http://www.apha.org/codeofethics/ethics.htm. Accessed August 2005.

13. Gerzoff RB, Richards TB. The education of local health department top executives. *J Public Health Manage Pract.* 1997;3:50–56.

14. Turnock BJ, Hutchison KD. *The Local Public Health Workforce: Size, Distribution, Composition, and Influence on Core Function Performance, Illinois 1998–1999.* Chicago, IL: Illinois Center for Health Workforce Studies; 2000.

15. Turnock BJ. Public health workforce preparedness roadmap. *J Public Health Manage Pract.* 2003;9:471–480.

16. Tilson H, Gebbie KM. The public health workforce. *Ann Rev Public Health.* 2004;25:341–356. Available at arjournals.annualreviews.org/doi/full/10.1146/annurev.publhealth.25.102802.124357. Accessed August 2005.

17. American Medical Association. Editorial. *JAMA.* 1893;20:189.

# CHAPTER 2

# Public Health Occupations and Organizations

This chapter defines and describes several key dimensions of public health occupations and organizations that provide the framework for examining specific positions and careers for public health workers in later chapters. Information on the full spectrum of occupations in the public health workforce is available from a variety of sources, including federal health and labor agencies and national public health organizations. Table 2–1 previews the public health titles, occupational categories, and careers examined in Chapters 3 through 9. The first column identifies the public health job titles and careers addressed in each chapter. The second column lists specific Bureau of Labor Statistics standard occupational categories (SOCs) included in each chapter. Standard occupation categories are explained later in this chapter.

## CHARACTERISTICS OF PUBLIC HEALTH OCCUPATIONS

There are many aspects of an occupation or career that are important to current and prospective public health workers. The framework used in this book includes:

- Occupational classification: These are based on job titles and whether the duties of the job are primarily administrative, professional, technical, or supportive in nature. Many positions in public

**Table 2–1** Public Health Occupations and Careers Addressed in Chapters 3 Through 9.

| Chapter Number | Career Category with Specific Public Health Titles Described | Bureau of Labor Statistics Standard Occupational Categories Relevant for Public Health |
|---|---|---|
| 3 | **Public Health Administration** | |
| | • Health services manager | • Health services manager/ administrator |
| | • Public health agency director | |
| | • Health officer | |
| 4 | **Environmental and Occupational Health** | |
| | • Environmental engineer | • Environmental engineer |
| | • Environmental health specialist (entry level) | • Environmental engineering technician and technologist |
| | • Environmental health specialist (midlevel) | • Environmental scientist and specialist |
| | • Environmental health specialist (senior level) | • Environmental science technician and technologist |
| | • Occupational health and safety specialist | • Occupational health and safety specialist |
| | | • Occupational health and safety technician |
| 5 | **Public Health Nursing** | |
| | • Public health nurse (entry level) | • Registered nurse |
| | • Public health nurse (senior level) | • Licensed practical/ vocational nurse |
| | • Licensed practical/vocational nurse | |
| 6 | **Epidemiology and Disease Control** | |
| | • Disease investigator | • Epidemiologist |
| | • Epidemiologist (entry level) | • Statistician |
| | • Epidemiologist (senior level) | |
| 7 | **Public Health Education and Information** | |
| | • Public health educator (entry level) | • Health educator |
| | • Public health educator (senior level) | • Public relations/public information/health communications/media specialist |
| | • Public information officer | |
| 8 | **Other Public Health Professionals** | |
| | • Public health nutritionist/dietician | |
| | • Public health social, behavioral, and mental health workers | |
| | • Public health laboratory workers | |
| | • Public health physicians | |
| | • Public health veterinarians | |
| | • Public health pharmacists | |

*continues*

**Table 2-1** *continued*

| | |
|---|---|
| • Public health dental workers | • Substance abuse and behavioral disorder counselor |
| • Administrative law judge/hearing officer | • Microbiologist |
| • Dietician/nutritionist | • Biochemist/biophysicist |
| • Dietetic technician | • Medical and clinical laboratory technologist |
| • Medical and public health social worker | • Medical and clinical laboratory technician |
| • Mental health and substance abuse social worker | • Public health physician |
| • Mental health counselor | • Public health veterinarian |
| | • Public health pharmacist |
| | • Public health dentist |
| | • Administrative law judge/hearing officer |

9  **Public Health Program Occupations**

- Public health program specialist/ coordinator
- Public health emergency preparedness and response coordinator
- Public health policy analyst
- Public health information specialists
- Community outreach and other technical occupations

health practice have a variety of job titles associated with them. Similarly, the same job title can have a variety of regular duties and day-to-day responsibilities.

- Public health practice profile: The public health functions and essential public health services addressed by each occupational grouping are presented in a public health practice profile.
- Important and essential duties: These are the defining characteristics of any position describing what the worker does on a daily basis. Examples are derived from a sampling of job and position descriptions from a variety of sources.
- Minimum qualifications: Some positions require a specific academic degree or credential; many don't. Some require previous experience, while others don't. All require some particular minimum level of knowledge, skills, and abilities. Many also require specific physical

capabilities. These characteristics will be identified for each public health occupation.

- Workplace considerations: This description will identify levels of government that employ significant numbers of workers in each occupational category as well as important nongovernmental work settings for public health workers. This section will also highlight considerations related to physical demands, work schedules, travel, and general working conditions.
- Salary estimates: Salary levels for public health workers are estimated based on information from current job postings and the May 2004 survey of employment and wages coordinated by the Labor Department's Bureau of Labor Statistics.
- Career prospects: Estimates as to current need and future demand for specific public health occupations and career paths are provided, based on the analyses performed by public health organizations and the Bureau of Labor Statistics' projections for various occupations.
- Additional information: Sources of additional information for each occupation or career are identified, including education and training opportunities.

The following sections briefly describe the type and source of information included for each of these characteristics.

## OCCUPATIONAL CLASSIFICATIONS

Throughout the economy, including the health sector, occupations are broadly classified as either white collar or blue collar depending on the degree of education and experience normally required. White collar occupations include five major occupational categories (professional, administrative, technical, clerical, and other), based on the subject matter of work, the level of difficulty or responsibility involved, and the educational requirements established for each occupation. Blue collar occupations are composed of the trades, crafts, and manual labor (unskilled, semiskilled, skilled), including foreman and supervisory positions entailing trade, craft, or laboring experience and knowledge as the paramount requirement.

The U.S. Office of Personnel Management tracks occupations in various industries using four general categories: professional, administrative, technical, and support.

- Professional occupations are those that require knowledge in a field of science or learning characteristically acquired through education or training equivalent to a bachelor's or higher degree with major study in or pertinent to the specialized field, as distinguished from general education. The work of a professional occupation requires the exercise of discretion, judgment, and personal responsibility for the application of an organized body of knowledge that is constantly studied to make new discoveries and interpretations, and to improve the data, materials, and methods. Professionals require specialized and theoretical knowledge. Well-known examples of professional job titles include physicians, registered nurses, dieticians, health educators, social workers, psychologists, lawyers, accountants, economists, system analysts, and personnel and labor relations workers. Professionals constitute the majority (56%) of public health workers (see Figure 2–1).

- Administrative occupations are those that involve the exercise of analytical ability, judgment, discretion, personal responsibility, and the application of a substantial body of knowledge of principles, concepts, and practices applicable to one or more fields of administration or management. While these positions do not require specialized educational

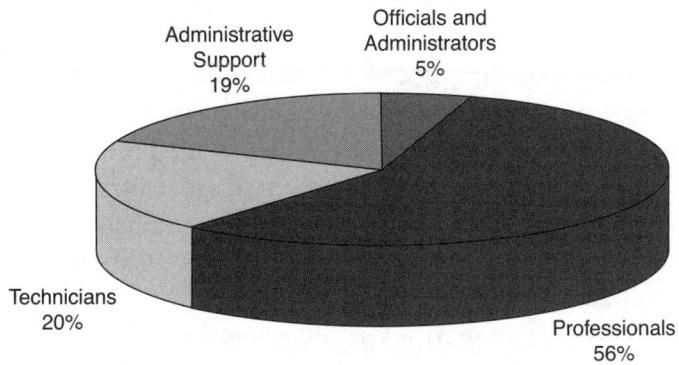

Source: Adapted from Health Resources and Services Administration (HRSA), Bureau of Health Professions, National Center for Health Workforce Information and Analysis and Center for Health Policy, Columbia School of Nursing. *The Public Health Workforce Enumeration 2000*. Washington, DC: HRSA; 2000. Available at http://www.phppo.cdc.gov/owpp/docs/library/2000/Public%20Health%20Workforce%20Enumeration%202000.pdf. Accessed August 2005.

**FIGURE 2–1** Percentage of Public Health Workers in Selected Occupational Categories, United States, 2000.

majors, they do involve the type of skills (analytical, research, writing, judgment) typically gained through a college-level general education, or through progressively responsible experience. Administrators set broad policies, oversee overall responsibility for the execution of these policies, direct individual departments or special phases of the agency's operations, or provide specialized consultation on a regional, district or area basis. Common job titles for administrators include department heads, bureau chiefs, division chiefs, directors, deputy directors, and similar titles. Administrators and managers comprise 5% of all public health workers.

- Technical occupations are those that involve work that is not routine in nature and is typically associated with, and supportive of, a professional or administrative field. Such occupations involve extensive practical knowledge gained through on-the-job experience, or specific training less than that represented by college graduation. Work in these occupations may involve substantial elements of the work of the professional or administrative field, but requires less than full competence in the field involved. Technical occupations require a combination of basic scientific or technical knowledge and manual skills. Titles include computer specialists, licensed practical nurses, inspectors, programmers, and a variety of technicians (environmental, laboratory, medical, nursing, dental, and so on). The technical occupations category also includes paraprofessionals who perform some of the duties of a professional or technician in a supportive role usually requiring less formal training and experience than that normally required for professional status. Included are outreach workers, research assistants, medical aides, child support workers, home health aides, ambulance drivers and attendants, and so on. Workers in technical occupations account for 20% of all public health workers.

- Administrative Support occupations are those that involve structured work in support of office, business, or fiscal operations; duties are performed according to established policies or techniques and require training, experience, or working knowledge related to the tasks to be performed. Clerical titles are often responsible for internal and external communication as well as recording and retrieval of data, information, and other paperwork required in an office. This category includes bookkeepers, messengers, clerk typists, stenographers, court transcribers, hearing reporters, statistical clerks, dispatchers, license distributors, payroll clerks, office machine and computer operators, telephone operators, legal assistants, and so on. In addition, workers in any of the blue collar occupational categories are considered support workers within the public health workforce. About 19% of public health workers are in the administrative support category.

As indicated in Figure 2–1, 81% of public health workers fall into the professional, administrative, and technical categories. More than half (56%) are classified as professionals, similar to the proportion of professionals among all 13 million health workers. Nursing and environmental health activities employ the largest number of public health workers when both professional and technical occupations are considered. Registered nurses (RNs) represent the largest professional category within the public health workforce.

The U.S. Department of Labor collects information on occupations throughout the economy, including the public sector. An official taxonomy for occupations allows the Department of Labor's Bureau of Labor Statistics (BLS) to track information on hundreds of standard occupational categories in terms of the number and location of jobs, salaries, and duties performed. BLS also develops projections for the number of future positions for these occupational categories based on economic and employment trends. Occupations generally can be found in a variety of industries making it difficult to pinpoint trends and needs specific to the public health system. For example, registered nurses are the largest occupational category in the overall health workforce with 2.3 million workers, but only a small percentage of all registered nurses (75,000) work in public health agencies. Many more work in hospitals and other health care organizations. This is also true for physicians, health services administrators, health educators, nutritionists, and many other occupations. Public health agencies, however, are the largest employers of several standard occupational categories, such as environmental health specialists and epidemiologists. For those occupational categories, BLS information is especially useful.

Standard occupational categories relevant for public health are identified in the second column of Table 2–1 with 28 specific categories listed.[1] Each of these categories is addressed in subsequent chapters, with the greatest attention on those with the largest numbers of workers in the public health workforce. These 28 occupational categories clearly do not cover all titles found in public health organizations. Nor do they capture the entire scope of work undertaken by public health workers. For these reasons, each chapter will focus specifically on job titles and job descriptions commonly found in public health organizations (see the first column of Table 2–1) with information on titles, duties, public health roles, and qualifications. Related job titles are addressed in the same chapter in order to demonstrate links and possible career pathways.

Estimates of the number of current workers in each occupational category are synthesized from two sources. The Bureau of Labor Statistics conducts surveys of all standard occupational categories twice yearly, including information on the industries and levels of government that employ workers in each standard occupational category. This source allows for estimates of the total number of workers in a particular standard occupational category who work for federal, state, and local agencies.

A second important source of estimates for public health workers in relevant standard occupational categories is the *Public Health Workforce Enumeration 2000* commissioned by the federal Health Resources and Services Administration (HRSA).[2] This enumeration collected information on workers of federal, state, and local public health agencies in the year 2000 based on existing data, reports, and surveys. As such, it was more of a qualitative and descriptive enumeration than a quantitative one. The year 2000 public health workforce enumeration identified a total of 450,000 public health workers, including 15,000 workers in voluntary sector organizations and 15,000 public health students. Occupational categories could not be established for 112,000 public health workers, making it difficult to project the actual number of workers in specific categories, such as public health nurses or epidemiologists.

To compare information with BLS data, the year 2000 public health enumeration numbers were adjusted to assign an occupational category to all workers. Table 2–2 provides both the actual number of workers identified in specific occupational categories and the adjusted number after those in the "unreported" group are assigned to a category and title. Each chapter then uses information from both sources to estimate the number of existing positions for each occupational category and title.

**Table 2-2** Number of Public Health Workers in Selected Occupational Categories and Titles, United States, 2000

| Gov PH Workers | Reported # | Adjusted # |
|---|---|---|
| Administrators | 15,920 | 21,247 |
| Professionals | 176,980 | 236,202 |
| Technicians | 61,088 | 81,530 |
| Other support | 59,085 | 69,283 |
| Unreported | 104,763 | |
| | 417,836 | 417,836 |
| *Occupational Categories* | | |
| Health administrators | 15,920 | 21,247 |
| Admin support staff | 37,805 | 62,981 |
| Admin/business prof | 4,725 | 7,306 |
| Attorney/hearing officer | 601 | 929 |
| Biostatistician | 1,164 | 1,800 |
| Environmental engineer | 4,549 | 7,034 |
| Environmental specialist | 14,882 | 23,013 |
| Epidemiologist | 927 | 1,433 |
| Policy analyst/plan/econ | 3,678 | 5,687 |
| Disease investigator | 783 | 1,211 |
| License/inspection spec | 13,780 | 21,309 |
| Social, behavioral, mental | 3,762 | 5,817 |
| Occ. health and safety spec | 5,593 | 8,649 |
| PH dental worker | 2,032 | 3,142 |
| PH educator | 2,230 | 3,448 |
| PH lab professional | 14,088 | 21,785 |
| PH nurse | 41,232 | 63,759 |
| PH nutritionist | 6,680 | 10,330 |
| PH pharmacist | 1,496 | 2,313 |
| PH physician | 6,008 | 9,290 |
| PH program specialist | 7,820 | 12,092 |
| PH veterinarian/animal cont spec | 2,037 | 3,150 |
| Public relations/public info | 563 | 871 |
| Other PH professional | 14,119 | 21,833 |
| Computer specialist | 4,326 | 6,210 |
| Environmental eng technician | 414 | 594 |
| En health technician | 501 | 719 |

*continues*

**Table 2–2** *continued*

| | | |
|---|---|---|
| HEALTH INFO SYSTEM/DATA ANALYST | 605 | 868 |
| Occ health and safety technician | 95 | 136 |
| PH laboratory technician | 5,700 | 8,182 |
| Other PH technician (LPN, etc.) | 26,953 | 38,690 |
| Community outreach/field worker | 676 | 902 |
| Other paraprofessional | 18,902 | 25,227 |

*Source:* Reported column adapted from Health Resources and Services Administration (HRSA), Bureau of Health Professions, National Center for Health Workforce Information and Analysis and Center for Health Policy, Columbia School of Nursing. *The Public Health Workforce Enumeration 2000.* Washington, DC: HRSA; 2000. Available at http://www. phppo.cdc.gov/owpp/docs/library/2000/Public%20Health%20Workforce%20Enumeration %202000.pdf. Accessed August 2005.

# PUBLIC HEALTH PRACTICE PROFILE

Individual workers, as well as occupational categories, produce work important to achieving public health goals and objectives. As noted in Chapter 1, key public health goals and objectives address preventing disease and injury, promoting healthy behaviors, protecting against health risks and threats, responding to emergencies, and assuring the quality of health services.[3] This overall public health practice framework provides the basis for channeling contributions both by individuals and organizations toward common goals. The specific work tasks of different occupations and individuals generally fall into one or more of the 10 essential public health services. Chapter 1 characterized the essential public health services as the means to achieving public health ends, or how the work of public health is accomplished. It is useful to view these functions and essential public health services as an aggregate job description for the entire public health workforce with the workload then divided among the many different professional and occupational categories composing the total public health workforce. In that light, each chapter will identify several purposes and essential public health services that form the core of the duties and job descriptions for each occupational category and public health career. A summary, in checklist format, appears in each chapter. Chapter 10 provides a composite profile by aggregating the profiles from Chapters 3 through 9. An example of this format is provided in Table 2–3.

**Table 2-3** Public Health Profile Example

| | (Example)<br>Public Health Practitioners<br>Make a Difference by: |
|---|:---:|
| **Public Health Purposes** | |
| Preventing epidemics and the spread of disease | ✔ |
| Protecting against environmental hazards | |
| Preventing injuries | ✔ |
| Promoting and encouraging healthy behaviors | ✔ |
| Responding to disasters and assisting communities in recovery | |
| Assuring the quality and accessibility of health services | |
| **Essential Public Health Services** | |
| Monitoring health status to identify community health problems | ✔ |
| Diagnosing and investigating health problems and health hazards in the community | ✔ |
| Informing, educating, and empowering people about health issues | ✔ |
| Mobilizing community partnerships to identify and solve health problems | |
| Developing policies and plans that support individual and community health efforts | |
| Enforcing laws and regulations that protect health and ensure safety | |
| Linking people with needed personal health services and assuring the provision of health care when otherwise unavailable | |
| Assuring a competent public health and personal health care workforce | |
| Evaluating effectiveness, accessibility, and quality of personal and population-based health services | ✔ |
| Researching new insights and innovative solutions to health problems | ✔ |

In this example, the public health occupational category is primarily involved in addressing three public health goals: preventing epidemics, preventing injuries, and promoting healthy behaviors. This public health occupational category works to address these goals largely through performing five essential public health services: monitoring health status, investigating health problems, educating people about health, evaluating effectiveness, and researching new solutions to health problems.

In this example, and in later chapters, the assignment of specific public health purposes and essential public health services may appear somewhat arbitrary. In each case, however, judgments are made as to which purposes and essential services are most closely associated with each occupational category. Some occupational categories may appear to have a relatively limited focus (such as public health laboratory workers) in comparison to others (such as public health nurses) which may have very broad roles that could conceivably cover all purposes and services. For each occupational category and title, however, the number of purposes and essential services identified for each occupational category is limited to no more than half the number possible (3 of 6 purposes, 5 of 10 essential public health services).

Characterizing the work of an occupational category in this manner proves a functional view of the work performed. It also facilitates an understanding of how the work of one occupational category relates to the work of another category, and how it relates to the overall work performed across all public health occupational categories (see Chapter 10).

## IMPORTANT AND ESSENTIAL DUTIES

The most important aspect of any job or career is what workers do day in and day out. It is those basic and routine duties that best define positions in public health or any other field of endeavor. This list varies enormously from one position to another and often from one level of the same position to a higher level (such as from an entry level environmental health specialist to a midlevel environmental health specialist). Important and essential duties for various titles within each chapter are based on information from a sampling of job and position descriptions from a variety of public health organizations. Each chapter also provides an example of a daily schedule for the occupational category addressed in that chapter.

## MINIMUM QUALIFICATIONS

Another key dimension of a position is a statement of the minimum qualifications necessary for that job. Often these minimum qualifications must be met in order for a worker to apply for a particular position. Minimum qualifications may emphasize experience or education or both. In any event, there is a battery of skills or competencies that are expected of those applying for and those working in public health positions. Minimum levels of knowledge, skills, and abilities are presented for public health job titles addressed in each chapter. Additional qualifications, such as physical capabilities appropriate for specific jobs or job locations, are also presented. These qualifications are synthesized from a sampling of current position descriptions.

The range of public health occupations and careers extends from those requiring considerable education and training to those that require relatively little. For example, some state and local health officials may hold several degrees such as a bachelor degree in science, a master's degree in public health, and a doctoral degree in medicine. At the same time, key staff performing investigations of communicable disease or environmental threats may have only an associate or bachelor's degree at the undergraduate level. It is not uncommon for some technical and clerical staff to have no more than a high school diploma with on-the-job training. As this book largely targets undergraduate and graduate-degree students, particular emphasis will be on occupations and careers requiring at least an undergraduate degree.

## WORKPLACE CONSIDERATIONS

Public health work takes place in many organizations and settings other than governmental public health agencies such as state health agencies or local public health departments. Many community and voluntary organizations collaborate with governmental public health agencies and employ staff whose work parallels that of workers in governmental public health agencies. This is true both for nongovernmental public health efforts here in the United States and those on the international level. Not much is known about public health workers and career opportunities in community and voluntary organizations. There is some information available for local, state, and federal public health agencies on measures such as numbers employed, occupational categories, work locations, salary, and specific duties. This book summarizes work setting information for each public health occupational category or career grouping.

Another important workplace consideration relates to special physical capabilities, travel requirements, and other unique aspects of specific jobs. For example, some positions may require the ability to lift and move items weighing up to 50 pounds. Other jobs may require the ability to walk great distances or to have normal vision or hearing. Others may require the ability to work outside in cold and inclement weather, or to work unusual hours.

## SALARY ESTIMATES

Detailed and specific salary information is not widely available. Information will be provided based on limited sources, including BLS data and current job postings. This information should not be considered to be definitive or completely accurate. Variations in salary scales are wide from agency to agency depending on a variety of circumstances and conditions. Figure 2–2 indicates that the average salary of a full-time worker employed by a state or local health agency increased by nearly 40% to nearly $42,000 between 1994 and 2004. One trend contributing to this increase is a higher proportion of workers in professional and technical occupational titles in 2003 than a decade earlier.

## CAREER PROSPECTS

Current and future opportunities for public health careers, as do careers in all fields, depend on relationships among the population, the labor force, and the demand for public health programs and services.[4] The size and composition of the population strongly influences both the size of the workforce and the types of services needed by the population.

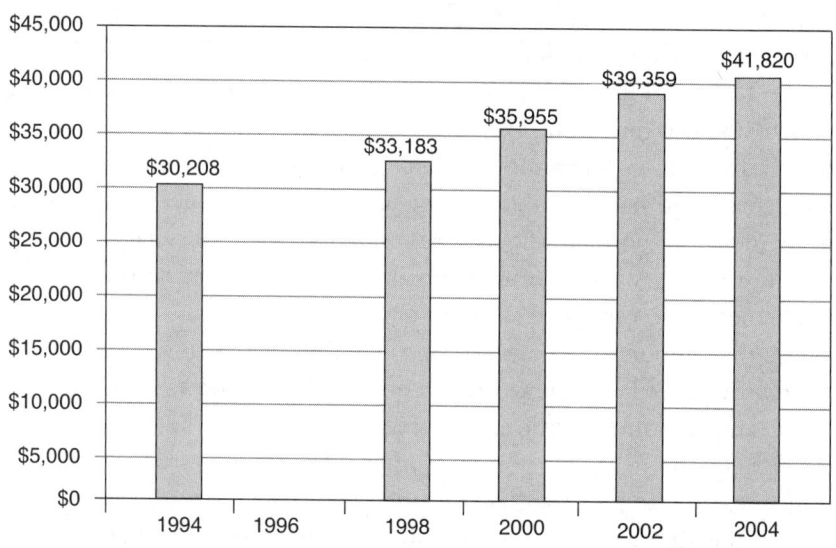

Due to changes in the data collection process, comparable data for 1996 are not available.
Source: Bureau of the Census. Federal, State, and Local Governments, Public Employment and Payroll Data. Available at http://www.census.gov/govs/www/apes.html. Accessed August 2005.

**FIGURE 2–2** Mean Salary for Full-Time Equivalent Workers of State and Local Health Agencies, 1994–2004, United States.

The U.S. population continues to increase, although at a slower rate than in recent decades. The average age of the population continues to increase as well, and the proportion of the population in the 55–64 year age category will increase more than 40% over the next 10 years. As this age group nears retirement, replacement of workers will create job opportunities and career advancement possibilities in addition to those created by the continued growth of the overall population.

Among the various sectors of the U.S. economy, the health sector is projected to grow faster and add more jobs than other sectors. About one in every four new jobs will be in the health sector. In the health sector, and in the overall economy, professional and related categories will exhibit the greatest growth and offer the greatest opportunities for new jobs and career advancement. In sum, the overall outlook for professional and technical occupations in public health is very bright for those now in or about to enter the job market.

The optimal number of public health workers is controversial and uncertain. There is widespread concern within the public health community that there will soon be a shortage of public health workers. Several key public health occupational categories are currently in short supply, such as public health nurses and epidemiologists. The information provided in this text will identify specific occupational categories that have been identified (rightly or wrongly) as being in greatest need.

Each chapter focuses on a specific public health occupation or career. But careers in public health, like those in many fields, are not always straightforward. Individual workers can begin in one career pathway and then move into another. For example, administrators of public health agencies could come up through the ranks of program and agency management or from one of the public health professional categories, such as environmental health, nursing, or health education. This section will identify some of these paths and career ladders for public health workers.

## ADDITIONAL INFORMATION

Only basic information is provided in the chapters that follow. Most public health occupational categories and careers, however, have excellent sources for more detailed information. Several sources, often professional associations or organizations, will be identified in each chapter. Career development opportunities through education, training, and credentialing are also provided for each public health workforce category.

## PUBLIC HEALTH ORGANIZATIONS AND AGENCIES[5]

### Federal Health Agencies

Three levels of government provide public health services in the United States: federal health agencies, state health agencies, and local public health agencies. Governmental public health agencies work with a myriad of other organizations and agencies to protect and promote health for specific populations. In addition to federal, state, and local public health agencies, other contributors include tribal health organizations, voluntary sector organizations focusing on health (such as the American Heart Association and the Red Cross), community health centers, hospitals, academic institutions, and many others. At the core of this complex public health system are the federal, state, and local public health agencies. Because many public health professionals are employed in the public sector, the characteristics of governmental public health agencies are important considerations for career planning.

The U.S. Public Health Service (PHS) within the U.S. Department of Health and Human Services (DHHS) serves as the focal point for public health concerns at the federal level with eight operating agencies and regional offices in 10 federal regions. In 2003 many emergency preparedness and response activities were moved out of DHHS into the newly established Department of Homeland Security. An Office of Public Health Emergency Preparedness and Response remained at DHHS to coordinate bioterrorism and other public health emergency activities managed by various PHS agencies. The eight PHS agencies, although only a small part of DHHS, address a wide range of public health activities, from research and training to primary care and health protection, as described in Table 2–4.

The organization of federal health responsibilities within DHHS is quite complex fiscally and operationally. In federal fiscal year 2004, the overall DHHS budget was about $500 billion.[6] DHHS has nearly 65,000 employees and is the largest grant-making agency in the federal government, with some 60,000 grants each year. DHHS manages more than

### Table 2–4  U.S. Public Health Service Agencies

| | |
|---|---|
| Health Resources and Services Administration (HRSA) | HRSA helps provide health resources for medically underserved populations. The main operating units of HRSA are the Bureau of Primary Health Care, Bureau of Health Professions, Maternal and Child Bureau, and the HIV/AIDS Bureau. A nationwide network of 643 community and migrant health centers and 144 primary care programs for the homeless and residents of public housing serve more than eight million Americans each year. HRSA also works to build the health care workforce and maintains the National Health Service Corps. The agency provides services to people with AIDS through the Ryan White Care Act programs. It oversees the organ transplantation system and works to decrease infant mortality and improve maternal and child health. HRSA was established in 1982 by bringing together several existing programs. HRSA has more than 1300 employees at its headquarters in Rockville, Maryland, and another 750 employees in 10 regional offices throughout the United States. |
| Indian Health Service (IHS) | The IHS is responsible for providing federal health services to American Indians and Alaska Natives. The provision of health services to members of federally recognized tribes grew out of the special government-to-government relationship between the federal government and Indian tribes. This relationship, established in 1787, is based on Article I, Section 8 of the Constitution, and has been given form and substance by numerous treaties, laws, Supreme Court decisions, and executive orders. The IHS is the principal federal health care provider and health advocate for the Indian population with the goal of raising their health status to the highest possible level. The IHS currently provides health services to approximately 1.5 million American Indians and Alaska Natives who belong to more than 557 federally recognized tribes in 35 states. IHS was established in 1924; its mission was transferred from the Interior Department in 1955. Agency headquarters are in Rockville, Maryland. |
| Centers for Disease Control and Prevention (CDC) | Working with states and other partners, CDC provides a system of health surveillance to monitor and prevent disease outbreaks, including bioterrorism events and threats, and maintains national health statistics. CDC also provides for immunization services, supports research into disease and injury prevention, guards against international disease transmission, and has personnel stationed in more than 25 foreign countries. CDC was established in 1946 with its headquarters in Atlanta, Georgia. CDC has 8500 employees. |
| National Institutes of Health (NIH) | Begun as a 1-room Laboratory of Hygiene in 1887, today the NIH is one of the world's foremost medical research centers and the federal focal point for health research. NIH is the steward of medical and behavioral research for the nation. Its mission is science in pursuit of fundamental knowledge about the nature and behavior of living systems and the application of that knowledge to extend healthy life and reduce the burdens of illness and disability. |

*continues*

**Table 2–4** *continued*

| | |
|---|---|
| | In realizing its goals, the NIH provides leadership and direction to programs designed to improve the health of the nation by conducting and supporting research: in the causes, diagnosis, prevention, and cure of human diseases; in the processes of human growth and development; in the biological effects of environmental contaminants; in the understanding of mental, addictive, and physical disorders; in directing programs for the collection, dissemination, and exchange of information in medicine and health, including the development and support of medical libraries and the training of medical librarians and other health information specialists. Though the majority of NIH resources sponsor external research, there is also a large in-house research program. NIH includes 27 separate health institutes and centers; its headquarters are in Bethesda, Maryland. NIH has more than 16,000 employees. |
| Food and Drug Administration (FDA) | FDA ensures that the food we eat is safe and wholesome, that the cosmetics we use won't harm us, and that medicines, medical devices, and radiation-transmitting products such as microwave ovens are safe and effective. FDA also oversees feed and drugs for pets and farm animals. Authorized by Congress to enforce the Federal Food, Drug, and Cosmetic Act and several other public health laws, the agency monitors the manufacture, import, transport, storage, and sale of $1 trillion worth of goods annually, at a cost to taxpayers of about $3 a person. FDA has more than 9000 employees located in 167 U.S. cities. Among its staff, FDA has chemists, microbiologists, and other scientists, as well as investigators and inspectors who visit 16,000 facilities a year as part of their oversight of the businesses that FDA regulates. FDA, established in 1906, has its headquarters in Rockville, Maryland. |
| Substance Abuse and Mental Health Services Administration (SAMHSA) | SAMHSA was established by Congress on October 1, 1992, to strengthen the nation's health care capacity to provide prevention, diagnosis, and treatment services for substance abuse and mental illnesses. SAMHSA works in partnership with states, communities, and private organizations to address the needs of people with substance abuse and mental illnesses as well as the community risk factors that contribute to these illnesses. SAMHSA serves as the umbrella under which substance abuse and mental health service centers are housed, including: the Center for Mental Health Services (CMHS), the Center for Substance Abuse Prevention (CSAP), and the Center for Substance Abuse Treatment (CSAT). SAMHSA also houses the Office of the Administrator, the Office of Applied Studies, and the Office of Program Services. In fiscal year 2000, SAMHSA's budget was approximately $2.6 billion. The agency employs approximately 550 staff members. SAMHSA headquarters are in Rockville, Maryland. |

*continues*

**Table 2–4** *continued*

| | |
|---|---|
| Agency for Toxic Substances and Disease Registry (ATSDR) | Working with states and other federal agencies, ATSDR seeks to prevent exposure to hazardous substances from waste sites. The agency conducts public health assessments, health studies, surveillance activities, and health education training in communities around waste sites on the U.S. Environmental Protection Agency's National Priorities List. ASTDR also has developed toxicological profiles of hazardous chemicals found at these sites. The agency is closely associated administratively with CDC; its headquarters are also in Atlanta, Georgia. ASTDR has more than 400 employees. |
| Agency for Health Care Research and Quality (AHRQ) | AHRQ supports cross-cutting research on health care systems, health care quality and cost issues, and effectiveness of medial treatments. The agency has about 300 employees: its headquarters are in Rockville, Maryland. Formerly know as the Agency for Health Care Policy and Research, AHRQ was established in 1989, assuming broadened responsibilities of its predecessor agency, the National Center for Health Services Research and Health Care Technology Assessment. |

300 programs through its 11 operating divisions. The major share of the DHHS budget supports the Medicare and Medicaid programs within the Centers for Medicare and Medicaid Services (CMS). PHS activities accounted for less than one tenth of the fiscal year 2004 DHHS budget. In addition to CMS and the PHS agencies, DHHS also includes the Administration for Children and Families and the Administration on Aging.

Budgets for PHS operating divisions in federal fiscal year 2004 ranged from $28 billion for NIH to $300 million for AHRQ. Sixty percent of all PHS funds support NIH research activities, and another $18 billion support the remaining PHS agencies with HRSA and CDC together accounting for about $10 billion, which represents about 2% of total DHHS resources and about 0.5% of all federal spending. Federal grants-in-aid have long been the prime strategy and mechanism by which the federal government influences the priorities and services of state and local governments.

Beyond DHHS, several other federal agencies have health-related responsibilities, including the federal Environmental Protection Agency (EPA) and the Departments of Homeland Security, Education, Agriculture, Defense, Transportation, and Veterans Affairs, to name just a few.

## *State Health Agencies*

Several factors place states at center stage when it comes to health. The U.S. Constitution gives states primacy in safeguarding the health of their citizens. States carry out their health responsibilities through many different state agencies, although the overall constellation of health programs and services within all of state government is similar across states. Somewhere in the maze of state agencies is an identifiable lead agency for health. In many states this is a free standing agency; in others, the state health agency is part of a larger multipurpose human service agency, often with the state's social services and substance abuse responsibilities. The range of responsibilities for the official state health agency varies considerably in terms of specific programs and services. Staffing levels and patterns also show a wide range, reflecting the diversity in agency responsibilities. Comprehensive information on the resources and programs of state health agencies has not been available since the early 1990s, due to the demise of a national reporting system coordinated by the Association of State and Territorial Health Officials (ASTHO) and the Public Health Foundation. The data presented on state health agencies in this chapter are derived from the most recent compilation available, which was collected as part of a salary survey of state health officials in 2002.[7]

Figure 2–3 illustrates the variability in state health agencies' responsibilities for programs. In 2002, for example, 90% of the official state health agencies administered the Supplemental Food Program for Women, Infants and Children (WIC), vital statistics systems, public health laboratories, and tobacco prevention and control programs. Less than half of the state health agencies administered the state Medicaid Program, mental health and substance abuse services, and handled the licensing of health professionals. Most state health agencies administered programs for environmental health services, most frequently involving food and drinking water safety. However, only 25% of the state health agencies served as the environmental regulatory agency within their state, which often includes responsibility for clean air, resource conservation, clean water, superfund sites, toxic substance control, and hazardous substances.

The organizational placement and specific responsibilities of state health agencies largely determine the size of their budgets and workforce. Of 51 state health agencies (including the District of Columbia), 26 have

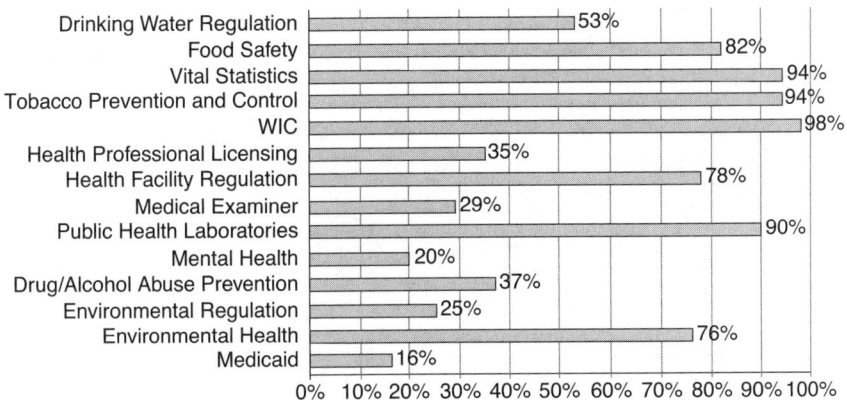

Source: Adapted from Association of State and Territorial Health Officials (ASTHO). *2002 Salary Survey of State and Territorial Health Officials*. Washington, DC: ASTHO; 2003.

**FIGURE 2–3** Selected Organizational Responsibilities of State Health Agencies, 2002.

1500 or fewer employees; these smaller agencies each have budgets averaging approximately $250 million. This group includes many free-standing agencies that have responsibility for traditional public health services but not for Medicaid, mental health, substance abuse, and environmental regulation. As these other responsibilities are added, the budgets and workforce of state health agencies increases substantially. Nine state health agencies have more than 4500 employees and average expenditures of almost $6 billion.

At the federal level, more than a dozen federal departments, agencies, and commissions (Transportation, Labor, Health and Human Services, Commerce, Energy, Defense, EPA, Homeland Security, Interior, Consumer Product Safety Commission, Agriculture, Nuclear Regulatory Commission, and Housing and Urban Development) have environmental health roles. State and local governments have largely replicated this web of environmental responsibility, creating a complex system often poorly understood by the private sector and general public. Federal statutes have driven the organization of state responsibilities. Key federal environmental statutes include:

- Clean Air Act (CAA)
- Clean Water Act (CWA)

- Comprehensive Environmental Response, Competition, and Liability Act (CERCLA) and Superfund Amendments and Reauthorization Act (SARA)
- Federal Insecticide, Fungicide, and Rodenticide Act (FIFRA)
- Resource Conservation and Recovery Act (RCRA)
- Safe Drinking Water Act (SDWA)
- Toxic Substance Control Act (TSCA)
- Food, Drug, and Cosmetic Act (FDCA)
- Federal Mine Safety and Health Act (MSHA)
- Occupational Safety and Health Act (OSHA)

States, however, have responded in no consistent manner in assigning implementation of federal statutes among various state agencies. The focus of federal statutes on specific environmental media (water, air, waste) has fostered the assignment of environmental responsibilities to state agencies other than official state health agencies. As a result, only a handful of states utilize their state health agency as the state's lead agency for environmental concerns. This role has shifted to state environmental agencies, although many other state agencies are also involved. Despite their diminished role in environmental concerns, state health agencies continue to address a very diverse set of environmental health issues and maintain epidemiologic and quantitative risk assessment capabilities not available in other state agencies.

The wide variation in organization and structure of state health responsibilities suggests that there is no standard or consistent pattern to public health practice among the various states. An examination of enabling statutes and state public agency mission statements provides further support for this conclusion. Only 11 of 43 state agency mission statements address the majority of the concepts related to public health purpose and mission in the *Public Health in America* document.[3,8] When state statutes enabling public health are examined for references to the essential public health services (also found in the *Public Health in America* document), the majority of the essential public health services can be identified in only one fifth of the states. The most frequently identified essential public health services reflect traditional public health activities, such as enforcement of laws, monitoring of health status, diagnosing and investigating health hazards, and informing and educating the public. The essential public health services least frequently referenced in these enabling statutes reflect more modern concepts of public health practice, including mobilizing community partnerships, evaluating the effects of health services, and research for innovative solutions. Only three states had both enabling statutes and state health agency mission statements highly congruent with the concepts advanced in the *Public Health in America* document.[8]

In sum, state health agencies face many challenges related to the fragmentation of public health roles and responsibilities among various state agencies. Central to these are two related challenges: how to coordinate public health's core functions and essential services effectively and how to leverage changes within the health system to instill greater emphasis on clinical prevention and population-based services.

## Local Public Health Agencies

In the overall structuring of governmental public health responsibilities, local public health agencies (LPHAs) are where the "rubber meets the road." These agencies are established to carry out the critical public health responsibilities embodied in state laws and local ordinances and to meet other needs and expectations of their communities. Although some cities had local public health boards and agencies prior to 1900, the first county health department was not established until 1911. At that time, Yakima County, Washington, created a permanent county health unit, based on the success of a county sanitation campaign to control a serious typhoid epidemic. The Rockefeller Sanitary Commission, through its support for county hookworm eradication efforts, also stimulated the development of county-based LPHAs. The number of LPHAs grew rapidly during the 1900s, although in recent decades, expansion has been tempered by closures and consolidations.

LPHAs should not be considered separately from the state network in which they operate. It is important to remember that states, through their state legislative and executive branches, establish the types and powers of local governmental units that can exist in that state. In this arrangement, the state and its local subunits, however defined, share responsibilities for health and other state functions. How health duties are shared in any given state depends on a complex set of factors that include state and local statutes, history, need, and expectations.

Local health agencies relate to their state public health systems in one of three general patterns.[9] In most states, LPHAs are formed and managed by local government, reporting directly to some office of local government, such as a local board of health, county commission, or city or county executive officer. In this decentralized arrangement, LPHAs often have considerable autonomy although they may be required to carry out specific state public health statues. Also, there are some states that share oversight of LPHAs with local government through the power to appoint local health officers or to approve an annual budget. In some states with decentralized LPHAs, some areas of the state lack coverage because the local government chooses not to form a local health agency, and the state must provide services in those uncovered areas. This mixed arrangement occurs in about 20% of the states. Another 30% of the states use a more centralized approach in which local health agencies are directly operated by the state, or there are no LPHAs and the state provides local health services.

Counties represent the most common form of subdividing states. In general, counties are geopolitical subunits of states that carry out various state responsibilities, such as law enforcement (sheriffs and state's attorneys) and public health. Counties largely function as agents of the state and carry out responsibilities delegated or assigned to them. In contrast, cities are generally not established as agents of the state. Instead, they have considerable discretion through home rule powers to take on functions that are not prohibited to them by state law. Cities can choose to have a health department or to rely on the state or their county for public health services. City health departments often have a wider array of programs and services because of this autonomy. As described previously, the earliest public health agencies developed in large urban centers, prior to the development of either state health agencies or county-based LPHAs. This status also contributes to their sense of autonomy. These considerations, as well as the increased demands and expectations to meet the needs of those who lack adequate health insurance, have made many city-based, especially big city-based, LPHAs qualitatively different from other LPHAs.

Both cities and counties have resource and political bases. Both rely heavily on property and sales taxes to finance health and other services, and both are struggling with the limitations of these funding sources. Political concerns over increasing property taxes are the major limitation for both. Relatively few counties and cities have imposed income taxes, the form of taxation relied upon by federal and state governments. However, both generally have strong political bases, although cities are generally more likely than counties to be at odds with state government on key issues.

NACCHO tracks public health activities of LPHAs; the most recent survey of LPHAs took place in 2005 with results to be available in 2006.[10,11] One limitation of information on LPHAs is that there is neither a clear nor a functional definition of what constitutes an LPHA. The most widely used definitions call for an administrative and service unit of local government, concerned with health, employing at least one full-time person, and carrying responsibility for health of a jurisdiction smaller than the state. By this definition, more than 3200 local health agencies operate in 3042 U.S. counties.[10] The number of local public health agencies varies widely from state to state; Rhode Island has none, whereas neighboring Connecticut and Massachusetts report more than 100 LPHAs.

Sixty percent of LPHAs are single-county health agencies, and about 75% operate out of a county base (single county, multicounty, or city-county).[11] Other LPHAs function at the city, town, or township levels; some state-operated units also serve local jurisdictions. Although the precise number is uncertain, it appears that the number has been increasing, from about 1300 in 1947 to about 2000 in the mid-1970s to somewhere over 3000 today.

Most LPHAs are relatively small organizations; more than two thirds (69%) serve populations of 50,000 or less, whereas less than one in five (18%) serves a population of 100,000 or more. Only 4% of LPHAs serve populations of 500,000 or more residents.[11]

Some states set qualifications for local health officers or require medical supervision when the administrator is not a physician. About four fifths of LPHAs employ a full-time health officer. Health officers have a mean tenure of about eight years and a median tenure of about six years. Approximately one half of all local health officers are physicians, about 15% are physicians with formal training in public health, and less than one fourth have graduate degrees in public health. LPHAs serving larger populations are more likely to have full-time health officers than are smaller LPHAs.

Similar to the situation with state health agencies, data on LPHA expenditures lack currency and completeness. Annual LPHA expenditures in 1999 ranged from zero to over $836 million. One half of LPHAs had budgets of $621,000 or less, and 25% had budgets over $2,250,000. Total expenditures increase with size of population. LPHAs located in metropolitan areas had substantially higher expenditures than their non-metropolitan-area counterparts.

In 1999, LPHAs derived their funding from the following sources: local funds (44%), the state (30%, including federal funds passing through the state), direct federal funds (3%), fees and reimbursements (19%), and other sources (4%). Metropolitan LPHAs and those serving smaller populations are more dependent on local sources of funding, but LPHAs in nonmetropolitan areas and those serving larger populations depend more on state sources.

The number of full-time equivalent employees also increases with the size of the population served. Only 10% of LPHAs employ 125 or more persons, and 50% have 17 or fewer employees. The number of employees and the number of different disciplines and professions are related to LPHA population size. Clerical staff, nurses, sanitarians, physicians, and nutritionists are the most common disciplines (in that order) and are all found in more than one half of all LPHAs.

There is considerable variety in the services provided by LPHAs. Top priority areas for LPHAs overall are communicable disease control, environmental health, and child health. LPHAs serving both large and small populations report similar priorities, although community outreach replaces environmental health as a top priority for the largest local health jurisdictions (those over 500,000 population). Slight differences in priorities are also apparent between metropolitan and nonmetropolitan-area LPHAs. LPHAs in metropolitan areas often include inspections as a high priority, but nonmetropolitan LPHAs are more likely to include family planning and home health care services as priorities.

Many LPHAs provide a common core battery of services that generally includes adult and childhood immunizations, communicable disease control, community assessment, community outreach and education, environmental health services, epidemiology and surveillance programs, food safety and restaurant inspections, health education, and tuberculosis testing (see Table 2–5). Less commonly, LPHAs provide services related to

---

**Table 2–5** Percent of Local Health Departments Directly Providing, Contributing Resources to, or Contracting for Public Health Programs and Services in the Community

| Prevent Epidemics and Spread of Disease | | Protects Against Environmental Hazards | |
|---|---|---|---|
| Communicable disease control | 94% | Indoor air quality | 44% |
| HIV/AIDS testing/counseling | 64% | Food safety | 85% |

*continues*

**Table 2–5** *continued*

| Prevent Epidemics and Spread of Disease | | Protects Against Environmental Hazards | |
|---|---|---|---|
| STD testing/counseling | 65% | Restaurant inspections | 80% |
| Tuberculosis testing | 88% | Lead screening and abatement | 74% |
| Childhood immunizations | 89% | Sewage disposal | 74% |
| EPSDT | 59% | Private water supplies | 72% |
| Influenza immunizations | 91% | Vector | 61% |
| Hepatitis B immunizations | 86% | Laboratory services | 45% |
| Cancer screening | 58% | Solid waste management* | 55% |
| Diabetes screening | 57% | Public water supplies* | 63% |
| High blood pressure screening | 81% | | |

| Prevents Injuries | | Promotes and Encourages Healthy Behaviors | |
|---|---|---|---|
| Occupational health and safety | 19% | Health education/risk reduction | 87% |
| Injury control | 37% | Tobacco prevention | 68% |
| | | Cardiovascular screening | 50% |
| | | WIC | 67% |
| | | School health | 46% |
| | | Dental health | 30% |
| | | Violence prevention | 22% |

| Responds to Disasters/Assists Recovery | | Assures Quality and Accessibility of Services | |
|---|---|---|---|
| Environmental emergencies | 61% | Linkage to needed care | 77% |
| Hazardous substances* | 57% | Primary care | 18% |
| Behavioral and mental health* | 26% | Prenatal care | 41% |
| | | Maternal health | 70% |
| | | Obstetrical care* | 31% |
| **Cross-cutting** | | Family planning | 58% |
| Community assessment | 79% | Case management | 67% |
| Community outreach and education | 90% | Health facilities licensing | 38% |
| | | Home health services | 36% |
| Epidemiology and surveillance | 84% | HIV treatment | 25% |
| | | Substance abuse* | 26% |
| | | School-based clinics* | 33% |
| | | TB treatment | 71% |
| | | Homeless health services | 10% |

*Source:* National Association of County and City Health Officials, Local Public Health Agency Infrastructure: A Chartbook. Washington, DC: NACCHO; 2001; except for * data, which is from National Association of County and City Health Officials. Profile of Local Health Departments 1996–1997 Dataset. Washington, DC: NACCHO; 1997.

primary care and chronic disease, including: cardiovascular disease, diabetes, and glaucoma screening; behavioral and mental health services; programs for the homeless; substance abuse services; and veterinary public health.[11]

LPHAs do not always provide these services themselves; increasingly, they contract for these services or contribute resources to other agencies or organizations in the community. Community partners for LPHAs include state health agencies, other LPHAs, hospitals, other units of government, nonprofit and voluntary organizations, academic institutions, community health centers, the faith community, and insurance companies. LPHAs increasingly interact with managed care organizations, although most do not have either formal or informal agreements governing these interactions.[9] Where agreements existed, they were more likely to be formal, to cover clinical and case management services, and to involve the provision (rather than the purchase) of services. More than one fourth of LPHAs had formal agreements for clinical services for Medicaid clients in 1996.

## Nongovernmental Organizations

This book focuses on public health workers employed in organizations whose primary mission tracks with improving health outcomes and quality of life for specific populations. Governmental public health agencies fit these criteria, for sure. But many other nongovernmental organizations and agencies also carry out this work and hire workers in occupational categories and titles similar to those used by governmental public health agencies. The list of nongovernmental organizations involved with public health efforts is a long one. It includes organizations such as the American Lung Association, American Cancer Society, American Heart Association, American Diabetes Association, the Red Cross, and all their state and local affiliates. It includes organizations such as home health agencies, migrant and community health centers, behavioral and mental health programs, teen pregnancy prevention and adolescent parent support services, and the many service and outreach efforts of educational institutions at all levels. It also includes the many international health and relief agencies, and many Peace Corps placements. The range of sites and services and opportunities is vast and cannot be adequately described here. The work done, however, and the occupational categories and titles used often parallel those used by governmental public health agencies.

## CONCLUSION

This chapter describes the framework that will be used in later chapters to examine various public health occupations and career pathways and key aspects of the agencies that employ most public health workers. For public health occupations and careers, key characteristics include occupational classification, public health roles, important and essential duties, minimum qualifications, workplace considerations, salary estimates, career prospects, and sources for additional information. For public health organizations, important features include governmental level, range of responsibilities, organizational structure, level and sources of funding, and relationships with nongovernmental organizations.

## REFERENCES

1. Bureau of Labor Statistics, U.S. Department of Labor, May 2004 National, State, and Metropolitan Area Occupational Employment and Wage Estimates. Available at http://www.bls.gov/oes/current/oes_nat.htm. Accessed August 2005.
2. Health Resources and Services Administration (HRSA), Bureau of Health Professions, National Center for Health Workforce Information and Analysis and Center for Health Policy, Columbia School of Nursing. *The Public Health Workforce Enumeration 2000.* Washington, DC: HRSA; 2000. Available at http://www.phppo.cdc.gov/owpp/docs/library/2000/Public%20Health%20 Workforce%20Enumeration%202000.pdf. Accessed August 2005.
3. Essential Public Health Services Working Group, Core Public Health Functions Steering Committee, U.S. Department of Health and Human Services. Public Health in America. Available at http://www.health.gov/phfunctions/public.htm. Accessed August 2005.
4. Bureau of Labor Statistics, U.S. Department of Labor. Occupational Outlook Handbook, 2004–2005 Edition. Available at http://www.bls.gov/oco/. Accessed August 2005.
5. Turnock BJ. *Public Health: What It Is and How It Works.* 3rd ed. Sudbury, MA: Jones and Bartlett; 2004. (Note: The section "Public Health Organizations and Agencies" is adapted from this text.)
6. U.S. Department of Health and Human Services (DHHS). *The Fiscal Year 2004 Budget.* Washington, DC: DHHS; 2003.
7. Association of State and Territorial Health Officials. *2002 Salary Survey of State and Territorial Health Officials.* Washington, DC: ASTHO; 2003.
8. Gebbie KM. State public health laws: An expression of constituency expectations. *J Public Health Manage Pract.* 2000;6(2):46–54.

9. Pickett G, Hanlon J. *Public Health Administration and Practice.* 9th ed. St. Louis, MO: Mosby; 1990.

10. National Association of County and City Health Officials. *Profile of Local Health Departments 1996–1997 Dataset.* Washington, DC: NACCHO; 1997.

11. National Association of County and City Health Officials. *Local Public Health Agency Infrastructure: A Chartbook.* Washington, DC: NACCHO; 2001.

# CHAPTER 3

# Public Health Administration

Public health organizations require leaders, managers, and administrators at various levels throughout the organization to plan, organize, direct, control, and coordinate health services, education, or policy. The people serving in these positions come from a wide variety of educational, professional, and work experience backgrounds. Many lack formal training and previous experience in public health. Nonetheless, they are the third largest occupational category within the public health workforce, behind environmental health professionals and public health nurses, and they represent a force even larger than their numbers. Table 3–1 provides a snapshot of an average day in the life of a public health administrator.

## OCCUPATIONAL CLASSIFICATION

There is no standard occupational category specific to public health administrators and managers. There is a more generic standard occupational category *health services administrator* that encompasses administrative positions in any health care or health services organization. This standard occupational category is one of the administrative occupations within the white collar grouping of occupations.

Public health administrators are health services administrators leading a public health agency, program, or major subunit. Public health administrators plan, analyze, organize, direct, coordinate, and evaluate the use of resources to deliver health services, education, or policy; they often manage or regulate health agencies and facilities. The category includes such job titles as director, administrator, chief, manager, or one of the many titles indicating chief public health official of a jurisdiction (e.g., secretary

**Table 3–1**  A Typical Day for a Public Health Administrator

| | |
|---|---|
| 7:30 a.m. | Breakfast with local hospital administrator and staff regarding diabetes screening |
| 8:30 a.m. | In office, follow-up call with state epidemiologist regarding recent outbreak of foodborne illness |
| 9:00 a.m. | Weekly meeting with senior staff |
| 10:15 a.m. | Meet with epidemiology, health education, and planning staff regarding completion of community needs assessment |
| 10:45 a.m. | Meet with county commissioner regarding West Nile virus concerns in her area |
| 11:15 a.m. | Review and update electronic slide presentation for today's lunch meeting |
| 11:45 a.m. | Meet with local Chamber of Commerce leadership before lunch, which includes public health presentation to business community |
| 1:00 p.m. | Discuss budget amendment proposal with fiscal and program staff |
| 1:30 p.m. | Media interview regarding West Nile virus concerns |
| 2:00 p.m. | Give welcoming remarks and overview for new employee orientation |
| 3:00 p.m. | Conference call for committee of National Association County and City Health Officials task force on workforce and leadership development |
| 4:00 p.m. | Review information suggested by senior staff for presentation to board of health |
| 4:30 p.m. | Drop by the clinic to see how things went today |
| 5:15 p.m. | Prepare remarks for board of health meeting |
| 7:00 p.m. | Attend monthly meeting of board of health |

of health, health officer, health commissioner, health official). Titles that include the term *coordinating* or *senior* are generally not classified as public health administrators but are included with the profession referenced (e.g., coordinating nutritionist with public health nutritionist, senior public health nurse with public health nurse).

Data from the Bureau of Labor Statistics indicate there are 225,000 health services administrators in the United States.[1] There were 25,000 working for federal, state, and local public health agencies in 2004. The *Public Health Workforce Enumeration 2000* identified 21,000 working in governmental public health agencies.[2] Data from these two sources are used throughout this chapter.

In addition to public health administrators and managers, there are several occupational classifications involved with public health administration. These include administrative business professionals and administrative support staff.

Administrative business professionals are trained at a professional level in their field of expertise prior to entry in public health and perform work in business, finance, auditing, management, and accounting. The *Public Health Workforce Enumeration 2000* identified 7500 administrative business professionals working in governmental public health agencies. Administrative business staff, including bookkeepers, accounting clerks, and auditing clerks, performs support work in areas of business and financial operations. In addition, there are another 80,000 administrative support workers (such as receptionists, typists, and stenographers) who perform nontechnical support work in all areas of agency management and program administration. Administrative business professionals and administrative support staff titles fall within the administrative chain of command of an agency but are not classified within the public health administrator category. Nonetheless, these titles can serve as steps along the career development path leading to a public health administrator position.

## PUBLIC HEALTH PRACTICE PROFILE

Public health administrators work at a level within an organization that often bears responsibility for achieving organizational goals and objectives. This means they may be involved with addressing any or all six public health responsibilities although their background and experience may provide greater expertise in some of these roles than others. For example, administrators of local public health agencies who worked their way to the top of the organization through the ranks of environmental health may continue to be directly involved in protecting against environmental hazards or responding to disasters. An administrator from the ranks of the nursing staff may remain more directly involved in disease prevention and quality assurance of health services. For most public health administrators, managing responses to public health emergencies and assuring the quality of health services require their personal attention. If these administrators also have professional training in epidemiology, disease and injury prevention, environmental health, or health education, they may be directly involved in these duties as well. Otherwise, the professional and program staff of the organization guide activities for these roles.

Similarly, among the 10 essential public health services, administrators may have more personal expertise in some services than others. There are several essential public health services, however, that all administrators must address. These include developing and mobilizing collaborative relationships and partnerships within the community, developing policies and plans, enforcing laws and regulations, assuring a competent workforce, and evaluating the effectiveness, accessibility, and quality of health services. Table 3–2 summarizes public health purposes and essential public health services at the core of positions for public health administrators.

## IMPORTANT AND ESSENTIAL DUTIES

There are many possible job titles and positions for public health administrators. The focus in this chapter will be on three positions: (1) health services manager; (2) local public health agency director; and (3) health

**Table 3–2**  Public Health Practice Profile for Public Health Administration

Public Health Administrators
Make a Difference by:

| | |
|---|---|
| **Public Health Purposes** | ✔ |
| Preventing epidemics and the spread of disease | |
| Protecting against environmental hazards | |
| Preventing injuries | |
| Promoting and encouraging healthy behaviors | |
| Responding to disasters and assisting communities in recovery | ✔ |
| Assuring the quality and accessibility of health services | ✔ |
| **Essential Public Health Services** | |
| Monitoring health status to identify community health problems | |
| Diagnosing and investigating health problems and health hazards in the community | |
| Informing, educating, and empowering people about health issues | |
| Mobilizing community partnerships to identify and solve health problems | |
| Developing policies and plans that support individual and community health efforts | ✔ |
| Enforcing laws and regulations that protect health and ensure safety | ✔ |
| Linking people with needed personal health services and assuring the provision of health care when otherwise unavailable | |
| Assuring a competent public health and personal health care workforce | |
| Evaluating effectiveness, accessibility, and quality of personal and population-based health services | ✔ |
| Researching new insights and innovative solutions to health problems | |

officer. Each of these positions and a representative panel of their important and essential duties are described in this section.

## *Health Services Manager*

This is an administrative and management position that directs, plans, analyzes, and coordinates health, public health, and regulatory programs and services. A worker in this or a similar title (such as health administrator) is often responsible for directing or assisting in the overall planning, directing, and coordinating of assigned health, public health, and regulatory programs and services, including the identification of program priorities and the development and implementation of new programs and services. This position could be located at a variety of managerial levels. Responsibilities may be in areas such as chronic disease prevention; environmental health and communicable disease prevention; health standards and licensure; maternal, child and family health; nutritional health and services; health information; regulation; senior services; health improvement; emergency response; or closely related areas. Positions have program management and decision-making authority, and usually have policy, assessment, planning, budget, and supervisory responsibilities. Direction is received from a designated administrative superior who reviews work through conferences, reports, and evaluation of operational results. The health services manager, however, is expected to exercise considerable initiative and judgment in planning and carrying out assignments.

Important and essential duties for health services managers may include:

- Directs or assists in the overall planning, development, and administration of assigned health, public health, and regulatory programs and services in such areas as chronic disease prevention; maternal, child and family health; environmental health and communicable disease prevention; nutritional health and services; health standards and licensure; health information; regulations; health improvement; or emergency response
- Develops and coordinates comprehensive public health systems for a specific geographic area, such as a county, city, or district
- Provides consultation to doctors, health care providers, hospitals, local health departments, and other agencies linked with health care in the effective delivery of health, public health, and regulatory programs and services

- Ensures individuals receive program services appropriate to their needs and program eligibility
- Oversees or assists in the development of community-based coalitions and works with coalitions, advocacy groups, and others interested in program issues to develop plans and outcomes on how to address specific health, public health regulatory, and senior programs and services concerns
- Prepares new or revises existing legislation and develops standards, regulations, and policies to implement the legislation
- Directs or assists administrative personnel in general management aspects of policy development and program planning and coordination as related to assigned responsibilities; assists in the evaluation of the effect of policy and organizational changes and new programs
- Reviews and revises programs in area of responsibility to ensure compliance of operations with laws, regulations, policies, plans, and procedures
- Supervises staff to carry out the strategies of the organization or program
- Participates in meetings with agency administrators to develop, coordinate, implement, and interpret new or revised initiatives
- Participates in conferences and meetings relating to areas of assigned responsibility
- Participates in the development of budget requests and the monitoring of expenditures according to budget allocations and appropriations
- Conducts research, institutes special studies, and prepares or reviews reports and related information to evaluate existing organizations, policies, procedures, and practices as related to the assigned program
- Maintains contact, cooperates with, and addresses local and community organizations and other interested groups pertaining to the assigned programs

## *Local Public Health Agency Director*

Under administrative direction, a local public health agency director plans, organizes, directs, manages, and supervises public health programs for the jurisdiction; directs the enforcement of federal, state, and local health laws and regulations; directs staff providing public health and education programs; represents agency activities, programs, and services with community organizations and other governmental agencies; performs special assignments as directed; and provides administrative support for its governing bodies (such as a board of health or a city or county board of supervisors). Local public health agency directors often serve as department head with general responsibility for the administration of the jurisdiction's public health programs and functions and may serve as the health officer for the jurisdiction. Many of the nonmedical duties of health officers are also performed by local public health agency directors. This position may report to a municipal or county board of health or board of supervisors (or perhaps a city council) through the municipal or county administrative officer or chief elected official. As agency head, this position often directly supervises positions such as director of nursing, fiscal officer, director of environmental health, director of health education, and sometimes a medical health officer.

Important and essential duties for local public health agency directors may include:

- Plans, organizes, directs, coordinates, and administers public health programs for the jurisdiction, such as communicable disease control, immunization, environmental health, health education, maternal and child health, vital statistics, and health programs for adults, children, handicapped children, and schools
- Enforces public health laws and regulations within the jurisdiction
- Develops and recommends agency goals, objectives, and policies
- Provides strategic direction and leadership in identifying community health needs and developing and implementing community health improvement plans that meet identified needs
- Prepares and administers agency budgets recommended by the jurisdiction's executive officer and approved by the governing board or entity
- Controls fiscal expenditures and revenues
- Monitors and evaluates overall agency and program performance and directs change to improve quality and effectiveness
- Hires, supervises, evaluates, and ensures proper training of agency staff in accordance with personnel rules
- Administers a variety of categorical programs
- Provides direction and develops policies for clinical services through protocol development

- Develops policies and protocols for the control and prevention of communicable diseases
- Plans and develops new program efforts
- Develops and administers grants
- Initiates appropriate epidemiological investigations of communicable disease outbreaks
- Provides health information to the public, community organizations, and other county staff
- Maintains contact with the press and community organizations
- Interprets policies and regulations for the public
- Supervises administration, program development, fiscal management, and provision of direct client services at agency clinic sites
- Represents the agency with other government agencies

### Health Officer

Health officers, often physicians, plan, organize, direct, and provide medical oversight over public health programs for the jurisdiction; provide technical consultation to citizens, public officials, staff, and community organizations and agencies on public health and preventive medicine issues; and serve as the designated health officer. A health officer provides medical supervision for the local public health agency by coordinating public health care services with external agencies and health care providers and providing ongoing communication with the local medical community. This position is also responsible for providing medical oversight and enforcement of public health regulations for a variety of public health programs and services including environmental health, vital records, communicable disease control, public health nursing, emergency and disaster medical planning, public health education, and state maternal and child health services. This title is distinguished from the local public health director in that the latter has overall management responsibility for the local public health agency's programs and services, whereas the health officer directs the medical oversight for all public health programs. In some instances, the health officer also serves as local public health director; in others, this position reports to the public health director or to the director of a higher-level health and human services agency. Some states (about half) require the health officer to be a licensed physician; the other half allow nonphysicians to act as health officers or set no requirements. Health officers often supervise titles such as the director of public health nursing, the director of environmental health, director of health education, and other professional and program directors.

Important and essential duties for health officers may include:

- Plans, organizes, directs, and evaluates the medical oversight of public health programs
- Assures enforcement of applicable public health, environmental health, and sanitation orders, ordinances, and statutes
- Analyzes legislative changes; evaluates and develops medical and public health policies, programs, and procedures; and formulates improvements
- Serves as an advocate to promote statewide public health policies, which also benefit the local jurisdiction
- Disseminates and interprets policies, laws, regulations, and state and federal directives regarding medical and public health issues to physicians, department staff, and representatives of hospitals, nursing homes, medical clinics, and schools by written means and personal contacts; acts as medical epidemiologist for public health diseases
- Consults and coordinates with federal and state officials and representatives of local public and private health agencies in the enforcement of health laws and the development of programs to meet public health needs
- Plans, organizes, directs, coordinates, and administers public health programs for the jurisdiction, such as communicable disease control, immunization, environmental health, health education, maternal and child health, vital statistics, and programs for adults, children, handicapped children, and schools
- Provides direction and advice regarding policies and procedures directed by the state immunization board
- Works closely with the agency director and health services managers to monitor performance and effect changes in practice to improve quality of services
- Confers with members of the public and representatives of federal, state, and local agencies regarding health department programs; cooperates with federal and state public health groups in the enforcement of health and sanitary matters
- Supervises, directs, and evaluates assigned staff, to include assigning work, handling employee concerns and problems, and counseling

- Reviews technical requirements, reports, and procedures generated by the health department
- Prepares public health information materials and news releases
- Consults with physicians, nurses, patients, staff members, other governmental agencies, or other individuals in the diagnosis of, and investigation of, cases of suspected communicable diseases and exchanges information or provides recommendations; takes measures to prevent and control epidemics
- Serves on emergency medical services and public health emergency preparedness committees
- Represents the jurisdiction on committees, boards, at meetings, or otherwise as assigned

## MINIMUM QUALIFICATIONS

Public health administrators can emerge from either a professional occupational category or from a career in other management positions. Those arising from the professional ranks may acquire management skills either as part of their education, such as in a master's degree program (such as a master's of public health, master's of public administration, master's of health administration, or master's of business administration degree) or, less commonly, in a doctoral degree program. Schools of public health commonly offer the doctor of public health (DrPH) degree for high-level public health practitioners. PhD and ScD degrees in public health sciences and disciplines are also offered by many institutions.

More commonly, however, public health administrators and managers lack formal training at the master's or doctoral level in public health. For example, only one in five chief administrators of local public health agencies reported formal training in public health in the mid-1990s. This includes administrators whose public health training was in their primary profession (such as nursing, environmental health, medicine, or health education) suggesting that few received public health training in programs preparing administrators. Many public health administrators acquire public health practice management skills on a nondegree basis through a variety of means including management academies and leadership development institutes. Nearly 20 states have developed such institutes for workers in their own and collaborating states. There are also several national public health leadership institutes and a national public health management academy.

Public health administrators represent a significant portion of the public health workforce for which career pathways are particularly unclear. Efforts to establish a greater professional identity for public health administrators are receiving increased attention. Management and leadership development programs are one example. Credentialing of public health administrators is another option under consideration. Several states license public health administrators, and one program credentials public health administrators through an independent review board. Some public health administrators view degrees from programs accredited by the Accrediting Commission on Education for Health Services Administration (ACHESA) or subsequent recognition from the American College of Healthcare Executives as meaningful credentials.

To be considered as qualified for a position as a public health administrator, both experience and education are important. Typical minimum qualifications for health services managers, local public health administrators, and health officers are detailed in the next section.

## *Typical Minimum Qualifications for Health Services Manager*

### Knowledge, Skills, and Abilities

A health services manager will generally have knowledge of:

- Principles and practices involved in the administration of health, public health, and regulatory programs and services
- The organization and operation of public agencies at the national, state, and local levels that are involved in health, public health, and regulatory programs and services
- The philosophy and objectives of state health and public health regulatory programs and services
- Programs and objectives of state and local public health agencies and of the interprofessional relationships in the implementation of their programs
- Current human service issues and theories
- The organization and functions of advocacy groups, voluntary agencies, civic organizations, and similar groups interested in health, public health, and regulatory programs and services and activities

- Managerial techniques and administrative practices

A health services manager will generally have the skills and ability to:

- Plan, promote, and direct complex public health programs or services at the state level.
- Analyze complex health data and formulate plans for coordinating and establishing new or improved health services and programs.
- Secure active cooperation from other public and private agencies in developing and guiding health, public health, regulatory, and senior programs and services.
- Develop, implement, and administer assigned programs or services to achieve positive program and client outcomes.
- Establish and maintain working relationships with departmental officials, legislators, staff associates, the general public, and others.
- Analyze and evaluate policies and operations and formulate recommendations.
- Communicate effectively.
- Provide leadership and supervision to professional, technical, and related program staff.
- Manage change, provide program management, and achieve results.
- Develop short- and long-range plans that meet established objectives and contribute to the overall goals and mission of the agency.

### Experience and Education

In many personnel systems, any combination of training and experience that provides the required knowledge and abilities qualifies an individual for this position. A typical career pathway for health services managers is through three or more years of professional experience in public health, health care delivery, environmental health or regulation, protective services for adults or the disabled, in-home services, or long-term care. In addition, a qualified applicant would have graduated from an accredited four-year college or university with specialization in public health; health care administration; public, personnel, or business administration; biological, physical, environmental, or social sciences; nursing; nutrition/dietetics; social work; human services; gerontology; physical rehabilitation; education; or closely related areas. Graduate work in specified educational areas may sometimes be substituted on a year-for-year basis for one or more years of the required experience. Additional qualifying experience in the specified areas may be substituted on a year-for-year basis for any deficiencies in the stated education.

## Typical Minimum Qualifications for Local Public Health Agency Director

### Knowledge, Skills, and Abilities

The local public health agency director generally has knowledge of:

- Basic principles of medical science and their application to local public health programs
- Public health problems and issues and their relationship to the development and operations of public health programs and services
- Federal, state, and local laws, ordinances, and regulations applicable to public health programs and communicable disease control
- Clinical skills and procedures
- Grant development and administration
- Principles, techniques, and practices of business and public health administration
- Budget development and expenditure control
- Principles and techniques of effective employee supervision, training, and development
- Public personnel management

The local public health agency director generally has the skills and ability to:

- Plan, organize, supervise, and administer the functions and programs of the local public health agency.
- Ensure proper enforcement of public health statues, laws, and regulations.
- Provide direction, supervision, and training for agency staff.
- Develop and administer budgets and control expenditures.
- Develop and administer grants.
- Review the work of agency staff and resolve problems.
- Oversee the development, maintenance, and preparation of public health statistics, medical records, and reports.
- Direct the preparation of and prepare clear, concise reports.
- Effectively represent the local public health agency in contact with the public, community organizations, and other government agencies.

- Establish and maintain cooperative working relationships.
- Coordinate assigned activities with community organizations and other government agencies.

### Experience and Education

Any combination of training and experience that provides the required knowledge and abilities can qualify an individual for this position. A typical way to obtain the required knowledge and abilities is through broad and extensive experience in the development, analysis, and administration of public health programs and services with three years of the background and experience in a management or full supervisory capacity. Ideally this experience includes work in the areas of fiscal management, personnel management, and program development. In addition, a master's degree in public health, public administration, or health care administration is highly desirable.

## *Typical Minimum Qualifications for Health Officer*

### Knowledge, Skills, and Abilities

The health officer generally has knowledge of:

- Principles, practices, and responsibilities of medicine and of contemporary public health programs and service needs
- Applicable federal and state laws and regulations
- Organization, purpose, and function of federal and state health agencies
- Local medical associations and community health groups
- Principles and methods of public and community relations, and public information practices and techniques
- Principles and methods of determining and servicing public health needs
- Socioeconomic and psychological factors that can impact the effectiveness of health services delivery
- Communicable diseases and methods of control of sexually transmitted diseases
- Basic principles of budgeting
- Principles and practices of management necessary to plan, analyze, develop, evaluate, and direct diverse and complex activities of major health programs

The health officer generally has the skills and ability to:

- Plan, organize, and direct public health programs within professional standards, legal requirements, and financial constraints.
- Direct and supervise professional and technical personnel.
- Analyze situations accurately and take effective actions.
- Interpret laws, regulations, and standards pertaining to public health.
- Prepare clear and comprehensive records and reports.
- Maintain accurate records.
- Communicate effectively, both orally and in writing.
- Speak effectively in public.
- Establish and maintain effective working relationships with staff members, other departments, agencies, public groups, and organizations.

### Education and Experience

Any combination of training and experience that provides the required knowledge and abilities will qualify an individual for this position. A typical way to obtain the required knowledge and abilities is through three years of administrative or supervisory public health medical experience or possession of a master's degree in public health from an accredited school of public health and one year of public health medical experience. In some states, health officers must be a graduate of a medical school in good standing and possess a valid license to practice medicine in that state.

## WORKPLACE CONSIDERATIONS

Every organization has a management structure with various levels of management positions. Larger and more complex organizations have greater numbers of managers and administrators although their scope of responsibility is often limited to a specific program or constellation of programs. Smaller organizations are more likely to be dominated by professionals with administrative positions often filled by workers with professional backgrounds and credentials. For example, more than half of the directors of the approximately 3000 local public health agencies in the United States have a health professional degree but no degree in public health. For several decades there has been a general trend toward more nonprofessional managers rather than elevating professionals into top management positions. This has been occurring at all governmental levels, but somewhat more frequently among state and federal health agencies than for local public health agencies. In 2004, there were 25,170 health administrators working for federal (9530), state (6420) and local (9220) governmental agencies (see Table 3–3).

Work settings also influence the typical physical requirement for positions in this occupational category. Similar to administrators and managers throughout the health sector, public health administrators work long and irregular hours. Most public health administration positions call for workers to be able to sit for extended periods and to frequently stand and walk short distances. Normal manual dexterity and eye-hand coordination, hearing, and vision corrected to within the normal range are also important considerations. Normally, public health administrators will be able to communicate verbally and use office equipment including computers, telephones, calculators, copiers, and fax machines. Although much of the work is performed in an office environment, frequent and/or

**Table 3–3** Number and Mean Salary for Health Administrators Working in Federal, State, and Local Governmental Agencies, May 2004

| Occupational Category | Federal Workers | Federal Worker Mean Salary | State Workers | State Worker Mean Salary | Local Workers | Local Worker Mean Salary | Total Federal, State, and Local Workers | Adjusted PH Enum. 2000 Workers |
|---|---|---|---|---|---|---|---|---|
| Administrators | 9530 | $86,470 | 6420 | $72,650 | 9220 | $69,150 | 25,170 | 21,247 |
| Administrative Business Professionals | NA | NA | NA | NA | NA | NA | NA | 7306 |
| Administrative, Business, and Other Support | NA | NA | NA | NA | NA | NA | NA | 77,162 |

*Source:* Data for federal, state, and local governmental agency workers from Bureau of Labor Statistics. *May 2004 National, State, and Metropolitan Area Occupational Employment and Wage Estimates.* Available at http://www.bls.gov. Accessed August 2005. See Chapter 2 for adjusted number of public health workers from *Year 2000 Public Health Workforce Enumeration.*

continuous contact with staff and the public is also necessary. In many situations, administrators may be required to possess a valid driver's license.

## SALARY ESTIMATES

The mean annual salary for medical and health administrators working in all settings was $75,000 in 2004 with the middle 50% earning between $53,000 and $89,000. The range between the 10th and 90th percentile was $41,000 and $119,000. Entry-level salaries are likely around $40,000. Mean salaries are higher for administrators working for hospitals and physician practices and lower for those working in the public and voluntary sector.

Salaries for public health administrators vary widely based on the type and size of the organization as well as the credentials and experience of the administrator. Mean salaries for health administrators working for federal agencies were $87,500 in 2004, but salaries for state and local health administrators averaged $72,500 and $69,000 respectively (Table 3–3). Small local public health agencies have notoriously low salary scales (often in the $35,000–$55,000 range) making it difficult to attract administrators with graduate degrees or with extensive previous experience. Larger governmental public health agencies can often offer salaries somewhat competitive of those found in the private and voluntary sector ($65,000–$85,000 range). Administrators with professional credentials, especially physicians, dentists, veterinarians, epidemiologists, and nurses, may be able to attract salaries in the 6-figure category.

## CAREER PROSPECTS

In 2004 there were nearly 225,000 medical and health services managers in the United States with 25,000 employed by federal, state, and local public health agencies. This large pool of health managers, in addition to the wide range of qualifications required by potential employers, often results in vacant administrative and management positions being filled even when there are not many applicants with the optimal desired qualifications. This is easy to appreciate as organizations must have people in leadership and management positions.

It is not uncommon to hear public health officials express concerns over difficulties in filling administrative positions with qualified candidates. It is not clear, however, whether this is a supply and demand issue or whether there are not adequate systems in place to recognize, reward, and value competent performance. Because administration and management require fairly nonspecific and generic skills, these positions are many times filled with individuals who are new to the field of public health. Public health professionals within such organizations often view such administrators as not necessarily committed to the same values and ethics as the professional staff. In any event, overall demand for public health administrators appears to be relatively steady and stable.

It is not uncommon for a public health administrator to have a general academic degree at the bachelor's or associate degree level and to have risen through the ranks of public service in the governmental sector. It is also common for an experienced public health professional such as an environmental health practitioner or public health nurse to be promoted into an agency leadership position. In sum, career pathways are many and varied for public health administration positions.

## ADDITIONAL INFORMATION

There are many good sources of information on public health administration as a career. Several sources are available for information on educational programs for health administration as well as for continuing education and leadership development for practicing public health administrators.

The Association of University Programs in Health Administration (AUPHA) Web site (http://www.aupha.org/index.php) provides information on approximately 150 undergraduate and graduate degree programs in health administration in the United States. AUPHA works closely with the Commission on Accreditation of Healthcare Management Education (http://www.cahmeweb.org) and the Accrediting Commission on Education for Health Services Administration (ACHESA), the organization that accredits master's-level programs. Only ACHESA accredited programs can become a full member of AUPHA.

Both AUPHA and ACHESA are linked with the American College of Healthcare Executives (http://www.ache.org/career.cfm), which credentials health administrators. A similar, but considerably smaller, program that certifies public health administrators is operated by the Public Health Practitioner Certification Board (http://www.phpcb.org).

Schools of public health are among the institutions offering graduate degrees in health administration. The Association of Schools of Public Health (http://www.asph.org) has identified a battery of core health administration competencies appropriate for all students receiving the master's of public health (MPH) degree (Table 3–4). These competencies provide a useful baseline for professional public health administration and indicate what, upon graduation, a student with an MPH should be able to do.

The American Public Health Association's Health Administration Section is another good source of information for public health administration. Its Web site can be accessed through the main APHA site (http://www.apha.org). The Health Administration Section has a nearly 100 year history, beginning as a section for medical health officers but expanding to include a broader spectrum of public health administrators.

The Public Health Leadership Society (http://www.phls.org/) includes graduates of the National Public Health Leadership Institute (http://www.phli.org/), operating from the University of North Carolina School of Public Health, as well as alumni of approximately 20 state and regional public health leadership development institutes (http://www.heartland centers.slu.edu/nln/). These programs serve public health practitioners

---

**Table 3–4** Health Administration Competency Expectations for Graduates of MPH Degree Programs

1. Identify the main components and issues of the organization, financing, and delivery of health services and public health systems in the United States.
2. Discuss the policy process for improving the health status of populations.
3. Describe the legal and ethical bases for public health and health services.
4. Apply quality and performance improvement concepts to address organizational performance issues.
5. Demonstrate leadership skills for building partnerships.
6. Apply "systems thinking" for resolving organizational problems.
7. Apply principles of strategic planning and marketing to public health.
8. Apply the principles of program planning, development, budgeting, management, and evaluation in organizational and community initiatives.
9. Communicate health policy and management issues using appropriate channels and technologies.
10. Explain methods of ensuring community health safety and preparedness.

*Source:* Association of Schools of Public Health (ASPH). MPH Core Competency Development Process, Version 1.2. Available at http://www.asph.org. Accessed August 2005.

through an intensive leadership development curriculum undertaken on a continuing education basis. The University of North Carolina also offers a Management Academy for Public Health serving public health managers and administrators from states in the southeast region of the United States.

## CONCLUSION

Public health administrators are one of the largest and most important of the professional occupational categories in the public health workforce. There are more than 20,000 health administrators working in public health settings. This group is also one of the most diverse in terms of academic credentials and previous work experiences. Public health administration offers a variety of work settings, especially at the local level, and a broad range of career pathways that are open to both individuals trained in public health and those new to the field. Because of the diverse backgrounds and skill levels, ongoing education and training are especially relevant issues for this occupational category. Demand for these positions is steady to slightly increasing and likely to remain so over the near term.

## REFERENCES

1. Bureau of Labor Statistics, U.S. Department of Labor. May 2004 National, State, and Metropolitan Area Occupational Employment and Wage Estimates. Available at http://www.bls.gov/oes/current/oes_nat.htm. Accessed August 2005.
2. Health Resources and Services Administration (HRSA), Bureau of Health Professions, National Center for Health Workforce Information and Analysis and Center for Health Policy, Columbia School of Nursing. *The Public Health Workforce Enumeration 2000*. Washington, DC: HRSA; 2000. Available at http://www.phppo.cdc.gov/owpp/docs/library/2000/Public%20Health%20Workforce%20Enumeration%202000.pdf. Accessed August 2005.

# CHAPTER 4

# Environmental and Occupational Health

Environmental health is an expansive field that has been an important part of public health practice for more than 150 years. The exploits of John Snow in battling cholera in England in the 1850s demonstrated the link between communicable disease and sanitary conditions. As briefly described in Chapter 1, the pioneering efforts of Chadwick in England and Shattuck in the United States resulted in blueprints for early public health responses and systems. Many public health successes in the latter part of the 1800s and the early years of the 1900s were the direct result of environmental engineering and sanitation advances. The people carrying out these duties have been an integral part of the public health workforce and remain so. These workers are employed in public health and environmental protection agencies at all levels of government and throughout the private sector as well. An accurate count of their numbers is not available although the Bureau of Labor Statistics reports 163,000 workers in environmental engineering, specialist, and technician positions and another 47,000 in occupational health and safety positions.[1] There were 75,000 environmental and occupational health workers employed by federal, state, and local governmental agencies in 2004. The *Public Health Workforce Enumeration 2000* identified 40,000 working for federal, state, and local public health agencies.[2] Data from these two sources are used throughout this chapter. The difference between these two sources indicates that many environmental and occupational health personnel work in nonhealth agencies at all levels of government, such as environmental protection agencies, departments of natural resources, and sanitation agencies. In any event, environmental health workers are one of the largest occupational groupings within the public health workforce today. Environmental public health workers, for many decades working primarily in local and state public health agencies, are increasingly finding positions in private sector organizations that offer a wide variety of environmental and occupational health services. Table 4–1 provides a snapshot of an average day in the life of an environmental health practitioner.

## OCCUPATIONAL CLASSIFICATION

There are six specific standard occupational categories for environmental health workers. These include environmental engineer, environmental engineering technician, environmental scientist/specialist, environmental science and protection technician, occupational health and safety specialist, and occupational health and safety technician.

**Table 4–1**   A Typical Day for an Environmental Health Practitioner

| | |
|---|---|
| 7:30 a.m. | Visit septic field inspection site to assist environmental health specialists on site |
| 8:30 a.m. | Office time for paperwork and information sharing with staff |
| 9:00 a.m. | Staff meeting to review priorities for week |
| 10:15 a.m. | Interview candidates for vacant entry-level environmental health specialist position |
| 10:45 a.m. | Meet with communicable disease control, epidemiology, and public health nursing staff regarding community concerns over West Nile virus threat |
| 11:45 a.m. | Brown bag lunch with other environmental health staff; today's guest is professor from state university undergraduate degree program in environmental health |
| 1:00 p.m. | Brief agency director regarding status of West Nile virus threat |
| 1:30 p.m. | Supervise inspection of food services, swimming pools, and septic systems at county fair site |
| 3:00 p.m. | Conference call meeting with epidemiology and environmental health staff of neighboring jurisdictions and state health department regarding current status of West Nile virus |
| 4:00 p.m. | Review information suggested by staff for tonight's community meeting |
| 4:30 p.m. | More paperwork related to permit approvals |
| 5:15 p.m. | Prepare remarks for tonight's community meeting |
| 7:00 p.m. | Represent agency at community meeting regarding West Nile virus concerns |

Three of these titles are professional occupations (environmental engineer, environmental scientist/specialist, and occupational health and safety specialist). The others are technical occupations.

- Environmental engineers (such as water supply or waste water engineers, solid waste engineers, air pollution engineers, and sanitary engineers) apply engineering principles to control, eliminate, ameliorate, and/or prevent environmental health hazards. There are 48,000 environmental engineers in the United States. Private-sector companies (architectural and engineering companies, management and technical consulting firms) employ the largest numbers of environmental engineers. Federal, state, and local government agencies employ 13,000 environmental engineers. The *Public Health Workforce Enumeration 2000* identified 7000 in governmental public health agencies.
- Environmental engineering technicians (such as water or waste water plant operators, water or waste water testing technicians, and air pollution technicians) assist environmental engineers and other environmental health professions in controlling, eliminating, ameliorating, and/or preventing environmental health hazards. There are 20,000 environmental engineering technicians working in the United States. Architectural and engineering companies employ the largest number of environmental engineering technicians, followed by local government and scientific research and development companies. Governmental agencies employ only 3000 environmental engineering technicians, 600 of which were identified in the *Public Health Workforce Enumeration 2000*.
- Environmental scientists or specialists (such as environmental researchers, environmental health specialists, food scientists, soil and plant scientists, air pollution specialists, hazardous materials specialists, toxicologists, water or waste water or solid waste specialists, sanitarians, and entomologists) apply biological, chemical, and public health principles to control, eliminate, ameliorate, and/or prevent environmental health hazards. There are 67,000 environmental specialists working in the United States. State governments are the leading source of employment for environmental specialists. Local government and private-sector companies also employ large numbers of environmental specialists. Governmental agencies employ

32,000 environmental specialists; the *Public Health Workforce Enumeration 2000* identified 23,000 in federal, state, and local public health agencies.

- Environmental science and protection technicians (such as air pollution technicians and vector control workers) assist environmental scientists and specialists and other environmental health professionals in the control, elimination, and/or prevention of environmental health hazards. There are 28,000 workers in the United States in environmental science and engineering technician positions. Local governments are the largest employer of environmental science technicians. Private companies and state governments are other important employment sources. Nearly 11,000 environmental science and protection technicians work for government agencies. The *Public Health Workforce Enumeration 2000* identified 700 working in governmental public health agencies.

- Occupational safety and health specialists (such as industrial hygienists, occupational health specialists, radiologic health inspectors, and safety inspectors) review, evaluate, and analyze workplace environments and exposures. They design programs and procedures to control, eliminate, ameliorate, and/or prevent disease and injury caused by chemical, physical, biological, and ergonomic risks to workers. There are 37,000 occupational health and safety specialists in the United States. Local and state governments are the largest employment sources for occupational safety and health specialists; hospitals are another large employer. Government agencies employ 14,000 occupational health and safety specialists. The *Public Health Workforce Enumeration 2000* identified nearly 9000 working in governmental public health agencies.

- Occupational health and safety technicians collect data on workplace environments and exposures for analysis by occupational safety and health specialists; they also implement programs and conduct evaluation of programs designed to limit chemical, physical, biological, and ergonomic risks to workers. There are 11,000 occupational health and safety technicians in the United States, with 3000 working for federal, state, and local governmental agencies. The *Public Health Workforce Enumeration 2000* identified only 150 working in governmental public health agencies.

As is apparent from these occupational categories, both professional and technical positions are common in the environmental health component of the public health workforce. Among the 40,000 positions identified in the *Public Health Workforce Enumeration 2000*, more than half were professional titles. Among professional positions, environmental health ranks second only to nursing within the public health workforce. Professional titles include engineers, scientists, and specialists. Technical titles include technicians and technologists.

## PUBLIC HEALTH PRACTICE PROFILE

Environmental and occupational health workers generally function at a program or unit level within public health agencies at all levels of government, but especially those at the local and state level. They are most frequently involved in public health responsibilities that focus on protecting against environmental hazards, preventing injuries, and preventing epidemics and the spread of disease. Environmental and occupational health workers may also be key components of efforts to prepare and respond to public health emergencies, especially natural disasters for which protection of water and food supplies can be critical.

Among the 10 essential public health services, environmental and occupational health workers are most likely to be involved in diagnosing and investigating health problems and health hazards in the community, enforcing laws and regulations that protect health and ensure safety, monitoring health status to identify community health status, and evaluating the effectiveness and quality of environmental and occupational health services in the community. With much of their work done in community settings, environmental and occupational health workers also inform, educate, and empower people about important health issues. Table 4–2 summarizes public health purposes and essential public health services at the core of positions for environmental and occupational health workers.

## IMPORTANT AND ESSENTIAL DUTIES

There are many different job titles and positions used for environmental and occupational health workers. The focus in this chapter will be on five representative positions: (1) environmental engineer; (2) entry-level

---

**Table 4–2** Public Health Practice Profile for Environmental Health

Environmental and Occupational Health Workers
Make a Difference by:

**Public Health Purposes**

| | |
|---|---|
| Preventing epidemics and the spread of disease | ✓ |
| Protecting against environmental hazards | ✓ |
| Preventing injuries | ✓ |
| Promoting and encouraging healthy behaviors | |
| Responding to disasters and assisting communities in recovery | |
| Assuring the quality and accessibility of health services | |

**Essential Public Health Services**

| | |
|---|---|
| Monitoring health status to identify community health problems | ✓ |
| Diagnosing and investigating health problems and health hazards in the community | ✓ |
| Informing, educating, and empowering people about health issues | ✓ |
| Mobilizing community partnerships to identify and solve health problems | |
| Developing policies and plans that support individual and community health efforts | |
| Enforcing laws and regulations that protect health and ensure safety | ✓ |
| Linking people with needed personal health services and assuring the provision of health care when otherwise unavailable | |
| Assuring a competent public health and personal health care workforce | |
| Evaluating effectiveness, accessibility, and quality of personal and population-based health services | ✓ |
| Researching new insights and innovative solutions to health problems | |

---

environmental health specialist; (3) midlevel environmental health specialist; (4) senior-level environmental health specialist; and (5) midlevel occupational health and safety specialist. Each of these positions and a representative panel of their important and essential duties are described in this section.

## Environmental Engineer

This is a professional environmental engineering position with duties within an assigned environmental program involving the protection of public health and/or the protection or restoration of the environment. There are often several grades for this position. Entry-level titles generally do not have any supervisory responsibilities. Higher-level environmental engineer titles may supervise or lead assigned engineers and/or other staff.

Workers in this title are responsible for the performance of professional engineering duties in performing field surveys and investigations of water supplies, sewage systems, streams, industrial waste facilities, solid and hazardous waste facilities, air pollution control systems, and/or dams and reservoirs. Work includes preparing reports of findings, and making recommendations to improve the public health, safety, and the environment. Environmental engineers work under general technical supervision and receive work assignments from a designated superior. There may be several levels of positions with this title.

Important and essential duties for environmental engineers include:

- Participates in the engineering review of the hydraulics and details of water supply systems and plants, industrial and domestic waste treatment systems, solid and hazardous waste management systems, air pollution control systems, dams and reservoirs, and so on
- Gathers and interprets data on pollution, contamination, and construction and design features relevant for environmental engineering projects
- Reviews engineering plans and specifications for sewage and industrial waste treatment plants, water supply systems, solid and hazardous waste disposal areas, air pollution control systems, and dams and reservoirs for compliance with approved standards
- Confers with officials and owners/operators of plants and establishments with regard to laws, regulations, and engineering requirements of appropriate state and local agencies
- Collects samples of water and sewage for bacteriological, chemical, or biological analysis
- Examines and prepares charts, tables, and maps for the interpretation of engineering data, and prepares reports of findings and analysis
- Prepares papers and lectures on subjects relating to the environment and/or dam safety
- Prepares technical and detailed reports of engineering surveys
- Participates in special investigations of fish kills and unusual stream conditions with representatives of other agencies
- Supervises, assigns, and assists in the work of a unit composed of a small group of professional personnel
- Trains subordinate engineers and other technical staff

## Environmental Specialist (Entry Level)

This position serves as an entry-level environmental specialist performing one or more of the following functions under close direction and supervision: conducting routine compliance and enforcement activities; assisting in the development of draft legislation, policies, and regulations; conducting routine scientific analyses and technical services on assigned office or field projects; providing regulatory assistance; providing project administration and environmental technical assistance for grants, contracts, or loans; interpreting policy and technical assistance; conducting less complex surveys and analyses; recording field conditions; gathering and analyzing information to assist in developing recommendations and decision making; and assisting in permit development. The number of levels for this position varies from one personnel system to another. In many systems there are three to five levels of environmental health specialist positions that allow for career advancement.

Important and essential duties for entry-level environmental health specialists include:

- Assists in the installation, operation, and maintenance of environmental monitoring/sampling equipment; assists in performing field and office surveys and studies; performs surveillance and other special projects
- Assists in routine repairs and calibrations of environmental monitoring/sampling equipment, in accordance with specifications and standard operating procedures; performs basic sampling data review for precision and accuracy
- Assists in responding to complaints, routine inspections/surveillance, and permit review to meet compliance requirements
- Assists in the research and compilation of basic information for use in regulation or policy development
- Enters and maintains basic databases or inventories
- Assists in preparing for public meetings, hearings, and workshops
- Assists with routine inspections or investigations of facilities or project sites that require specialized knowledge of industry processes, pollutant sources, or natural processes
- Responds to routine inquiries or requests for technical assistance regarding the scientific background and technical implementation of agency programs

- Reviews plans for technical accuracy and makes recommendations to higher-level staff
- Conducts routine sampling and testing; analyzes, evaluates, and interprets data; writes reports; and assists higher-level staff
- Maintains and utilizes computerized environmental databases in support of technical projects
- Reviews routine permit applications for technical accuracy and makes recommendations regarding the scientific merit of proposals
- Provides technical and administrative assistance to grant, contract, or loan recipients in the planning, design, construction, and implementation of environmental protection projects

### Environmental Specialist (Midlevel)

This position serves as a staff environmental specialist performing one or more of the following functions independently with little direction and supervision: conducting compliance and enforcement activities; developing draft legislation; developing, performing, coordinating, implementing, and evaluating scientific analyses, plans, or services involving office or field projects; conducting surveys, analyses, and recording field conditions; providing project administration and environmental technical assistance for grants, contracts, and loans; gathering and analyzing information to develop recommendations for decision making and permit development, review, and oversight. This position may lead or supervise assigned staff.

Important and essential duties for midlevel environmental specialists include:

- Independently performs the installation, operation, and maintenance of environmental monitoring/sampling equipment; on an area or site list basis performs and/or provides guidance for surveys, field studies, or other special data-gathering activities
- Performs complex equipment repair and calibrations; reviews monitored data for evaluation of equipment performance
- Responds to and investigates complex or highly technical complaints or violations; performs complex inspections or field investigations; coordinates complaint and enforcement priorities, schedules, and assists in negotiating agreements and settlements; prepares final permit evaluation or report for approval; may impose on-site enforcement

action; performs follow-up inspections to ensure corrective action is implemented

- Plans, develops, researches, and conducts or oversees technical data collection and analyzes, evaluates, and interprets data; analyzes or interprets information requirements and coordinates information gathering for a team or other assignment outside of a team; writes reports and reviews draft reports
- Determines database or inventory requirements; works with agency and nonagency sources on data submittals; evaluates databases or inventories for analysis, reporting, or compliance purposes; may design and/or develop databases or inventories to be utilized in support of technical projects
- Reviews permit applications for technical accuracy, negotiates permit conditions, conducts conflict resolution, and makes decisions regarding the scientific merit of proposals; serves as a senior permit writer or historical/institutional memory for geographic area or complex site
- Develops and/or implements project plans, consent decrees, orders, or scientific studies for cleanups, resource management, or policy/regulation development; conducts research for technical projects; reviews project plans for technical accuracy and makes decisions on the scientific merit of proposals
- Oversees contractor or consultant services for compliance and certifies performance; provides assistance to other staff, agencies, and the public
- Makes recommendations to senior staff regarding new or modified sampling and analytical testing methods, best management practices, and technical operating procedures
- Makes technical and scientific recommendations regarding the development, coordination, and implementation of environmental technical assistance programs involving pollution prevention, pollution control, or natural resource management
- Evaluates data to determine technical compliance with regulatory requirements
- Plans, facilitates, and represents the program or agency in public meetings, hearings, and workshops
- Conducts literature evaluations to assess evidence-based practice; formulates grant proposals; proposes and designs assessment and research projects

- Develops evidence-based protocols for specific program interventions and services
- Independently provides technical and administrative assistance to grant, contract, or loan recipients in the planning, design, construction, or implementation of environmental protection projects
- Coordinates the development of policies, procedures, statutes, and regulations of a high degree of complexity
- Directs or coordinates nonagency employees at large spills or complex sites

### Environmental Specialist (Senior Level)

This position serves as a senior program expert in one or more program subject areas as designated in writing by a program manager, agency director, or higher. A senior environmental specialist, performs, directs, implements, and evaluates activities that are of critical agency, regional, statewide, or national interest, sensitivity, or complexity. Such activities may include planning and directing surveys and analyses of projects that are a high priority for the agency or involve participation in the resolution of major environmental questions. In most circumstances, this position supervises five or more professional environmental staff.

Important and essential duties for senior-level environmental specialists include:

- Advises program management on monitoring and sampling policies, priorities, effectiveness, and cross-media or agency issues and requirements
- Evaluates equipment inventories for material readiness, amortization, and technology transfer; management of contracted services and equipment utilization; conducts equipment needs assessments
- Advises program management on violations of critical or controversial agency interest; evaluates rule effectiveness and recommends enforcement/compliance rule making; may represent the program on multimedia or highly complex or controversial enforcement/compliance actions involving other programs or agencies
- Works with other programs and agencies in identifying information required for policy development, legislation, regulations, and recommended priorities, scheduling requirements, and information parameters for program management

- Evaluates databases and inventories for policy or regulation development; determines new, changing, or emerging requirements for databases and inventories; may work with other programs or agencies on database/inventory requirements
- Conducts literature evaluations to assess evidence-based practice; formulates grant proposals; proposes and designs assessment and research projects
- Develops evidence-based protocols for specific program interventions and services
- Coordinates controversial or critical plans for resource management, policy or regulation development, or statewide cleanup priorities
- Advises program or agency management on the need for contractor or consultant services versus agency staff and expertise
- Identifies critical or emerging issues and recommends preventative or corrective measures
- Represents agency and testifies at legal or public hearings or conferences and before Congress
- Provides expertise or historical background not otherwise available to the agency that is used as a basis for agency management decisions
- Serves as an agency representative to regional and national commissions and environmental or professional organizations relevant to assigned responsibilities with the agency

## Occupational Health and Safety Specialist

This is midlevel professional scientific work in evaluating work and indoor environments for safety and health hazards. Occupational health and safety specialists make comprehensive safety and health hazard evaluations, including the more difficult evaluations, of all general industry and indoor environments, involving office buildings and factories. A comprehensive safety and health hazard evaluation may consist of the following: conducting a physical survey; establishing appropriate sampling techniques; collecting samples as necessary to assess the presence of chemical, physical, and microbial agents in accordance with the requirements of the Occupational Safety and Health Act; analyzing the data generated by sampling and making a professional judgment using accepted industrial hygiene practices and federal standards to determine the degree of hazard present; interviewing employers and employees and other potentially exposed individuals to determine possible sources of safety and health hazards; preparing a technical report of the safety and health hazard evaluation that can be understood and followed by lay personnel; and making recommendations within this report that will reduce or correct the health hazard. Occupational health and safety specialists receive minimal supervision from an administrative superior.

Important and essential duties for midlevel occupational health and safety specialists include:

- Conducts initial conferences with employers to introduce the services offered by the agency
- Consults with employers on the existence, utilization, and operating condition of powered mechanical ventilation devices, personal safety equipment and procedures, noise abatement equipment and procedures, material safety data sheets, hazardous chemical correction, and safety and health programs
- Performs difficult safety and health hazard evaluations requiring literature research, analysis, and scientific design
- Determines the magnitude of exposure or nuisance to workers and the public; selects or devises methods and instruments suitable for measurements; studies and tests materials associated with the work operation
- Collects samples from office buildings and other workplaces to determine the presence of toxic substances and other potential hazards; evaluates building ventilation systems for possible deficiencies; and provides technical advice on remedial action
- Interprets results of the examination of the work environment in terms of the potential of causing a community nuisance or damage or impairing worker safety, health, and efficiency; and presents specific conclusions to appropriate interested parties by means of a technical report
- Determines the need for, or effectiveness of, control measures, and when necessary, recommends procedures that will be suitable and effective in achieving those measures
- Interprets occupational safety and health laws, rules, and regulations; determines compliance with safety and health laws; holds conferences with management to discuss identified violations and deficiencies and recommends corrections

- Reviews facility safety and health programs required by the federal Occupational Safety and Health Administration (OSHA)

## MINIMUM QUALIFICATIONS

Environmental and occupational health includes a mix of professional and technical occupations both of which generally have several levels of positions. This provides a natural career pathway and allows environmental and occupational health workers to remain in this field for many years. Comparable positions exist in local public agencies of all sizes, making career advancement from a small to larger employer a common story for these workers.

Although environmental and occupational health professionals are produced by schools of public health, there are many undergraduate and graduate degree programs specializing in environmental sciences. It is these programs that are even larger producers of environmental and occupational health practitioners. Many workers in technical positions have less than a bachelor degree; some have no more than a high school degree.

As with virtually all public health positions, both experience and education are important considerations for hiring and promotion. Experience and education both contribute to necessary knowledge, skills, and abilities required for workers in this field. Typical minimum qualifications for environmental engineers, three levels of environmental health specialists, and occupational health and safety specialists are detailed below.

### *Typical Minimum Qualifications for Environmental Engineer*

#### Knowledge, Skills, and Abilities

An environmental engineer will generally have knowledge of:

- Principles and practices of environmental engineering and/or environmental sanitation
- Design, construction, and operation of air quality control, water supply and treatment, and sewage and industrial waste disposal systems
- Laws and regulations governing sanitation

- Physical and biological sciences, including chemistry, bacteriology, and physical properties of ambient air, water, sewage, and liquid waste as related to environmental engineering
- Mathematics, geometry, calculus, and engineering formulas

An environmental engineer will generally have the skills and ability to:

- Develop designs involving environmental engineering theory and judgment
- Establish and maintain cooperative working relationships with public officials and community groups
- Perform investigations involving the application of professional theory and interpretation of laws, regulations, and requirements
- Plan, promote, and conduct engineering projects
- Analyze significant environmental engineering and sanitation data
- Consult with and advise plant owners and operators on proper design, construction, and operation of plants
- Prepare engineering reports and papers and lectures related to the environment

### Experience and Education

Any combination of training and experience that provides the requisite knowledge and abilities will qualify an individual for this position. A typical way to obtain the required knowledge and abilities is through acquisition of a master's degree with major study in one of the engineering fields (such as sanitary, water resource, civil, geotechnical, environmental, chemical, or mechanical engineering) and one year of experience in environmental engineering. Another path is through acquisition of an engineer-in-training certificate or a bachelor degree with a major study in one of the engineering fields listed above and two years of environmental engineering experience. Some jurisdictions may require registration as a professional engineer within the state or another state with equivalent requirements for registration or an engineer-in-training certificate. In some instances a PhD degree in an engineering field may substitute for one or more years of environmental engineering experience. Requirements for professional registration as an engineer in some states may require up to eight years of professional experience (which may include up to four years of college-level engineering education) and successful completion of professional licensing exams.

## Typical Minimum Requirements for Entry-Level Environmental Specialist

### Knowledge, Skills, and Abilities

An entry-level environmental health specialist will generally have knowledge of:

- Field investigative techniques, including data gathering and basic research
- Practices and methods of environmental problem solving
- Soil, water, or air sampling methods and techniques
- Characteristics of pollutants
- Principles, practices, and methods of environmental science, natural resource management, pollution prevention, and pollution control
- Applicable federal, state, and local environmental regulations

An entry-level environmental health specialist will generally have the skills and ability to:

- Use sound judgment in performing assigned tasks.
- Understand and apply environmental regulations and related laws.
- Write clearly and concisely, and prepare maps, plans, charts, and graphs.
- Communicate effectively with agency staff, other agencies, industry, and the general public.

### Experience and Education

Entry-level environmental health specialists come from a wide range of educational levels and previous work experiences, which generally include:

- A bachelor degree involving major study in environmental, physical, or one of the natural sciences; environmental planning; or other allied field
- Experience at or above the environmental technician level or equivalent will substitute, year for year, for education

## Typical Minimum Requirements for Midlevel Environmental Specialist

### Knowledge, Skills, and Abilities

A midlevel environmental health specialist will generally have knowledge of:

- Principles, practices, and methods of environmental or resource management and environmental pollution prevention and pollution control
- Methods and techniques of field sampling, testing, data gathering, basic research, and field investigations
- Soil science, geology, hydrology, hydrogeology, metrology, and toxicology
- Applicable federal, state, and local environmental regulations and policies
- Characteristics and health effects of pollutants
- Technical report writing methods

A midlevel environmental health specialist will generally have the skills and ability to:

- Use sound, independent judgment in making decisions on environmental problems and completing assigned tasks.
- Understand and interpret plans, maps, and equipment specifications.
- Prepare clear and concise written reports and make oral presentations.
- Analyze and prepare plans and reports.
- Understand and communicate complex environmental regulations and statutes.
- Communicate effectively with agency staff, other agencies, industry, and the general public.

### Experience and Education

Any combination of training and experience that provides the requisite knowledge and abilities will qualify an individual for this position. A typical way to obtain the required knowledge and abilities is through acquisition of a bachelor degree involving major study in environmental, physical, or one of the natural sciences; environmental planning; or other allied field; and two years of professional-level experience in environmental analysis, control, or planning. Additional qualifying experience may substitute, year for year, for education. A master's degree in one of the above fields may also substitute for one year of the required experience. Another way to meet these qualifications is through acquisition of a PhD degree in one of the above fields or through one year of experience in the next lower-level environmental specialist position.

## Typical Minimum Qualifications for Senior-Level Environmental Specialist

### Knowledge, Skills, and Abilities

A senior-level environmental specialist will generally have knowledge of:

- Applicable federal, state, and local environmental regulations and policies
- Soil science, geology, hydrology, hydrogeology, metrology, and toxicology
- Methods for the development of an environmental program or complex study
- Multimedia environmental principles and practices

A senior-level environmental specialist will generally have the skills and ability to:

- Identify and assess program or agency service delivery needs and requirements.
- Recognize emerging issues and conduct advanced planning to address those issues.
- Represent program or agency management on complex or controversial issues with other agencies, jurisdictions, or interest groups.
- Effectively negotiate and resolve conflict.
- Effectively communicate technical information clearly, both orally and in writing.
- Demonstrate a high degree of technical expertise in a particular field or specialty as shown through the publication of papers in peer-reviewed, scientific or technical journals or the presentation of papers at professional conferences.

### Experience and Education

Any combination of training and experience that provides the requisite knowledge and abilities will qualify an individual for this position. A typical way to obtain the required knowledge and abilities is through a bachelor degree involving major study in environmental, physical, or one of the natural sciences; environmental planning; or other allied field; and six years of professional-level experience in environmental analysis, control, or planning, which includes two years equal to the midlevel environmental specialist position. Additional qualifying experience may substitute, year for year, for education. Another pathway to satisfy these qualifications is through acquisition of a master's degree in one of the preceding fields and four years of professional-level experience that include two years equal to a midlevel environmental specialist. Yet another way to satisfy these requirements is through acquisition of a PhD degree in one of the preceding fields and three years of professional-level experience that include two years equal to a midlevel environmental specialist.

## *Typical Minimum Qualifications for Occupational Health and Safety Specialist*

### Knowledge, Skills, and Abilities

A occupational health and safety specialist generally has knowledge of:

- Sampling and direct measuring techniques for gas, vapor, dust, noise, and radiation
- Microbiology, radiology, physiology, and chemistry
- Common diseases and health hazards related to indoor environments and industrial occupations and of their possible sources
- The standard types of machinery and equipment used in industrial and commercial establishments
- The Occupational Safety and Health Act and the applicable regulations of the Environmental Protection Agency that relate to workplace safety and health

A occupational health and safety specialist generally has the skills and ability to:

- Analyze complex problems of environmental hazard reduction and arrive at sound decisions regarding actions to be taken.
- Develop, organize, and present training through a comprehensive company-specific safety program.
- Analyze and interpret technical reports and criteria documents on exposure limits.
- Operate and maintain detection and measurement apparatus.
- Communicate thoughts and ideas clearly and concisely.
- Establish and maintain effective working relationships with plant managers, safety directors, employees, and the public.

### Experience and Education

Any combination of training and experience that provides the requisite knowledge and abilities will qualify an individual for this position. A typical way to obtain the required knowledge and abilities is through one year of experience as an entry-level occupational safety and health specialist or one year of professional experience in safety and health consultation in a governmental agency or program or in private industry as an industrial hygienist, industrial safety professional, safety manager, or other closely related position in the occupational safety or health field, and graduation from an accredited 4-year college or university with specialization in industrial hygiene or safety or a closely related area. In some instances, graduate work in industrial hygiene or safety may be substituted on a year-for-year basis for the stated experience. Certification as a certified industrial hygienist (CIH) by the American Board of Industrial Hygiene or as a certified safety professional by the Board of Certified Safety Professionals (CSP) may be substituted for six months of the stated experience. Some states may require specific certifications and licensing.

## WORKPLACE CONSIDERATIONS

State and local governmental agencies employ more than 60,000 environmental and occupational health workers (both professional and technical titles). Federal agencies employ another 12,000 workers, making governmental agencies the largest sources of jobs for environmental and occupational health workers.

Work settings and working conditions influence the typical physical requirement for positions in environmental and occupational health categories. For example, entry-level and midlevel environmental and occupational health specialists spend considerable time outside the office. Environmental health specialists often find themselves at various environmental sites; occupational health specialists often do their work at business sites. Environmental engineers and higher-level environmental and occupational health specialists spend somewhat more time in an office setting.

Most positions call for workers to be able to sit for extended periods and to frequently stand and walk extended distances. Normal manual dexterity and eye-hand coordination, hearing, and vision corrected to within the normal range are also important considerations. This work requires good vision to peruse and review correspondence, statutes, and related material and to perform visual inspections required for work activities conducted on site. Also important are the ability to stand, walk, and have full use of upper and lower extremities to effect investigations and collection efforts in business establishments and in the field. At times this work may require climbing ladders and entering confined areas for investigations.

Normally, environmental and occupational health workers can communicate verbally and use office equipment including computers, telephones, calculators, copiers, and fax machines. For work performed in an office environment, frequent or continuous contact with staff and the public is also necessary. In many situations, environmental and occupational health workers must be mobile and may be required to possess a valid driver's license. Important attributes are verbal and reasoning ability in order to read and understand a variety of written matter; to process directives, reports, and correspondence; and to initiate action required. These positions require emotional stability and good judgment to deal with the public and personnel whose business activities are being inspected or investigated.

## SALARY ESTIMATES

Salaries vary considerably across environmental and occupational health positions depending on whether they are professional or technical titles as well as on educational attainment and experience. Salaries for environmental engineers average $68,000 with the middle 50% ranging from $51,000 to $84,000. The mean salary for environmental engineers employed by federal agencies was $80,000 in 2004. Average salaries are lower for environmental engineers working in state ($57,000) and local ($63,500) governmental agencies (see Table 4–3). Mean salaries are somewhat higher for environmental engineers working in the private sector (architectural and engineering companies, and management and technical consulting companies).

Environmental engineering technicians have mean salaries of $41,000 with the middle 50% ranging from $30,000 to $51,000. Salaries are generally higher for those working in private-sector companies, although environmental engineering technicians employed by local governmental

**Table 4–3** Number and Mean Salary for Environmental and Occupational Health Workers in Federal, State, and Local Governmental Agencies, May 2004

| Occupational Category | Federal Workers | Federal Worker Mean Salary | State Workers | State Worker Mean Salary | Local Workers | Local Worker Mean Salary | Total Federal, State, and Local Workers | Adjusted PH Enum. 2000 Workers |
|---|---|---|---|---|---|---|---|---|
| Environmental Engineers | 4,160 | $79,930 | 5,440 | $57,040 | 3,670 | $63,530 | 13,270 | 7,034 |
| Environmental Engineering Technicians | NA | NA | 590 | $39,550 | 2,010 | $43,720 | 2,600 | 594 |
| Environmental Health Specialists | 5,210 | $73,320 | 17,130 | $48,420 | 10,010 | $51,310 | 32,350 | 23,013 |
| Environmental Health Technicians | 310 | $39,200 | 4,180 | $40,540 | 6,440 | $40,390 | 10,930 | 719 |
| Occupational Health and Safety Specialists | 1,260 | $72,670 | 5,490 | $44,890 | 7,010 | $49,910 | 13,760 | 8,649 |
| Occupational Health and Safety Technicians | 1,010 | $68,120 | 460 | $39,190 | 1,320 | $41,330 | 2,790 | 136 |

*Source:* Data for federal, state, and local governmental agency workers from Bureau of Labor Statistics. May 2004 National, State, and Metropolitan Area Occupational Employment and Wage Estimates. Available at http://www.bls.gov. Accessed August 2005. See Chapter 2 for adjusted number of public health workers from *The Public Health Workforce Enumeration 2000.*

agencies have mean salaries nearing $44,000. Salaries for environmental engineering technicians working for state governmental agencies averaged $40,000 in 2004.

For environmental health specialists, salaries average $56,000 with the middle 50% ranging from $39,000 to $68,000. Average salaries are well above the mean for environmental health specialists employed by the federal government ($73,500) and lower for those working in state ($48,500) and local ($32,500) governmental agencies.

The average annual salary for environmental technicians is $38,000 with the middle 50% earning between $28,000 and $46,000. Average salaries are similar (at $40,000) for those employed by federal, state, and local governmental agencies.

Occupational health and safety specialists have an average salary of $54,000 with the middle 50% ranging between $40,000 and $66,000. State and local governments are the leading employers for this category. Mean salaries for occupational health and safety specialists employed by federal agencies are well above those of workers at state and local agencies ($72,500 federal, $45,000 state, $50,000 local).

Occupational health and safety technicians average $45,000 per year with the middle 50% ranging between $30,000 and $57,000. Mean salaries for occupational health and safety technicians employed by federal agencies are well above those of workers at state and local agencies ($68,000 federal, $39,000 state, $41,500 local).

## CAREER PROSPECTS

Over the next 10 years, the Bureau of Labor Statistics projects that job growth will be greater than average for environmental engineers, environmental health specialists, occupational health and safety specialists, and environmental technicians. There are several reasons for these projections. There is increasing recognition of environmental engineering as a specialty distinct from civil and other engineering fields of endeavor. In addition, there has been a steady increase in recognition of the importance of regulatory compliance for industries and businesses in order to protect and maintain the environment and assure the safety of workers. An increasing emphasis on prevention as an overall strategy to safeguard environmental and human resources also fosters new job opportunities for these occupations. Finally, as many of these positions are in the public sector, they are somewhat insulated from economic shifts and downturns.

Although environmental and occupational health is a broad category, career pathways are somewhat limited. Specific academic preparation and experience are necessary for environmental engineers. For example, there is little opportunity for a technician in this field to advance to engineer status without completing the academic degrees required for the field. The academic requirements for environmental and occupational health and safety specialists are somewhat less restrictive. It is possible for technicians to advance into some of these professional positions through continuing education and work experience.

Technicians often begin work as trainees in routine positions under the direct supervision of a professional title or a more experienced senior technician. Technicians with previous hands-on experience with equipment used in that field usually require shorter periods of on-the-job training. As they become more experienced and proficient, technicians progress to become more independent in carrying out their duties. Their ability to move beyond technical titles, however, may be limited unless they acquire additional education or secure specific professional certifications.

Most of these occupational categories do provide their own job ladder with several levels of titles for entry-level to midlevel to senior-level positions. Over a span of several decades, these can comprise a satisfactory framework for a career. At higher levels, professional titles can lead to appointments into management and leadership positions. A substantial number of local public health agency directors, for example, come from the ranks of environmental health professionals.

## ADDITIONAL INFORMATION

There are many good sources of information on environmental and occupational health as a career. Several sources are available for information on educational programs for environmental and occupational health as well as for continuing education and leadership development for practitioners.

The National Environmental Health Association (NEHA) (http:// www.neha. org) offers several nationally recognized credentials within the environmental health profession. Each credential signifies a level of expertise and competence based on education and experience. Eligibility to sit for these credentialing exams is determined by the NEHA. Certifications and credentials available through NEHA include:

- Onsite wastewater system installers: This credential is being developed through a cooperative agreement with the USEPA and will be completed by early 2006. Credentialing and licensing is one of the goals of the *USEPA Voluntary Management Guidelines* and is also recommended by the *National Onsite Wastewater Recycling Association (NOWRA) Model Code.*
- Registered environmental health specialist/registered sanitarian (REHS/RS): The REHS/RS is the premiere NEHA credential. It is

available to a wide range of environmental health professionals. Individuals holding the REHS/RS credential show competency in environmental health issues, direct and train personnel to respond to routine or emergency environmental situations, and frequently provide education to their communities on environmental health concerns. The advantages of NEHA's REHS/RS registration program are: the nationwide recognition of the REHS/RS credential, the continual update of the REHS/RS examination and study guide based on an ongoing assessment of the environmental health field, and the tracking of an individual's continuing education by NEHA.

- Certified food safety professional (CFSP): NEHA has created a credential especially for food safety professionals. The CFSP is designed for individuals within the public and private sectors whose primary responsibility is the protection and safety of food. The exam for this prestigious credential integrates food microbiology, HACCP principles, and regulatory requirements into questions that test problem-solving skills and knowledge.
- Certified environmental health technician (CEHT): The CEHT is for individuals who are interested in field-intensive environmental health activities—such as testing, sampling, and inspections—and who are required to provide information on safe environmental health practices and to eliminate environmental health hazards.
- Registered environmental technician (RET): NEHA's RET is a baseline credential for entry-level hazardous materials professionals. The credential is a excellent way for recent, 2-year graduates (AA) or career changing professionals to demonstrate competency in the core requirements of hazardous materials handling and management.
- Registered hazardous substances professional (RHSP): The RHSP provides technically qualified professionals with national recognition for proven expertise in hazardous materials and toxic substances management.
- Registered hazardous substances specialist (RHSS): The RHSS credential is for individuals who follow protocols for field-intensive hazardous materials activities—such as testing, sampling and handling—and who ensure personal, public, and site safety.
- Board of Certified Safety Professionals (BCSP) offers the Certified Safety Professional (CSP) credential.

- American Board of Industrial Hygiene (ABIH) offers the Certified Industrial Hygienist (CIH) and Certified Associate Industrial Hygienist (CAIH) credentials.
- Council on Certification of Health, Environmental, and Safety Technologist (OHST) has requirements that are less stringent than for CSP, CIH, or CAIH credentials. This remains a voluntary credential although many employers encourage or require certification.

In addition to NEHA, the Web site of the American Academy of Environmental Engineers (http://www.aaee.net) is a useful resource for environmental engineers. The Environmental Health Section of the American Public Health Association's Web site (http://www.apha.org) is another good source of information for environmental health. Schools of public health are among the institutions that offer graduate degrees in environmental and occupational health. The Association of Schools of Public Health (http://www.asph.org) has identified a battery of core environmental health competencies appropriate for all students receiving the master's of public health (MPH) degree. These competencies provide a useful baseline for professional practice and summarize what an MPH graduate should be able to do (Table 4–4).

---

**Table 4–4** Environmental Health Competency Expectations for Graduates of MPH Degree Programs

1. Specify approaches for assessing, preventing, and controlling environmental hazards that pose risks to human health and safety.
2. Describe the direct and indirect human, ecological, and safety effects of major environmental and occupational agents.
3. Specify current environmental risk assessment methods.
4. Describe genetic, physiologic, and psychomotor factors that affect susceptibility to adverse health outcomes following exposure to environmental hazards.
5. Discuss various risk management and risk communication approaches relating to issues of environmental justice and equity.
6. Explain the general mechanisms of toxicity in eliciting a toxic response to various environmental exposures.
7. Develop a testable model of environmental injury.
8. Describe federal and state regulatory programs, guidelines, and authorities that control environmental health issues.

---

*Source:* Association of Schools of Public Health (ASPH) MPH Core Competency Development Process, Version 1.2. Available at http://www.asph.org. Accessed August 2005.

# CONCLUSION

Environmental and occupational health covers a wide range of duties and roles at a variety of levels. Career development opportunities in this area of public health practice are plentiful. A mix of education and experience prepares environmental health workers for increasing responsibility in public-sector agencies as well as the private sector. The field is increasingly moving toward competency-based credentials and certifications. Ongoing education and training are especially relevant concerns for this occupational category. Demand for these positions is steady, and prospects will likely increase over the near term.

# REFERENCES

1. Bureau of Labor Statistics, U.S. Department of Labor. May 2004 National, State, and Metropolitan Area Occupational Employment and Wage Estimates. Available at http://www.bls.gov/oes/current/oes_nat.htm. Accessed August 2005.
2. Health Resources and Services Administration (HRSA), Bureau of Health Professions, National Center for Health Workforce Information and Analysis and Center for Health Policy, Columbia School of Nursing. *The Public Health Workforce Enumeration 2000*. Washington, DC: HRSA; 2000. Available at http://www.phppo.cdc.gov/owpp/docs/library/2000/Public%20Health%20 Workforce%20Enumeration%202000.pdf. Accessed August 2005.

# CHAPTER 5

# Public Health Nursing

The title *public health nurse* designates a nursing professional with educational preparation in public health and nursing science with a primary focus on population-level outcomes. The primary aim of public health nursing is to promote health and prevent disease for entire population groups. This may include assisting and providing care to individual members of the population. It also includes the identification of individuals who may not request care but who have health problems that put themselves and others in the community at risk, such as those with infectious diseases.

The focus of public health nursing is not on providing direct care to individuals in community settings. Public health nurses support the provision of direct care through a process of evaluation and assessment of the needs of individuals in the context of their population group. Public health nurses work with other providers of care to plan, develop, and support systems and programs in the community to prevent problems and provide access to care.

As defined by the Public Health Nursing section of the American Public Health Association (APHA), public health nursing is the practice of promoting and protecting the health of populations using knowledge from nursing, social, and public health sciences. Public health nursing practice is a systematic process by which:

- The health and health care needs of a population are assessed in order to identify subpopulations, families, and individuals who would benefit from health promotion or who are at risk of illness, injury, disability, or premature death.

- A plan for intervention is developed with the community to meet identified needs that takes into account available resources, the range of activities that contribute to health and the prevention of illness, injury, disability, and premature death.
- The plan is implemented effectively, efficiently, and equitably.
- Evaluations are conducted to determine the extent to which the interventions have an impact on the health status of individuals and the population.
- The results of the process are used to influence and direct the delivery of care, deployment of health resources, and the development of local, regional, state, and national health policy and research to promote health and prevent disease.

Table 5–1 provides a snapshot of an average day in the life of a public health nurse.

**Table 5–1  A Typical Day for a Public Health Nurse**

| | |
|---|---|
| 7:30 a.m. | Breakfast meeting with visiting nursing agency to discuss interagency coordination |
| 8:30 a.m. | Consult with clinic staff on issues requiring follow-up, such as missed appointments |
| 9:00 a.m. | Visit home of family missing recent appointments |
| 10:15 a.m. | Back in office for meeting to update director of nursing |
| 10:45 a.m. | Meeting with communicable disease control and epidemiology staff regarding community concerns over West Nile virus threat |
| 11:45 a.m. | Informal lunch meeting with community college faculty and students to promote interest in public health nursing careers |
| 1:00 p.m. | Back in office to discuss referrals from clinic and communicable disease staff |
| 1:30 p.m. | Visit patient receiving directly supervised therapy for tuberculosis; identify need for job training assistance and assist with referral |
| 3:00 p.m. | Back in office, assist clinic staff with back-to-school physicals and immunizations |
| 4:30 p.m. | Time to complete paperwork and follow-up phone calls for today's activities |
| 5:15 p.m. | Review and plan tomorrow's schedule |
| 7:00 p.m. | Attend community meeting regarding West Nile virus concerns to assist epidemiology and environmental health staff |

# OCCUPATIONAL CLASSIFICATION

There is no standard occupational category specific to public health nurses. There is a more generic standard occupational category *registered nurse* that encompasses professional nursing positions in any health care or health services organization. This standard occupational category is one of the administrative occupations within the white collar grouping of occupations.

Public health nurses plan, develop, implement, and evaluate nursing and public health interventions for individuals, families, and populations at risk of illness or disability. This category covers all positions identified at the registered nurse level, unless specified as performing work defined under some other professional occupational category (such as epidemiologist or occupational health and safety specialist) and includes graduates of diploma and associate degree programs with the RN license. Common job titles for public health nurses include community health nurse, nurse consultant, school nurse, public health nurse, occupational health nurse, home health nurse, and RN case manager. Public health nurses holding administrative positions have titles such as supervising nurse, nursing coordinator, program director, and director of nursing. Public health nurses who provide clinical services often function with titles such as staff nurse, nurse clinician, or nurse practitioner. Licensed practical (or vocational) nurses (LPNs/LVNs) are considered as technical rather than professional workers in this classification.

There are 2.3 million registered nurses and 700,000 licensed vocational/practical nurses in the United States. Only 13% of registered nurses (300,000) work in community or public health settings. Bureau of Labor Statistics data indicate that more than 175,000 nurses (135,000 registered nurses and 42,000 licensed practical nurses) work for federal, state, and local governmental agencies.[1] The *Public Health Workforce Enumeration 2000* identified 64,000 public health nurses and an estimated 15,000–20,000 licensed vocational/practical nurses working for governmental public health organizations with another 8000 registered nurses working for voluntary-sector agencies.[2] Data from these two sources are used throughout this chapter.

# PUBLIC HEALTH PRACTICE PROFILE

Nurses have long been the professional core of the public health workforce. Nurses provide both clinical and community health services in a wide variety of public and private organizations. Services are provided within maternal and child health programs, communicable disease prevention and control, immunization, and school health programs, to name just a few. Many nurses trained in public health take on supervisory and management roles and serve as chief administrator or as part of the senior management team for many local public health agencies. Nurses also serve as program coordinators and consultants for state and federal health agencies. Their broad expertise and professional credibility assists in advocacy and coalition-building activities and in the evaluation of programs within the community. Public health nurses are also active in community health planning and community health improvement initiatives across the United States. Nurses are directly involved in a wide variety of health promotion and disease and injury prevention efforts. Their skills are critical to achieving community health objectives and broader public health goals through performing one or more of the essential public health services. As a result, public health nurses are involved in a wider array of public health purposes and essential public health services than most other public health occupational categories. It is somewhat misleading to highlight only a few public health purposes and essential public health services that are most closely associated with public health nursing. Virtually all fit within the scope of their professional expertise. For the sake of consistency with other public health occupations and titles addressed in this book, three public health purposes and five essential public health services are identified for public health nurses in Table 5–2.

## IMPORTANT AND ESSENTIAL DUTIES

Nursing positions within public health organizations have many different titles. In some organizations, all registered nurses are covered by one series usually called public health nurse. In other organizations, registered nurses performing clinical duties may be distinguished from those performing community and public health nursing duties. Some organizations employ nurse practitioners to provide primary medical care. In addition to registered nurses, some public health organizations employ licensed practical nurses or licensed vocational nurses to provide supportive nursing services for clinical care programs. The focus in this chapter will be on three nursing positions: entry-level public health nurse, senior-level public health nurse, and licensed vocational nurse.

---

**Table 5–2** Public Health Practice Profile for Public Health Nurses

---

Public Health Nurses
Make a Difference by:

**Public Health Purposes**

| | |
|---|---|
| Preventing epidemics and the spread of disease | ✔ |
| Protecting against environmental hazards | |
| Preventing injuries | |
| Promoting and encouraging healthy behaviors | ✔ |
| Responding to disasters and assisting communities in recovery | |
| Assuring the quality and accessibility of health services | ✔ |

**Essential Public Health Services**

| | |
|---|---|
| Monitoring health status to identify community health problems | ✔ |
| Diagnosing and investigating health problems and health hazards in the community | |
| Informing, educating, and empowering people about health issues | ✔ |
| Mobilizing community partnerships to identify and solve health problems | |
| Developing policies and plans that support individual and community health efforts | |
| Enforcing laws and regulations that protect health and ensure safety | |
| Linking people with needed personal health services and assuring the provision of health care when otherwise unavailable | ✔ |
| Assuring a competent public health and personal health care workforce | |
| Evaluating effectiveness, accessibility, and quality of personal and population-based health services | ✔ |
| Researching new insights and innovative solutions to health problems | ✔ |

---

## *Public Health Nurse (Entry Level)*

Under direction, entry-level public health nurses provide public health nursing services, including health education, the promotion of health awareness, and the prevention and control of diseases. This is the entry and first working level in the public health nurse class series. Incumbents must have requisite public health nursing certification, but have limited public health nursing work experience. As experience is gained, incumbents learn to perform the full scope of public health nursing duties. Entry-level public health nurses are distinguished from midlevel public health nurses who carry responsibility for more independently performing a larger scope of public health nursing duties and activities. Midlevel public health nurses perform a larger range of duties and activities on a more independent basis and are distinguished from senior public health nurses in that senior public health nurses perform more complex, specialized assignments, as well as provide lead direction, work coordination, and training for other professional nursing and support staff. Entry-level and midlevel public health nurses generally report to a senior public health nurse or the director of nursing services. Entry-level positions do not supervise other staff.

Important and essential duties for entry-level public health nursing positions may include:

- Participate in planning, organizing, and providing public health nursing services, health instruction, counseling, and guidance for individuals, families, and groups regarding disease control, health awareness, health maintenance, and rehabilitation in a clinic setting.
- Identify and interact with local care providers in the coordination of health care.
- Provide referrals to other community-based health and social services.
- Teach and demonstrate health practices to individuals and groups.
- Instruct clients in immunization procedures, family planning, and sexually transmitted disease prevention and follow-up.
- Identify individual and family problems that are detrimental to good health.
- Make home visits to assess a patent's progress and intervene accordingly.
- Work with families to alleviate health problems and promote good health habits.
- Refer and coordinate the care of individuals and families with other public and private agencies.
- Identify special health needs for assigned cases, recommending and implementing services to meet those needs.
- Assist individuals and families with implementing physician recommendations.
- Participate in planning, directing, and performing epidemiological investigations in homes, schools, workplaces, the community, and public health clinics.
- Prepare appropriate records and case documentation, arranging follow-up services based on findings.

- Confer with physicians, nursing staff, and other staff regarding public health programs, patient reports, evaluations, medical tests, and related items.
- Participate in multidisciplinary teams for the purpose of creating a plan of service for at-risk families.
- Participate and collaborate with community groups to identify public health needs, develop needed public health services, and improve existing public health services.
- Prepare reports and maintain records.
- Compile statistical information for appraisal and planning purposes.

## Public Health Nurse (Senior Level)

Under direction, senior public health nurses provide lead direction and work coordination for other professional nursing and support staff. Senior public health nurses plan and conduct a variety of public health nursing clinics and services and provide complex, specialized, and general nursing, health education, and health consulting services, including the prevention and control of diseases and the promotion of health awareness. This is the advanced level and lead class in the public health nurse series. Incumbents provide the more complex public health nursing services in a specialized public health program, as well as provide lead direction and coordination for other professional nursing staff. This class is distinguished from the midlevel public health nurse by assignment of a higher level of public health program responsibilities and the performance of lead responsibilities for other professional nursing staff. Senior public health nurses report to the director of nursing services and, in turn, provide lead direction and work coordination for entry-level and midlevel public health nurses.

Important and essential duties for senior-level public health nurses may include:

- Investigate outbreaks of communicable diseases.
- Plan and implement programs for the prevention and control of communicable disease, including tuberculosis, sexually transmitted diseases, and AIDS.
- Develop procedures to control the spread of communicable diseases and identify people needing public health services.
- Provide interpretations of public health laws and regulations for others.

- Assess individuals and families, using health histories, observations of physical condition, and a variety of evaluative methods to identify health problems, health deficiencies, and health service needs.
- Identify psychosocial, cultural background, and environmental factors that may hinder the use of or access to health care services.
- Assist with determining funding needs for specific programs, and monitor budget expenditures within those programs.
- Plan and coordinate services for special programs such as family planning, or perinatal, maternal, child, or adolescent programs.
- Perform public health nursing activities to promote perinatal, child, and adolescent health.
- Provide local case management and coordination within specific programs.
- Participate in programs to enhance school children health.
- Work with community groups to identify needs, develop and facilitate a variety of health services, and improve existing programs.
- Refer individuals and families to appropriate agencies and clinics for health services.
- Participate in programs to enhance community health services and education.
- Attend conferences and workshops related to community health issues.
- Assist with the preparation of program and service policies and procedures.
- Supervise paraprofessional staff and volunteers.
- Prepare reports and maintain records.
- Compile and analyze statistical information for appraisal and planning purposes.
- Provide lead direction, training, and work coordination for other professional nurses.

### Licensed Vocational/Practical Nurse

Under general supervision, licensed vocational (or practical) nurses perform a variety of health-related activities in the provision of basic nursing care, including administering immunizations and vaccinations, hearing and vision screening, basic skin and blood tests, and blood pressure monitoring. Licensed vocational nurses assist with a variety of activities related to implementation of various agency health programs. Workers in this title do not have the necessary education, experience, or license requirements to qualify as either a registered nurse or a public health nurse. Workers perform a variety of clinical and basic nursing duties consistent with their license and experience. Licensed vocational nurses report to a midlevel or senior-level public health nurse or to the director of nursing. These positions do not carry supervisory responsibility.

Important and essential duties for licensed vocational nursing positions may include:

- Perform, read, and evaluate skin, hearing, vision, and blood tests.
- Perform and evaluate blood pressure readings.
- Provide health education sessions.
- Administer immunizations and vaccinations.
- Participate in health care clinics, coordinating activities as assigned.
- Maintain a current inventory of clinic supplies.
- Operate a mobile health van.
- Evaluate medical records and determine the need for immunization or vaccination.
- Prepare patients for physical examinations.
- Weigh and measure patients.
- Assist with examinations.
- Refer clients to other health care providers.
- Prepare specimens for mailing.
- Provide basic health information and instruction to individuals and families.
- Answer health-related questions from the public.
- Sterilize equipment.
- Maintain safety requirements in a clinical setting.
- Triage requests for information.

## MINIMUM QUALIFICATIONS

Nurses working in public health come from a wide variety of backgrounds and academic preparation. The number of registered nurses (RNs) produced by 4-year baccalaureate programs is increasing, but there are many RNs from diploma programs in the public health workforce as well. Many nursing schools offer master's-level preparation in community health nursing, school health, and other public health specializations. As described later in this chapter, there is a highly respected, competency-based credential that is offered for community health nurses. Nonetheless, many of those working as nurses in public health settings, including those holding public health nursing titles, do not qualify for this credential because of inadequate educational attainment.

## Typical Minimum Qualifications for Entry-Level Public Health Nurse

### Knowledge, Skills, and Abilities

The typical entry-level public health nurse generally has knowledge of:

- Principles, methods, practices, and current trends of general and public health nursing and preventive medicine
- Community aspects of public nursing including community resources and demography
- Federal, state, and local laws and regulations governing communicable disease, public health, and disabling conditions
- Environmental, sociological, and psychological problems related to public health nursing programs
- Child growth and development
- Causes, means of transmission, and methods of control of communicable disease
- Methods of promoting child and maternal health and public health programs
- Principles of health education

A typical entry-level public health nurse has the skills and ability to:

- Learn to organize and carry out public health nursing activities in an assigned program.
- Collect, analyze, and interpret technical, statistical, and health data.
- Analyze and evaluate health problems of individuals and families, and take appropriate action.
- Provide instruction in the prevention of diseases.
- Develop and maintain health records, and prepare clear and concise reports.
- Communicate effectively orally and in writing.

- Interact tactfully and courteously with the public, community organizations, and other staff when explaining public health issues and providing public health services.
- Establish and maintain cooperative working relationships.
- Effectively represent the agency and nursing division in contacts with public, other staff, and other governmental agencies.

### Experience and Education

Any combination of training and experience that provides the required knowledge and abilities will qualify an individual for this position. A typical way to obtain the required knowledge and abilities is to complete a bachelor degree and have adequate work experience to meet existing state certification requirements. These often call for one year of previous public health nursing experience comparable to an entry-level public health nurse with the hiring organization. Special requirements include possession of a valid state license as a registered nurse. A state-issued certificate as a public health nurse and possession of a valid state driver's license may also be required by some agencies.

## Typical Minimum Qualifications for Senior-Level Public Health Nurse

### Knowledge, Skills, and Abilities

In addition to those required for entry-level public health nurses, senior-level public health nurses generally have knowledge of:

- Unique psycho-social and cultural issues encountered in a rural health program
- Principles of health education
- Program planning, evaluations, and development principles
- Principles of lead direction, program and work coordination, and training
- Community health assessment principles, strategies, and tools

A senior-level public health nurse generally has the skills and ability to:

- Plan, organize, and carry out public health nursing activities and services for an assigned service area or program.

- Develop and maintain effective working relationships with clients, staff, community groups, and other government organizations.
- Collect, analyze, and interpret technical, statistical, and health data.
- Analyze and evaluate health problems of individuals and families, and take appropriate action.
- Provide work direction and coordination for other staff.
- Provide instruction in the prevention and control of diseases.
- Communicate effectively in writing and orally.
- Develop and maintain health records and prepare clear and concise reports.

### Experience and Education

Any combination of training and experience that provides the required knowledge and abilities will qualify an individual for this position. A typical way to obtain the required knowledge and abilities is to complete sufficient education and experience to meet state certification requirements. This may require one year of public health nursing experience comparable to a midlevel public health nurse. In addition, special requirements may include possession of a valid state license as a registered nurse, state certification as a public health nurse, and a valid state driver's license.

## Typical Minimum Qualifications for Licensed Practical/Vocational Nurses

### Knowledge, Skills, and Abilities

A licensed practical/vocational nurse generally has knowledge of:

- Principles, methods, and procedures of general nursing
- Causes, means of transmission, and methods of controlling communicable diseases
- Basic medical terminology
- Principles and procedures of medical record keeping
- Health problems and requirements of infants, children, adolescents, and the elderly
- State laws relating to reporting child abuse and neglect

A licensed practical/vocational nurse generally has the skills and ability to:

- Operate a variety of standard medical testing equipment.
- Communicate effectively in writing and orally.

- Follow oral and written instructions.
- Provide responsible nursing care and services.
- Maintain confidentiality of material.
- Interview patients and families to gather medical history.
- Perform skin tests and interpret results.
- Prepare medical forms and records.
- Work responsibly with physicians and other members of the health care team.
- Effectively represent the agency in contacts with the public, community organizations, and other government agencies.
- Establish and maintain cooperative working relationships with patients and others.

### Experience and Education

Any combination of training and experience that provides the required knowledge and abilities will qualify an individual for this position. A typical way to obtain the required knowledge and abilities is through one year of vocational nursing experience and completion of nursing studies and curriculum sufficient to obtain requisite state licenses. In addition, special requirements may include possession of a valid state license as a licensed vocational nurse and a valid driver's license.

## WORKPLACE CONSIDERATIONS

Public health nurses have long been one of the most important, and most numerous, categories within the professional public health workforce. Public health nurses are especially prominent in local public health agencies where they are involved in a wide range of disease prevention, health promotion, and health service programs. They are also found in state and federal health agencies, although not as frequently today as in past decades. Public health nurses play key roles in maternal and child health services, WIC programs, immunization and communicable disease control programs, and in the clinical operations of local public health agencies. Their professional background also makes them effective links with other community health organizations and agencies, especially local hospitals and schools. Public health nurses need to know medical terminology and how to perform various medical screening tests and basic nursing procedures.

Work is performed in clinics and health care offices, at work site, and in home environments with occasional exposure to communicable diseases and blood-borne pathogens as well as saliva, urine, and feces. Nurses are expected to understand and follow recommended practices and precautions for prevention of disease transmission. Ongoing contact with other staff and the public is part of the daily routine for public health nurses. Public health nurses may need to travel to various locations within the community, including to remote or unsafe areas in all weather conditions in order to perform their duties. Personal safety is enhanced through safety training, use of cell phones and identification badges, and not traveling alone to neighborhoods with high crime rates.

Typical physical requirements for nurses at all levels include the ability to sit and stand for extended periods, normal manual dexterity and eye-hand coordination, the ability to lift and move objects weighing up to 50 pounds, hearing and vision corrected to normal range, verbal communications skills, and the ability to properly use medical and office equipment, including computer, telephone, calculator, copiers, and fax machines.

## SALARY ESTIMATES

Salary levels for public health nurses depend in part on academic degrees, credentialing, experience, as well as on market conditions related to the shortage of nurses in the area. At the lower end of these criteria, salaries of $10–12 an hour are not uncommon. At the higher levels of these criteria, salaries may be in the $35–40 per hour range. It is common for public health nurses to move up into unit and agency leadership positions and higher salaries. It is not uncommon for the public health agency director of a small agency to be an experienced public health nurse.

Registered nurses in the United States have a mean salary of $55,000 with 50% earning between $44,000 and $64,000. As indicated in Table 5–3, registered nurses working for federal agencies have higher average salaries than those working for state or local governmental agencies ($65,000 federal, $50,500 state, $53,000 local) but far lower than those working in acute care settings.

Licensed practical/vocational nurses have an average annual salary of $35,000 with 50% earning between $29,000 and $41,000. Mean salaries are similar for LPNs or LVNs working for the different levels of government ($37,000 federal, $34,000 state, $34,500 local).

**Table 5–3** Number and Mean Salary for Nurses in Federal, State, and Local Governmental Agencies, May 2004

| Occupational Category | Federal Workers | Federal Worker Mean Salary | State Workers | State Worker Mean Salary | Local Workers | Local Worker Mean Salary | Total Federal, State, and Local Workers | Adjusted PH Enum. 2000 Workers |
|---|---|---|---|---|---|---|---|---|
| Registered Nurses | 48,490 | $64,780 | 35,540 | $50,520 | 51,320 | $53,200 | 135,350 | 63,753 |
| Licensed Vocational/ Practical Nurses | 12,690 | $37,060 | 13,170 | $34,240 | 16,620 | $34,310 | 42,480 | (est) 25,000 |

*Source:* Data for federal, state, and local governmental agency workers from Bureau of Labor Statistics. May 2004 National, State, and Metropolitan Area Occupational Employment and Wage Estimates. Available at http://www.bls.gov. Accessed August 2005. See Chapter 2 for adjusted number of public health workers from *The Public Health Workforce Enumeration 2000.*

## CAREER PROSPECTS

Nurses remain in short supply throughout the health sector, making the recruitment and retention of public health nurses an issue for potential employers, both public and private. Public-sector agencies, such as local and state health departments as well as community and national not-for-profit organizations, often are not able to match salary and benefit levels available through private employers (such as hospitals, clinics, and health plans). Competition with private-sector employers has increased nursing salaries to some extent, although public health agencies generally are not able to match the salaries and benefits (including signing bonuses) available within the acute care and primary care sectors.

As the largest professional category employed by public health agencies, and due to the growing shortage of registered nurses, there are many opportunities for all levels of nurses within the public health workforce. Working hours and conditions for nurses working in public health agencies can be attractive, and many nurses appreciate the importance and impact of working in public health. Still, public health nurses are the number one worker category identified as needed now and in the future for public health agencies. The *Public Health Workforce Enumeration 2000* found 50,000 public health nurses, nearly of all of whom worked in state and local public health agencies.

The number of undergraduate and graduate students entering nursing training programs has been increasing steadily in recent years. As noted earlier, the demand for public health nurses is also increasing, probably even faster than the supply.

## ADDITIONAL INFORMATION

There are many good sources of information on public health nursing. Several sources of information are available on educational programs for these occupations as well as for continuing education and leadership development for public health nurses.

The Public Health Nursing section of the American Public Health Association's (http://www.apha.org) Web site is a great source of information on public health nursing. The Public Health Nursing section has a long history and currently has many members, making it one of APHA's largest and most active sections.

Schools of public health are among the institutions offering master's and doctoral degrees in public health for nurses. The Association of Schools of Public Health (http://www.asph.org) provides information on accredited schools of public health and on the characteristics of public health students and degree concentrations.

State licensing boards (which license registered nurses), schools of nursing, the American Nursing Association, and its many state affiliates are rich sources for additional information on public health nurses. The American Nursing Credentialing Center (ANCC) is the credentialing arm of the American Nurses Association (http://www.nursingworld.org/ancc/cert/eligibility/CommHealth.html) and awards a RN, BC (registered nurse, board certified) certification. ANCC certifies community health nurses who meet all the following requirements:

- Active registered nurse license in the United States
- Two full years of public heath nursing practice in the United States
- Bachelor or higher degree in nursing
- Two thousand or more hours of clinical practice within the past three years (can include nursing administration, education, client care, and research)
- Thirty contact hours of continuing education within the past three years

The Quad Council of Public Health Nursing Organizations is an alliance of the four national nursing organizations that address public health nursing issues: the Association of Community Health Nurse Educators (ACHNE), the American Nurses Association's (ANA) Congress on Nursing Practice and Economics, the American Public Health Association (APHA) Public Health Nursing Section, and the Association of State and Territorial Directors of Nursing (ASTDN). The *Quad Council PHN Competencies* is designed for use with others documents. It complements the *Definition of Public Health Nursing* adopted by the APHA's Public Health Nursing Section in 1996 and the American Nurses Association's *Standards of Public Health Nursing Practice.*[3]

In developing the competencies the Quad Council members concurred that the generalist level would reflect preparation at the bachelor level. Although recognizing in many states much of the public health nursing workforce does not have a bachelor degree, the Quad Council believes that those nurses may require job descriptions that reflect a different level of practice or may require extensive orientation and education to achieve the competencies identified. Further, the specialist-level competencies described in this document reflect preparation at the master's level in community/public health nursing or public health. Again, while recognizing that there may be other public health nurses who are promoted or appointed to managerial or consultant positions that require specialist competencies, a master's degree prepares public health nurses for the specialist-level competencies identified in this document. At both levels, it is expected that on-the-job training and continuing education for nurses hired for these positions who have less than a bachelor or master's degree (as appropriate to the level) will assure these competencies are attained.

The Quad Council based its competency framework on several relevant assumptions. Public health nurses must first possess the competencies common to all nurses with bachelor degrees and then demonstrate additional competencies specific to their roles in public health. The progression from awareness to knowledge to proficiency is a continuum, and there are no discrete boundaries between those levels of competence. Both levels reflect competencies for a reasonably prudent public health nurse who has experience in the role (i.e., not a novice and not in a specialized or limited focus role). Defined competencies are intended to reflect the standard for public health nursing practice, not necessarily what is occurring in practice today. Importantly, in any practice setting

---

**Table 5–4** American Nurses Association Public Health Nursing Standards of Practice and Professional Performance

**Standards of Practice**

1. Assessment: The public health nurse assesses the health status of populations using data, community resource identification, input from the population, and professional judgment.
2. Population diagnosis and priorities: The public health nurse analyzes the assessment data to determine population diagnoses or priorities.
3. Outcomes identification: The public health nurse identifies expected outcomes for a plan that is based on population diagnoses or priorities.
4. Planning: The public health nurse develops a plan that identifies strategies, action plans, and alternatives to attain expected outcomes.
5. Implementation: The public health nurse implements the identified plan by partnering with others.
   a. Coordination: The public health nurse coordinates programs, services, and other activities in implementing the identified plan.
   b. Health education and health promotion: The public health nurse employs educational strategies to promote health, prevent disease, and ensure a safer environment for populations.
   c. Consultation: The public health nurse provides consultation to various community groups and officials to facilitate the implementation of programs and services.
   d. Regulatory activities: The public health nurse identifies, interprets, and implements public health laws, regulations, and policies.
6. Evaluation: The public health nurse evaluates the health status of the population.

**Standards of Professional Performance**

7. Quality of practice: The public health nurse systematically enhances the quality and effectiveness of nursing practice.
8. Education: The public health nurse attains knowledge and competency that reflects current nursing and public health practice.
9. Professional practice evaluation: The public health nurse evaluates one's own nursing practiced in relation to professional practice standards and guidelines, relevant statutes, rules, and regulations.
10. Collegiality and professional relationships: The public health nurse establishes collegial partnerships while interacting with representatives of the population, organizations, and health and human services professionals, and contributes to the professional development of peers, colleagues, and others.
11. Research: The public health nurse puts research findings into practice.
12. Resource utilization: The public health nurse considers factors related to safety, effectiveness, cost, and impact on practice and on the population in the planning and delivery of nursing and public health programs, policies, and services.
13. Leadership: The public health nurse provides leadership in nursing and public health.
14. Advocacy: The public health nurse advocates and strives to protect the health, safety, and rights of the population.

---

*Source:* American Nurses Association. Public Health Nursing: Scope and Standards of Practice. Available at http://www.nursingworld.org/practice/publichealthnursing.pdf. Accessed September 2005.

the job descriptions may reflect components from each level, depending on the agency's structure, size, leadership, and services. Table 5–4 outlines the American Nurses Association *Standards of Public Health Nursing Practice*. Detailed information on core public health nursing competencies are available at http://www.nursingworld.org/anp/palpha.cfm, in various ANA publications, and in documents with the full scope and standards of public health nursing practice.

## CONCLUSION

Public health nurses are the largest category of health professionals in the public health workforce. They are active in community as well as clinical services and at all levels of public health organizations, including serving as public health managers and administrators. Although there are more than 2 million nurses in the United States, only an estimated 75,000 work for governmental public health organizations, and relatively few of those have formal training in public health. The national nursing shortage, particularly acute for nursing positions in hospitals and long-term care facilities, also affects the ability of public health organizations to attract and retain qualified nurses. Recruitment and retention initiatives are widely discussed within the public health community, a testimony to the continuing importance of public health nurses if public health goals and objectives are to be achieved.

## REFERENCES

1. Bureau of Labor Statistics, U.S. Department of Labor. May 2004 National, State, and Metropolitan Area Occupational Employment and Wage Estimates. Available at http://www.bls.gov/oes/current/oes_nat.htm. Accessed August 2005.
2. Health Resources and Services Administration (HRSA), Bureau of Health Professions, National Center for Health Workforce Information and Analysis and Center for Health Policy, Columbia School of Nursing. *The Public Health Workforce Enumeration 2000*. Washington, DC: HRSA; 2000. Available at http://www.phppo.cdc.gov/owpp/docs/library/2000/Public%20Health%20 Workforce%20Enumeration%202000.pdf. Accessed August 2005.
3. American Nurses Association. Public Health Nursing: Scope and Standards of Practice. Available at http://www.nursingworld.org/practice/publichealthnursing .pdf. Accessed September 2005.

# Epidemiology and Disease Control

Epidemiology is often called the mother science of public health practice. Epidemiologists investigate and describe the determinants and distribution of disease, disability, and other health outcomes and help develop the means for their prevention and control. Epidemiology works hand in hand with biostatistics and field investigations to provide information and insights into factors that contribute to health and disease in a population. John Snow's methods of examining cholera outbreaks in 1854 demonstrated the usefulness of epidemiological methods even when little was known about the microorganism causing these outbreaks. Epidemiology and biostatistics are essential tools for research and evaluation into causative factors as well as into the effectiveness of clinical and community interventions.

Recent concerns over bioterrorism threats and events have raised awareness of the important role played by epidemiologists and related occupations. One of the major objectives of increased funding for bioterrorism preparedness and response is to rapidly increase the number of epidemiologists working in state and local public health agencies. Table 6–1 provides a snapshot of an average day in the life of an epidemiologist.

## OCCUPATIONAL CLASSIFICATION

Two standard occupational categories used for public health workers (epidemiologist and statistician) are addressed in this chapter. Epidemiologist is a standard occupational category that is commonly found in public health organizations. Biostatisticians are a subset of statisticians. Both

**Table 6-1** A Typical Day for an Epidemiologist

| | |
|---|---|
| 7:30 a.m. | Phone discussion from home with state epidemiologist regarding current status of West Nile virus and follow up on last week's foodborne illness outbreak involving local fast-food establishment |
| 8:30 a.m. | Meeting with public health student completing internship project analyzing childhood asthma morbidity |
| 9:00 a.m. | Staff meeting to review priorities for week |
| 10:15 a.m. | Meet with agency director, health education, and planning staff regarding completion of community health assessment |
| 10:45 a.m. | Meet with communicable disease control and public health nursing staff regarding community concerns over West Nile virus threat |
| 11:45 a.m. | Interview candidates for vacant entry-level epidemiologist position |
| 12:15 p.m. | Lunch at desk while catching up with e-mail and phone messages |
| 1:00 p.m. | Grand Rounds presentation at community hospital on nosocomial infections |
| 2:30 p.m. | Office time to respond to e-mail and phone messages |
| 3:00 p.m. | Conference call with epidemiologists and environmental health staff of neighboring jurisdictions and state health department regarding current status of West Nile virus |
| 4:00 p.m. | Review information suggested by staff for tonight's community meeting on West Nile virus |
| 4:30 p.m. | Brief agency director on West Nile virus |
| 5:15 p.m. | Complete final report on last week's foodborne illness outbreak involving local fast-food establishment |
| 7:00 p.m. | Represent agency at community meeting regarding West Nile virus concerns |

categories are professional white collar categories. Another important and related occupational category, disease investigators, is not included among the standard occupational titles but will also be described in this chapter as their work complements that of epidemiologists and biostatisticians.

- The role of epidemiologist encompasses positions that investigate, describe, and analyze the distribution and determinants of disease, disability, and other health outcomes, and develop the means for their prevention and control. Epidemiologists also describe and analyze the efficacy of programs and interventions. This category includes individuals specifically trained as epidemiologists as well as those trained in another discipline (such as medicine, nursing, or environmental health) working as epidemiologists under such job titles as nurse epidemiologist. Bureau of Labor Statistics data indicate that there are 4600 epidemiologists in the United States, with state and local governments employing 1800 of these positions.[1] The *Public Health Workforce Enumeration 2000* identified 1400 epidemiologists working in federal, state, and local governmental public health agencies.[2] Data from these two sources are used throughout this chapter. Hospitals, scientific research and development companies, and educational institutions are also important sources of employment for epidemiologists. A 2004 survey conducted by the Council of State and Territorial Epidemiologists identified 2600 epidemiologists working in state and local public health agencies, although it is likely that this number included some disease investigator positions.[3]

- The role of infection control/disease investigator includes positions that assist in identifying and locating individuals or groups at risk of specified health problems and incorporating those people into appropriate health promotion and disease prevention programs. This category includes public health investigators or sexually transmitted infection investigators without reference to educational preparation. Disease investigators may be undercounted if individuals with specific professional preparation (such as nursing, environmental health, or laboratory science) are primarily performing investigations but are employed under another professional title. As this title is not one of the standard occupational categories tracked by the Bureau of Labor Statistics, it is not clear how many disease investigator positions exist. The *Public Health Workforce Enumeration 2000* identified 1200 infection control and disease investigator positions in governmental public health agencies. It is likely that there is some overlap between these positions and those designated as epidemiologists or general program specialists (see Chapter 9).

- Biostatisticians apply statistical reasoning and methods in addressing, analyzing, and solving problems in public health, health care, and biomedical, clinical, and population-based research. The precise number of biostatisticians is not known. Bureau of Labor Statistics data indicates there are 17,000 statisticians in the United States, with nearly 6000 working for governmental agencies. The federal government alone employs over 3500 statisticians. The *Public Health Workforce Enumeration 2000* identified 1800 biostatisticians in governmental public health agencies, the majority working for federal and state agencies.

## PUBLIC HEALTH PRACTICE PROFILE

Epidemiologists, biostatisticians, and disease investigators primarily address public health responsibilities for preventing disease and injury and protecting against environmental hazards. These occupational groups may also be involved in emergency preparedness and response and, not infrequently, with assessing the impact and quality of health services within a community.

Among the 10 essential public health services, epidemiologists and related occupations are especially important for four: monitoring health status, diagnosing and investigating health events and threats in the community, assessing the impact and quality of services, and researching innovative solutions to health problems. Table 6–2 summarizes public health

**Table 6–2**  Public Health Practice Profile for Epidemiology and Disease Control

| | Epidemiology and Disease Control Professionals Make a Difference by: |
|---|:---:|
| **Public Health Purposes** | |
| Preventing epidemics and the spread of disease | ✓ |
| Protecting against environmental hazards | ✓ |
| Preventing injuries | ✓ |
| Promoting and encouraging healthy behaviors | |
| Responding to disasters and assisting communities in recovery | |
| Assuring the quality and accessibility of health services | |
| | |
| **Essential Public Health Services** | |
| Monitoring health status to identify community health problems | ✓ |
| Diagnosing and investigating health problems and health hazards in the community | ✓ |
| Informing, educating, and empowering people about health issues | |
| Mobilizing community partnerships to identify and solve health problems | |
| Developing policies and plans that support individual and community health efforts | |
| Enforcing laws and regulations that protect health and ensure safety | |
| Linking people with needed personal health services and assuring the provision of health care when otherwise unavailable | |
| Assuring a competent public health and personal health care workforce | |
| Evaluating effectiveness, accessibility, and quality of personal and population-based health services | ✓ |
| Researching new insights and innovative solutions to health problems | ✓ |

purposes and essential public health services at the core of positions for epidemiologists and disease control professionals.

## IMPORTANT AND ESSENTIAL DUTIES

There are many job titles and positions in the public health workforce that investigate and analyze health problems and risks. The focus in this chapter will be on four positions: communicable disease investigator, entry-level epidemiologist, senior-level epidemiologist, and biostatistician. Each of these positions and a representative panel of their important and essential duties are described in this section.

### Communicable Disease Investigator

This position investigates confirmed or suspected cases of communicable diseases to ensure patient treatment and follow-up. Duties are often characterized by the responsibility to implement key aspects of a communicable disease control program. This position performs communicable disease investigative work, bringing to treatment those patients with positive laboratory tests and providing information on sexually transmitted and other communicable diseases. Communicable disease investigator titles may include higher-level titles responsible for supervising the work of communicable disease investigators and providing the more difficult and sensitive pre- and posttest counseling to patients and families. Entry-level and midlevel communicable disease investigators exercise no supervision over other workers.

Operational duties related to identifying and obtaining treatment for carriers of communicable diseases include identifying target populations, conducting epidemiological investigations, testing patients, and making referrals for social or community services. This position administers tuberculin skin tests, obtains laboratory samples, and performs epidemiological investigations. Many personnel systems have several levels for disease investigators.

Important and essential duties of a communicable disease investigator include:

- Interviews clients and contacts; performs risk assessment and counseling; performs disease testing; performs partner counseling and referral service to contacts of infected persons; counsels patients diagnosed as having a communicable disease regarding the disease process (such as the sequence of symptoms), appropriate medications, complications, and prevention so that they will be encouraged to be treated and give names, addresses, and phone numbers of contacts who have been exposed when this is appropriate

- Provides referrals to service providers
- Provides transportation for infected clients and their partners to get appropriate medical care
- Manages cases to closure including successful treatment or failure to comply
- Locates contacts by phone or field visits and informs contacts of infected persons of possible exposure to a sexually transmitted or other communicable disease; maintains confidentiality of information
- Reviews information (such as epidemiological reports) from other jurisdictions regarding persons exposed to sexually transmitted and other communicable disease; initiates and provides such information for use by other agencies; consults with medical providers regarding specific clients' diagnosis, treatment plan, infection history, and location; consults with laboratory microbiologist regarding complex test results
- Attends meetings and in-service training on identification, testing, and treatment protocols for sexually transmitted and other communicable diseases; may serve as an agency resource or act on behalf of the program coordinator in that person's absence in an assigned program area
- Maintains professional knowledge in applicable areas and keeps abreast of changes in job-related rules, statutes, laws, and new business trends; makes recommendations for the implementation of changes; reads and interprets professional literature; attends training programs, workshops, and seminars as appropriate
- Identifies, contacts, and recruits high-risk patients for participation in communicable disease education and prevention programs
- Provides health education to community organizations, schools, and groups about risky lifestyles and contracting communicable diseases
- Maintains epidemiological control record of patients, contacts, and suspects
- Maintains a central record file on communicable diseases
- Maintains records of locations where high-risk activity occurs

- Participates as member of a multidisciplinary team on disease surveillance and investigations with epidemiologists, biostatisticians, health care professionals, environmental health practitioners, health information specialists, and staff of regulated industries (such as restaurants, hospitals, and nursing homes)
- Maintains cooperative relationships with officials of the armed forces, state department of public health, and local police departments

### Epidemiologist (Entry Level)

This position performs epidemiological investigations of human morbidity and mortality; compiles, maintains, and analyzes health data and reports; identifies causative agents resulting in adverse health conditions and proposes corrective actions; and provides public health information and consultative services. This is the entry-level professional epidemiologist performing duties under the direct supervision of a higher-level epidemiologist.

Entry-level epidemiologists work in the investigation, analysis, prevention, and control of injuries or communicable, chronic, or environmentally induced diseases. An entry-level epidemiologist is responsible for conducting ongoing epidemiologic studies in order to investigate, identify, and analyze incidence, prevalence, trends, and causes of injuries or communicable, chronic, or environmentally induced diseases. An entry-level epidemiologist is also responsible for assisting with the development of intervention strategies, policies, and procedures and the evaluation of new and existing prevention and control programs based on epidemiologic findings. Work involves communicating with health care providers; social service agencies; schools; federal, state, and local officials; the media and others concerning disease and injury investigation, prevention, and control. This position may supervise subordinate staff, such as communicable disease investigators. Work is subject to general review and direction by a higher-level epidemiologist, program administrator, or other designated superior; however, an entry-level epidemiologist works with considerable independence within established policies and procedures.

Important and essential duties of an entry-level epidemiologist include:

- Assists in the design of or conducts epidemiologic studies of disease or injury occurrence, including evaluation of behavioral and clinical interventions

- Reviews and evaluates disease or injury reporting and surveillance systems and advises program administrators of important incidence or prevalence changes within reporting areas
- Conducts or assists in in-depth investigations of disease clusters using epidemiologic methods, including gathering information and biological specimens
- Conducts field interviews of case subjects, potential case and control subjects, government officials, and others to ascertain disease incidence and prevalence
- Maintains contact with community physicians, hospital staff, and other health care professionals to encourage proper reporting of injuries and communicable, chronic, or environmentally induced diseases and conditions
- Participates as member of a multidisciplinary team on disease surveillance and investigations with disease investigators, biostatisticians, health care professionals, environmental health practitioners, health information specialists, and staff of regulated industries (such as restaurants, hospitals, and nursing homes)
- Communicates with health care providers; social service agencies; schools; federal, state, and local officials; the media; and others concerning disease and injury investigation, prevention, and control
- Conducts epidemiologic investigations, surveys, and special studies relating to public health, including assessment of risk behaviors or continuing risk of exposure to specific agents
- Conducts evaluations of control measures related to communicable, chronic, or environmentally induced diseases or injuries
- Prepares investigation reports, statistical analyses, and summaries on completed epidemiologic studies and evaluations
- Participates in preparing grant applications, research reports, and other public health documents

## *Epidemiologist (Senior Level)*

This position coordinates, conducts, analyzes, interprets, and reports the findings from public health surveillance systems and advanced epidemiologic studies that identify the causes of morbidity and mortality; designs and coordinates appropriate preventive health measures based upon investigative results; and determines which specific public health issues require further epidemiologic studies. Medical epidemiologists (such as physicians, veterinarians, dentists, and nurses) provide professional medical consultation in the performance of these duties. This is the highest-level position in the series. Incumbents at this level independently propose and direct epidemiological investigations or act as the principal investigator on local, state, or federal health research grants. Positions at this level may supervise or lead lower-level epidemiologists or other research staff.

Important and essential duties of senior-level epidemiologists include:

- Conducts case control, cohort, or cross-sectional studies to identify the incidence, prevalence, or causes of human morbidity or mortality; prepares formal written reports of findings, including a description of the methods used, the findings, and the interpretation of the findings
- Conducts disease outbreak investigations to identify causative agents and environmental conditions resulting in disease outbreaks
- Performs statistical analyses of health data, such as analysis of variance, trend analysis, multiple logistic regression, survival analysis, and so on
- Trains interviewers and clerical staff in project-specific tasks as necessary
- Obtains, as necessary, approval from human subject review boards to conduct investigations or research
- Interacts during the course of investigations with health providers or other persons performing clinical or health research
- Collects surveillance information of reportable human morbidity and mortality as required by state law
- Compiles, maintains, and analyzes health data and reports using statistical methods
- Identifies corrective actions to environmental conditions resulting in adverse health conditions
- Independently proposes and supervises epidemiological investigations of human morbidity or mortality
- Participates as member of a multidisciplinary team on disease surveillance and investigations with disease investigators, biostatisticians, health care professionals, environmental health practitioners, health information specialists, and staff of regulated industries (such as restaurants, hospitals, and nursing homes)
- Collaborates with a broad spectrum of public health constituents and participants including federal, state, and local public health

officials, as well as government officials, private individuals, and senior researchers in academic settings

- Communicates health risks to public officials, the media, and the public
- Coordinates local, state, and federal health research programs
- Serves as principal investigator on local, state, and federal health research grants
- Supervises the work of lower-level epidemiologists

## Biostatistician

This position conducts statistical analyses of morbidity and mortality data, quality assurance, clinical data, surveillance and other data, and serves as a resource for epidemiology and other agency staff.

Important and essential duties of a biostatistician include:

- Provides usable reports to epidemiology, program, and clinical staff
- Advises and assists epidemiology staff with research design, statistical design, and statistical analysis of quantitative research projects and databases
- Designs research protocols
- Provides direction on sample size and distribution
- Directs appropriate measures for proper data handling and cleaning
- Analyzes statistical databases, such as birth, death, or disease records, for proper organization and treatment of data
- Suggests revisions based on statistical and research implications
- Writes research design and statistical portions of proposals and papers
- Works closely with epidemiologists to appropriately frame information for reports or papers
- Cultivates sources of population-based data and information available from other public and private agencies
- Participates as member of a multidisciplinary team on disease surveillance and investigations with epidemiologists, disease investigators, health care professionals, environmental health practitioners, health information specialists, and staff of regulated industries (such as restaurants, hospitals, and nursing homes)
- Assists with outbreak investigations, when needed; in unusual instances, such as a bioterrorism event or disease outbreak, the biostatistician may need to assist with interviewing victims, analyzing

data, arranging sample collection, and so on as directed by the agency leadership team

## MINIMUM QUALIFICATIONS

Epidemiologists come from a variety of professional and experiential backgrounds. Among 2500 positions in state health agencies, 12% are physicians, another 12% have some other doctoral degree (such as PhD, DrPH, DVM, or DDS), 42% have a master's degree, 23% have a bachelor degree, and 5% have less than a bachelor degree.[3]

Epidemiologists and communicable disease investigators work together in investigations of disease patterns and outbreaks. Epidemiologists often have graduate degrees, and some have other professional credentials such as an RN, MD, DDS, or DVM degree. Biostatistics is a specialized field in which master's and doctoral degrees are common. Communicable disease investigators may or may not have education and training equivalent to a bachelor degree. Typical minimum qualifications for communicable disease investigators, entry-level and midlevel epidemiologists, and biostatisticians are detailed below.

### *Typical Minimum Qualifications for Communicable Disease Investigator*

#### Knowledge, Skills, and Abilities

A typical communicable disease investigator generally has knowledge of:

- Transmission, diagnosis, and treatment of sexually transmitted and other communicable disease
- Symptoms of sexually transmitted and other communicable diseases
- Methods and techniques used to conduct disease investigations
- Methods of infection control
- Laws and legal issues related to the control of communicable diseases
- Diagnostic and therapeutic problems involved in the control of communicable diseases
- Basic medical terminology, clinical practices, and medical procedures
- Principles and practices of customer service
- Available community and social service agencies
- Diverse cultural practices and customs
- Personal computers and related software

A typical communicable disease investigator generally has the skills and ability to:

- Understand, interpret, and apply laws, regulations, policies, and procedures relating to communicable disease reporting.
- Interview tactfully and effectively, and work cooperatively with other agencies involved in the control of sexually transmitted and other communicable diseases.
- Deal firmly and fairly with clients of various socioeconomic backgrounds and temperaments.
- Maintain accurate records and document actions.
- Make referrals to local and regional providers of social, medical, and other specialized services.
- Maintain confidentiality of information; recognize and respect limit of authority and responsibility.
- Conduct interviews of a highly personal nature.
- Exercise initiative and tact in tracing contacts and bringing them in to seek treatment.
- Gain the confidence of many varied personalities.
- Communicate and work effectively with coworkers, supervisors, and the general public sufficient to exchange or convey information and to receive work direction.
- Communicate effectively both verbally and in writing.
- Understand program objectives in relation to departmental goals and procedures.
- Establish and maintain effective working relationships with officials, the general public, and personnel from other government agencies.
- Operate personal computers, including spreadsheet database, word processing, presentation, and other related software.

### Experience and Education

Any combination of training and experience that provides the required knowledge and abilities will qualify an individual for this position. A typical way to obtain the required knowledge and experience is through one year of experience in a clinical or other health care setting requiring contact with the general public, and at least an associate degree or trade school diploma, preferably as a medical assistant or a closely related field with college-level course work in psychology, health education, or social work.

Another path to these qualifications is through an associate degree in allied health or a related field and two years experience providing emergency medical treatment as an emergency medical technician (EMT), medical technician, military corpsman, or related experience; or an equivalent interchange of related education and experience sufficient to successfully perform the essential duties of the job. Still another path is through graduation from an accredited college with a degree in biological or behavioral sciences or a related field and one year of professional experience in public health, hospital services, or a related field. Qualifying experiences may substitute for the required education on a year-for-year basis.

Special requirements often necessary for this position include a valid driver's license, ability to travel independently, bilingual skills, and the ability to work in an environment that may include exposure to communicable diseases. Disease investigators may be required to work outside normal business hours and sign a statement agreeing to comply with state laws and regulations relating to child abuse reporting.

## Typical Minimum Qualifications for Entry-Level Epidemiologists

### Knowledge, Skills, and Abilities

A typical entry-level epidemiologist generally has knowledge of:

- Modern epidemiologic principles and practices including the symptoms, causes, means of transmission and methods of control of communicable and chronic diseases
- Microbiology and pathophysiology
- Basic medical terminology
- Modern research procedures including biostatistical methodology
- Computers and programming in database management and statistical software
- Community organizations and resources related to the field of public health and epidemiology
- Epidemiologic techniques, methods, and surveillance systems, particularly those related to communicable, chronic, or environmentally induced diseases or injury control
- Current research and analytical methods related to public health and epidemiology

- Scientific methods and the pathobiology of disease or injury occurrence
- Nature and objectives of statewide public health programs addressing individual and community health problems
- Organization and operation of federal, state, and local governmental agencies relating to public health

A typical entry-level epidemiologist generally has the skills and ability to:

- Apply laws, rules, and regulations to problems of disease control.
- Communicate clearly and concisely orally and in writing on both technical and nontechnical levels.
- Prepare grant proposals and budgets.
- Implement and evaluate program activities relating to the prevention and control of injuries and communicable, chronic, or environmentally induced diseases.
- Analyze and interpret epidemiologic data.
- Assess a disease outbreak situation and make appropriate decisions.
- Prepare or assist in preparing scientific articles, making presentations to professional groups, and clearly communicating the findings of epidemiologic studies.
- Establish and maintain effective working relationships with other employees, health care providers, social service agencies, schools, the media, the public, and federal, state, and local officials.

## Experience and Education

Any combination of training and experience that provides the required knowledge and abilities will qualify an individual for this position. A typical way to obtain the required knowledge and experience is through a master's degree in epidemiology or a master's degree in public health with specialization in epidemiology and one year of experience in epidemiology research and analysis. Another path is through one year of professional experience in chronic disease, communicable disease, human nutrition, injury control, environmental epidemiology, or infection control, which includes disease or injury investigation and risk assessment, and a master's degree from an accredited college or university in nursing, nutrition/dietetics, health care administration, biostatistics, sociology, psychology, anthropology, or a biological, physical or environmental science. Another pathway is through two years of professional experience above the entry level in chronic disease, communicable disease, human nutrition, injury control, environmental epidemiology, or infection control, which includes disease or injury investigation and risk assessment, such as a position as a research analyst, program specialist, environmental specialist, nutritionist, community health nurse, or health educator.

## Typical Minimum Qualifications for Senior-Level Epidemiologists

### Knowledge, Skills, and Abilities

In addition to the knowledge and abilities required for the entry-level epidemiologist just listed, this position requires knowledge of disease control methods, recent developments in the field of epidemiology, and basic management skills. It also requires the skill and ability to supervise and lead lower-level staff and develop grant proposals.

### Experience and Education

Any combination of training and experience that provides the required knowledge and abilities will qualify an individual for this position. A typical way to obtain the required knowledge and experience is through a doctoral degree in epidemiology or biostatistics and two years of experience in epidemiology research and analysis. Another pathway is through a doctoral degree in a health science field, with a master's degree in epidemiology or a master's degree in public health with specialization in epidemiology and two years of experience in epidemiology research and analysis. A third pathway is through a master's degree in epidemiology, or a master's degree in public health with specialization in epidemiology and six years of experience in epidemiology research and analysis. Yet another pathway is through a medical degree with a master's degree in epidemiology or a master's degree in public health with specialization in epidemiology and two years of experience in epidemiology research analysis. It is possible that completion of related training or experience such as with the Centers for Disease Control or the National Institute of Health could substitute for the MPH degree. When an MD is selected, a license to practice medicine in the state is necessary.

## Biostatistician

### Knowledge, Skills, and Abilities

A typical biostatician generally has knowledge of:

- Biostatistics and statistics with basic knowledge of medicine and epidemiology, including research designs, probability, distributions,

rates, proportions, odds, categorical variable analyses, regression, logistic regression, survival analysis, sample size calculations, and power analysis essentials
- Modern, high-level database management and statistical languages such as SAS and SPSS (and possibly S-Plus, StatXact and SigmaPlot), in addition to Microsoft Office software including Excel and Access
- Both parametric and nonparametric statistics
- Sample survey design and analysis including the survey software SUDAAN, FoxPro 2000, Dbase, Oracle, SQL, Visual Basic languages, and database formats

A typical biostatician generally has the skills and ability to:

- Effectively interact with multidisciplinary teams and outside investigators.
- Develop novel approaches for new situations, and exhibit the leadership skills needed for successful implementation.
- Prioritize conflicting tasks in a fast-paced environment with minimal supervision.
- Communicate easily and successfully both verbally and in writing, remain calm under pressure, work as part of a team, and meet deadlines while paying meticulous attention to detail.
- Relate well with others and be flexible in unpredictable, ever-changing work environments.

### Experience and Education

Any combination of training and experience that provides the required knowledge and abilities will qualify an individual for this position. A typical way to obtain the required knowledge and experience is through a master's degree in biostatistics, epidemiology, or a related field and four years of experience in research analysis and database management, either as part of an educational process or as paid employment. Experience should be in a science, social science, or community-based research setting and involve extensive use of statistical methodologies.

## WORKPLACE CONSIDERATIONS

Physical requirements for positions in this occupational category are similar to those for many other public health occupations. Most epidemiologist, biostatistician, and communicable disease investigator positions call for workers to be able to sit for extended periods and to frequently stand and walk short distances. Normal manual dexterity and eye-hand coordination and hearing and vision corrected to within the normal range are also important considerations. Normally, public health professionals must be able to communicate verbally and be able to use office equipment including computers, telephones, calculators, copiers, and fax machines. Although much of the work is performed in an office environment, frequent or continuous contact with staff and the public is also necessary. In some situations, a valid driver's license may be required.

Physical abilities necessary for most public health occupations include the ability to exert light physical effort in sedentary to light work, which may involve some lifting, carrying, pushing, and pulling of objects and materials of light weight (5–10 pounds). Tasks may involve extended periods of time at a keyboard or workstation. When epidemiologists and communicable disease investigators work outside the office, they must have the ability to work under conditions where exposure to communicable disease risks and environmental factors poses a risk of moderate injury or illness.

## SALARY ESTIMATES

Based on information from current job postings, salaries for communicable disease investigators fall in the $33,000–53,000 range (see Table 6–3).

The average annual salary for an epidemiologist is $58,000 with the middle 50% earning between $46,000 and $68,000. The mean salary for epidemiologists working for local governmental agencies is greater than that for epidemiologists working for state agencies ($54,000 local versus $49,500 state). Entry-level epidemiologists can expect salaries in the $35,000–45,000 range. Many small and medium-sized local public health agencies do not employ an epidemiologist. Larger local public health agencies and state health departments often have several. Larger governmental public health agencies can often offer salaries somewhat competitive of those found in the private and voluntary sectors ($65,000–85,000 range). Epidemiologists with professional credentials, especially physicians, dentists, veterinarians, epidemiologists, and nurses, may be able to attract salaries in the 6-figure category.

**Table 6–3** Number and Mean Salary for Epidemiologists and Statisticians in Federal, State, and Local Governmental Agencies, May 2004

| Occupational Category | Federal Workers | Federal Worker Mean Salary | State Workers | State Worker Mean Salary | Local Workers | Local Worker Mean Salary | Total Federal, State, and Local Workers | Adjusted PH Enum. 2000 Workers |
|---|---|---|---|---|---|---|---|---|
| Epidemiologists | NA | NA | 1,170 | $49,390 | 650 | $54,140 | 1,820 | 1,433 |
| Statisticians | 3,550 | $79,680 | 1,500 | $43,660 | 590 | $53,330 | 5,640 | 1,800 |
| Disease Investigators | NA | NA | NA | NA | NA | NA | NA | 1,211 |

*Source:* Data for federal, state, and local governmental agency workers from Bureau of Labor Statistics. May 2004 National, State, and Metropolitan Area Occupational Employment and Wage Estimates. Available at http://www.bls.gov. Accessed August 2005. See Chapter 2 for adjusted number of public health workers from *The Public Health Workforce Enumeration 2000.*

The 2004 CSTE survey found the highest ratios of epidemiologists to population on the East Coast and West Coast (1 per 10,000). The South and the Midwest lag behind with 0.7 and 0.8 epidemiologists per 100,000 population, respectively.

Salary information for biostatisticians is not very straightforward as biostatisticians are lumped with other types of statisticians in employment and wage surveys. Mean salaries for statisticians working for federal agencies are much higher than mean salaries of statisticians working for state and local governmental agencies ($79,500 federal, $43,500 state, $53,500 local).

## CAREER PROSPECTS

According to a recent survey of state and territorial health agencies, epidemiologic capacity needs to be increased by 50%.[3] Recent increases in epidemiologists have largely benefited bioterrorism preparedness and response efforts, often at the expense of communicable disease, chronic disease, injury, and environmental epidemiologic capacity. As a result, there is consensus that additional epidemiologists are needed, especially infectious disease, chronic disease, and terrorism-related epidemiologists. The Bureau of Labor Statistics also identifies epidemiologists as an occupation that will grow more rapidly than the average for all occupations over the next 10 years.

## ADDITIONAL INFORMATION

There are many good sources of information on epidemiologists, disease investigators, and biostatisticians. Several sources are available for information on educational programs for these occupations as well as for continuing education and leadership development for practitioners.

The Council of State and Territorial Epidemiologists (CSTE, http://www. cste.org) and the CDC Epidemiologic Intelligence Service (EIS) site (http://www.cdc.gov/eis/) head the list of useful information sources. CSTE has nearly 1000 members working in state and local public health agencies. The EIS is an elite unit of CDC that provides technical assistance and manpower to state and local governments during unusual or large outbreaks.

Schools of public health are among the institutions offering graduate degrees in health administration. The Association of Schools of Public Health (http://www.asph.org) has identified a battery of core epidemiology and biostatistics competencies appropriate for all students receiving the master's of public health (MPH) degree. These competencies provide a useful baseline for professional practice and summarize what an MPH graduate should be able to do (see Table 6–4).

The epidemiology section and statistics section of the American Public Health Association's Web site (http://www.apha.org) are also good sources of information for epidemiologists and biostatisticians. The epidemiology section has a long history and currently has 3000 members, making it one of APHA's largest and most active sections.

Additional sources of relevant information include the American College of Preventive Medicine (http://www.acpm.org), the American College of Epidemiology (http://www.acepidemiology2.org), the American Epidemiology Society (http://www.acepidemiology.org), the Association for Professionals in Infection Control and Epidemiology (http://www.apic.org), the International Epidemiologic Association (http://www.dundee.ac.uk), and the Society for Epidemiologic Research (http://www.epiresearch.org).

## CONCLUSION

Epidemiology is the virtual operating system of public health practice, and epidemiologists are in great demand. Although recent events have emphasized bioterrorism threats and events, epidemiologists, biostatisticians, and

---

**Table 6–4** Epidemiology and Biostatistics Competency Expectations for Graduates of MPH Degree Programs

---

1. Recognize the importance of epidemiology for informing scientific, ethical, economic, and political discussion of health issues.
2. Describe a public health problem in terms of magnitude, population affected, time, and place.
3. Use the basic terminology and definitions of epidemiology.
4. Identify key sources of data for epidemiologic purposes.
5. Calculate basic epidemiology measures.
6. Evaluate the strengths and limitations of epidemiologic reports.
7. Draw appropriate inferences from epidemiologic data.
8. Communicate epidemiologic information to lay and professional audiences.
9. Comprehend basic ethical and legal principles pertaining to the collection, maintenance, use, and dissemination of epidemiologic data.
10. Recognize the principles and limitations of public health screening programs.
11. Describe the role biostatistics serves in the discipline of public health.
12. Distinguish among the different measurement scales and the implications for selection of statistical methods to be used based on these distinctions.
13. Apply descriptive techniques commonly used to summarize public health data.
14. Use basic concepts of probability, random variation, and commonly used statistical probability distributions.
15. Apply common statistical methods for inference.
16. Describe preferred methodological alternatives to commonly used statistical methods.
17. Apply descriptive and inferential methodologies according to the type of study design for answering a particular research question.
18. Interpret results of statistical analyses found in public health studies.
19. Develop written and oral presentation based on statistical analyses for both public health professionals and educated lay audiences.
20. Use vital statistics and other public health records in the description of population health characteristics and in public health research and evaluation.

---

*Source:* Association of Schools of Public Health (ASPH) MPH Core Competency Development Process, Version 1.2. Available at http://www.asph.org. Accessed August 2005.

---

disease investigators work across the entire spectrum of diseases, conditions, and health risks. As the spotlight has focused on epidemiology, its visibility as a public health career has grown. As disease investigators acquire practical skills in the field, they often seek to complement their experience with additional education and training, establishing an effective partnership with public health epidemiologists in disease prevention and control efforts.

# REFERENCES

1. Bureau of Labor Statistics, U.S. Department of Labor. May 2004 National, State, and Metropolitan Area Occupational Employment and Wage Estimates. Available at http://www.bls.gov/oes/current/oes_nat.htm. Accessed August 2005.
2. Health Resources and Services Administration (HRSA), Bureau of Health Professions, National Center for Health Workforce Information and Analysis and Center for Health Policy, Columbia School of Nursing. *The Public Health Workforce Enumeration 2000.* Washington, DC: HRSA; 2000. Available at http://www.phppo.cdc.gov/owpp/docs/library/2000/Public%20Health%20 Workforce%20Enumeration%202000.pdf. Accessed August 2005.
3. Council of State and Territorial Epidemiologists (CSTE). *2004 National Assessment of Epidemiologic Capacity: Findings and Recommendations.* Washington, DC: CSTE; 2004. Available at http://www.cste.org/Assessment/ECA/ pdffiles/ECAfinal05.pdf. Accessed August 2005.

# CHAPTER 7

# Public Health Education and Information

Public health education is one of the fastest growing public health professions. Public health educators play important roles in a variety of public health programs and in community relations in general. Chronic disease prevention programs, injury prevention and control activities, and community health planning and community health improvement initiatives all rely heavily on the expertise of health educators. Recent concerns over bioterrorism threats and events have raised awareness as to the importance of risk communication and public information skills within the public health workforce. Table 7–1 provides a snapshot of an average day in the life of a public health educator.

## OCCUPATIONAL CLASSIFICATION

Two standard occupational categories for public health workers are addressed in this chapter: health educators and public information specialists.

A health educator is a white collar, professional category encompassing positions that promote, maintain, and improve individual and community health by assisting individuals and communities to adopt healthy behaviors. Health educators collect and analyze data to identify community needs prior to planning, implementing, monitoring, and evaluating programs designed to encourage healthy lifestyles, policies, and environments. Health educators serve as resources to individuals, other professionals, and the community, and may administer fiscal resources for health education programs. Bureau of Labor Statistics indicate that there are 47,000 health educators working in the United States.[1] Federal, state,

**Table 7–1** A Typical Day for a Public Health Educator

| | |
|---|---|
| 7:30 a.m. | Breakfast meeting with steering committee of community health coalition for community health improvement plan |
| 8:30 a.m. | Office time for phone messages and e-mail |
| 9:00 a.m. | Staff meeting to review priorities for week |
| 10:15 a.m. | Meeting with agency director, epidemiology, and planning staff on community health assessment |
| 10:45 a.m. | Set up conference room for satellite downlink program |
| 11:00 a.m. | Satellite downlink program on establishing a medical reserve corps unit, followed by staff discussion |
| 12:15 p.m. | Lunch at desk revising presentation slides for staff orientation |
| 1:00 p.m. | Staff orientation presentation on "What Is Public Health, and Where Do I Fit In?" |
| 2:00 p.m. | Review draft for agency press release if West Nile virus outbreak occurs |
| 3:00 p.m. | Conference call meeting with technical program committee for state public health association annual meeting |
| 4:00 p.m. | Review information to be distributed at tonight's community meeting on West Nile virus threat |
| 4:30 p.m. | Review and analyze participant evaluations from today's orientation program for new employees; revise presentation materials for next month's orientation |
| 5:15 p.m. | Prepare remarks for tonight's community meeting |
| 7:00 p.m. | Represent agency at community meeting regarding West Nile virus concerns |

and local governmental agencies are among the biggest employers of health educators; these agencies employ 13,000 health educators. The *Public Health Workforce Enumeration 2000* identified 3500 public health educator positions in governmental public health agencies.[2] Data from these two sources are used throughout this chapter. At the state and local level, less than one half of the public health educators are professionally certified.

Public information specialist is somewhat similar to the standard occupational classification public relations specialist, which includes positions that engage in promoting or creating goodwill for individuals, groups, or organizations by writing or selecting material and releasing it through various communications media. Public relations and media specialists present public health issues to the media and the public often serving as spokespersons for public health agencies. These positions may prepare and arrange displays and make speeches and other presentations. There are more than 16,000 public relations and public information positions in federal, state, and local governmental agencies. The *Public Health Workforce Enumeration 2000* identified 900 public information positions in governmental public health agencies.

## PUBLIC HEALTH PRACTICE PROFILE

Health educators and public information officers are primarily involved with addressing public health responsibilities for promoting healthy behaviors and preventing disease and injury. These occupational categories may also be involved in emergency preparedness and response and sometimes in assessing the impact and quality of health services within a community.

Among the 10 essential public health services, public health education and information professionals are especially important for four: informing and educating the public, mobilizing community partnerships, developing policies and plans that support community health improvement, and assuring a competent workforce. Table 7–2 summarizes public health purposes and essential public health services at the core of positions for public health educators.

## IMPORTANT AND ESSENTIAL DUTIES

There are several job titles and positions in the public health workforce that specialize in public health education and information services. The focus in this chapter will be on three positions: entry-level public health educator, senior-level public health educator, and public information specialist/coordinator. Each of these positions and a representative panel of their important and essential duties are described in this section.

### Public Health Educator (Entry Level)

This position encompasses entry-level professional work in the development and coordination of public health education and health promotion activities. Public health educators assist in the formulation of the health education plan and in the development and implementation of health promotion programs. Work includes providing technical assistance and training to local health professionals, schools, community organizations, government agencies, businesses, and individuals. Supervision is received from a higher-level health educator or other designated administrative

**Table 7–2** Public Health Practice Profile for Public Health Education and Information Professionals

| Public Health Education and Information Professionals Make a Difference by: | |
|---|---|
| **Public Health Purposes** | |
| Preventing epidemics and the spread of disease | ✓ |
| Protecting against environmental hazards | |
| Preventing injuries | ✓ |
| Promoting and encouraging healthy behaviors | ✓ |
| Responding to disasters and assisting communities in recovery | |
| Assuring the quality and accessibility of health services | |
| **Essential Public Health Services** | |
| Monitoring health status to identify community health problems | |
| Diagnosing and investigating health problems and health hazards in the community | |
| Informing, educating, and empowering people about health issues | ✓ |
| Mobilizing community partnerships to identify and solve health problems | ✓ |
| Developing policies and plans that support individual and community health efforts | ✓ |
| Enforcing laws and regulations that protect health and ensure safety | |
| Linking people with needed personal health services and assuring the provision of health care when otherwise unavailable | |
| Assuring a competent public health and personal health care workforce | ✓ |
| Evaluating effectiveness, accessibility, and quality of personal and population-based health services | |
| Researching new insights and innovative solutions to health problems | |

superior; however, the employee is expected to work with considerable independence within established policies and procedural guidelines.

Essential and important duties for an entry-level public health educator include:

- Assists in the development and implementation of health education, behavioral risk reduction, and health promotion programs for schools, worksites, communities, and individuals; provides healthy intervention strategies that meet specified and measurable objectives
- Collects, analyzes, and disseminates information regarding major health problems, behavioral risk factors, and health attitudes and

knowledge using epidemiological procedures; assists in the formulation of disease prevention and health promotion strategies

- Develops various educational materials such as brochures, exhibits, videotapes, and slides; employs mass media, group process, and counseling techniques in health education, health promotion, and behavioral risk reduction program activities
- Assists in development of training programs and works with others to plan and implement health promotion programs, policies, and legislation
- Maintains knowledge and skills in health education and health promotion research through review of professional literature, participation in conferences, and continuing education
- Provides assistance in the submission of applications for health education, behavioral risk reduction, and health promotion program funds; monitors existing programs for compliance with federal and state regulations

## Public Health Educator (Senior Level)

Under direction, this position plans, develops, supervises, evaluates, and monitors specific health education program(s) for the agency. Senior-level public health educators are distinguished from lower-level public health educators by their responsibility for the preparation, administration, and evaluation of specific public health education programs, grant contracts, and budgets. In addition, a senior public health educator supervises staff assigned to specific programs. This position is distinguished from the health education program manager in that the latter manages the overall agency public health education program, but this position is responsible for the preparation, administration, and evaluation of the public health education efforts of specific programs.

Essential and important duties of senior-level public health educators include:

- Plans, implements, and evaluates specific public health education programs
- Assesses and identifies community needs for educational services in specific program areas
- Plans, organizes, designs, develops, and evaluates public health education activities; carries out or directs others to carry out public

health education activities including educational presentations and workshops

- Assists in the development and adaptation of data collection instruments and designs for assessment and evaluation activities
- Develops educational literature and flyers and provides information to the community
- Selects, trains, directs, evaluates, and handles disciplinary problems of subordinate staff
- Seeks funding sources for specific public health education programs
- Prepares grant proposals
- Develops memoranda of understanding and budgets
- Negotiates and monitors contracts with funding agencies and other subcontractors
- Develops and maintains contact with state and local public health agencies, community organizations, and the media
- Serves as the community leader of public health education efforts for specific programs
- Inputs, accesses, and analyzes data in a computer database

## *Public Information Specialist/Coordinator*

This position is a midlevel informational and public relations professional for a public health organization. Public information specialists prepare and disseminate informational materials to support and promote the programs and services of their agency. Work includes composing and editing copy for press releases, articles, bulletins, newsletters, pamphlets, and other publications. Work may involve interpreting and communicating agency programs to employees, special interest groups, and the general public. Supervision is received from an administrative superior who reviews work in progress and upon completion.

Public health information coordinators perform more advanced duties coordinating informational and public relations activities in an agency or specialized program and serve as assistants to a public information administrator, or perform a comparable level of work. Work involves collecting, preparing, and disseminating informational material to support and promote agency programs and services, including composing and editing text and producing graphic and photographic illustrations for publication or distribution to the news media and other groups. Work includes interpreting and communicating agency programs to employees, special interest groups, and the general public. Supervision may be exercised over professional, technical, or clerical staff. General supervision is received from a public information administrator or other administrative superior; consequently, the employee is expected to work with considerable independence and technical skill in the area of communication and public relations.

Essential and important duties of public information specialists/coordinators include:

- Gathers, compiles, and verifies information; composes and edits copy for newsletters, brochures, Web pages and other publications
- Prepares news releases to inform and educate the public concerning agency programs and services
- Composes or edits articles for internal agency news bulletins; edits articles or correspondence for staff members
- Develops spot announcements and scripts for radio and television
- Answers requests for literature and information; maintains files of photographs, clippings, and agency publications
- Meets with agency officials and attends staff meetings for the purpose of discussing activities and securing newsworthy information
- Researches available material to assist in the preparation of speeches for agency officials
- Operates still and video cameras
- Creates illustrations and does layout work
- Assists with agency-sponsored and interagency public relations activities and special events
- Coordinates informational and public relations activities in a specialized program, serves as an assistant to a public information administrator, or performs work of comparable level and scope
- Provides assistance to higher-level management on matters pertaining to public relations and informational policy
- Develops and maintains working relationships with media representatives and public, private, labor, business, and civic organizations to ensure the effective dissemination of informational material
- Estimates costs, develops specifications, and makes recommendations on securing and accepting bids for printing; maintains contact with printing contractors to assure quality control; reviews and corrects printers' galley proofs

- Arranges public appearances and media engagements for agency officials; prepares or edits the material to be presented
- Makes presentations and serves as a spokesperson for assigned agency programs to special interest groups, employee groups, and the general public
- Informs management of public reaction to programs, suggests strategies for future communications, and makes recommendations for modified or new programs
- Coordinates special events and develops materials, displays, and programs to promote agency services, missions, and goals and to enhance consistency and accuracy in those efforts
- Provides training to improve the techniques of supervisory and professional staff in furthering public understanding of the services offered by the agency
- Supervises, trains, and evaluates subordinate staff

## MINIMUM QUALIFICATIONS

Public health educators and public information staff work in professional positions often supported by administrative support and clerical positions. There are generally several steps in the health educator and public information series that allow for advancement and career development. Comparable positions exist in local public health agencies of all sizes, making career advancement from a small to larger employer not uncommon for these workers.

Public health training programs in schools of public health and other academic institutions produce health educators and other communications specialists. The vast majority of current workers in these titles, however, do not have a public health degree. This allows for variability in the types of experience and training that agencies require when filling these positions. As with virtually all public health positions, both experience and education are important considerations for hiring and promotion. Experience and education both contribute to necessary knowledge, skills, and abilities required for workers in this field. Typical minimum qualifications for entry- and senior-level health educators and public information specialists/coordinators are detailed in this section.

## Typical Minimum Qualifications for Entry-Level Public Health Educator

### Knowledge, Skills, and Abilities

A typical entry-level public health educator generally has knowledge of:

- Current principles, practices, and processes employed in the health education and health promotion component of a public health program
- Principles, techniques, and application of behavioral epidemiology as related to health education and health promotion
- The psychological, social, economic, and cultural determinants of behavior and methods to promote healthy lifestyles
- Educational methods and techniques of developing and presenting health education to individuals and groups
- Community organization principles and resources, and community health needs
- Current trends and developments in public health, medical sciences, and health care
- Research methods as applied to health education and health promotion

A typical entry-level public health educator has the skills and ability to:

- Assist in the planning, development, implementation, and evaluation of effective health education and health promotion programs for various populations.
- Perform statistical computations.
- Explain complex medical information to civic and community groups and to public officials, and present ideas effectively.
- Establish and maintain effective working relationships with other employees, community groups, and the public.

### Experience and Education

Any combination of training and experience that provides the required knowledge and abilities will qualify an individual for this position. A typical way to obtain these knowledge and abilities is through graduation from an accredited 4-year college or university with a bachelor degree with major specialization in health education or health promotion, or a master's degree in health education, health promotion, or public health with specialization in health education.

## *Typical Minimum Qualifications for Senior-Level Public Health Educator*

### Knowledge, Skills, and Abilities

A typical senior-level public health educator generally has knowledge of:

- The principles of public health education including program planning and evaluation
- Public health education methods and materials including teaching methods and curriculum design
- Assessment techniques to identify community health problems in specific program areas
- Existing methods of intervention and control and the health education needs of various target groups
- Principles and practices of community organization for enhancing public health
- The philosophy, concepts, and principles of public health
- The functions and services of local community health agencies and community organizations
- Publicity and media practices and procedures
- Grant proposal writing and budgeting techniques
- Principles and practices of staff supervision and training

A typical senior-level public health educator has the skills and ability to:

- Plan, organize, implement, and evaluate public health education services.
- Design, effectively use, and evaluate public health education methods and materials.
- Provide public health education consultation, and develop cooperative relationships with a wide range of individuals and representatives of organizations and the news media.
- Prepare and present a variety of clear and concise written and oral reports.
- Develop and nurture funding sources.
- Analyze and prepare grant proposals, contracts, and related budgets.

- Negotiate and monitor contracts.
- Originate, prepare, and distribute informational and publicity materials.
- Plan, assign, direct, and evaluate the work of staff.
- Interpret legislation regulations, administrative policies, and procedures.
- Input, access, and analyze data in a computer database.

### Experience and Education

Any combination of training and experience that provides the required knowledge and abilities will qualify an individual for this position. A typical way to obtain such knowledge and abilities is through two years of experience in public health education, promotion, or a related field that provides the knowledge and abilities previously identified. Some agencies may require a master's degree in health education from an accredited college and a valid driver's license.

## Typical Minimum Qualifications for Public Information Specialist/Coordinator

### Knowledge, Skills, and Abilities

A typical public information specialist/coordinator generally has knowledge of:

- Journalism, photography, film/video production, graphic arts, publication, and printing
- News media operation and its proper utilization for dissemination of information
- Principles and methods of establishing and maintaining good public relations
- Community resources and organizations
- Commercial art methods and the general principles of layout and design
- Marketing and advertising practices and techniques
- Journalistic principles and practices including techniques of planning, composing, and editing informational materials
- Use of methods and techniques of disseminating information to the public
- Public relations techniques and procedures

- Agency organizational structure, including programs, administrative rules and regulations, and staff
- Community resources and organizations
- Marketing and advertising practices and techniques
- Commercial art methods and the general principles of layout and design
- Operation of still and video cameras and developing, processing, and editing the film or video

A typical public information specialist/coordinator generally has the skills and ability to:

- Compose and produce a variety of informational materials.
- Use a variety of desktop publishing software packages and Web formatting languages.
- Establish and maintain working relationships with media representatives, agency officials, other employees, and the general public.
- Communicate with special interest groups, employee groups, and the general public.
- Produce graphic art, photographs, and other materials.
- Interpret and explain agency policies, laws, and operations.
- Stimulate public interest and gain support for agency programs.
- Compose and produce a variety of informational materials for release to the media or other publications.
- Conduct research to find pertinent and newsworthy information.
- Advise and train agency staff in public relations methods and techniques.

### Experience and Education

Any combination of experience and training that results in the acquisition of the knowledge and skills described above will qualify an individual for this position. A typical way to acquire these qualifications is through graduation from an accredited 4-year college or university with specialization in journalism, communications, English, public relations, advertising, marketing, or closely related areas. Professional experience in the areas of journalism, advertising, marketing, film/video production, or public relations and information may be substituted on a year-for-year basis for the required education. For a public information coordinator, requirements may include one year as public information specialist or two years of professional experience in public relations, advertising, or journalism; and graduation from an accredited 4-year college or university with specialization in journalism, communications, English, public relations, advertising, marketing, or closely related areas. Professional experience in the areas of journalism, advertising, marketing, film/video production, or public relations and information may be substituted on a year-for-year basis for the stated education. Graduate work in the educational areas previously listed may be substituted on a year-for-year basis for one or more years of the stated experience.

## WORKPLACE CONSIDERATIONS

State and local governmental agencies employ more than 11,000 health educators, and there is every indication that even greater numbers will be employed by these agencies over the next decade.

Physical requirements for positions in this occupational category are similar to those for other professional public health positions. Most health educator and public information positions call for workers to be able to sit for extended periods and to frequently stand and walk short distances. Normal manual dexterity and eye-hand coordination and hearing and vision corrected to within the normal range are also important considerations. Normally, public health educators and public information staff will be able to communicate verbally and be able to use office equipment including computers, telephones, calculators, copiers, and fax machines. Although much of the work is performed in an office environment, frequent or continuous contact with staff and the public is also necessary. In many situations, people filling these positions may be required to possess a valid driver's license.

## SALARY ESTIMATES

The average annual salary for a health educator is $43,000 with the middle 50% earning between $30,000 and $53,000. Entry-level salaries for public health educators employed by public health agencies in the $25,000–30,000 range are common. As indicated in Table 7–3, average salaries for health educators working for federal agencies are considerably higher than mean salaries for health educators employed by state and local governmental agencies ($79,000 federal, $42,500 state, $41,000 local).

**Table 7-3** Number and Mean Salary for Health Educators and Public Relations/Public Information Workers in Federal, State, and Local Governmental Agencies, May 2004

| Occupational Category | Federal Workers | Federal Worker Mean Salary | State Workers | State Worker Mean Salary | Local Workers | Local Worker Mean Salary | Total Federal, State, and Local Workers | Adjusted PH Enum. 2000 Workers |
|---|---|---|---|---|---|---|---|---|
| Health Educators | 1,990 | $79,170 | 4,680 | $42,600 | 6,660 | $40,780 | 13,330 | 3,448 |
| Public Relations/ Public Information Specialists | 3,830 | $69,890 | 4,280 | $45,690 | 8,100 | $46,770 | 16,210 | 871 |

*Source:* Data for federal, state, and local governmental agency workers from Bureau of Labor Statistics. May 2004 National, State, and Metropolitan Area Occupational Employment and Wage Estimates. Available at http://www.bls.gov. Accessed August 2005. See Chapter 2 for adjusted number of public health workers from the *Public Health Workforce Enumeration 2000.*

The average salary for public relations specialists is $50,000 with the middle 50% earning between $33,000 and $60,000. Governmental agencies employ a relatively small number of public relations and public information officers. Entry-level salaries for public information specialists employed by public health agencies are often in the $25,000–35,000 range; public information coordinator salaries are often in the $32,000–47,000 range. Average salaries for public relations/public information specialists working for federal agencies are notably higher than average salaries at state and local governmental agencies ($70,000 federal, $45,500 state, $47,000 local).

## CAREER PROSPECTS

As is the case with several other public health occupations, health educators and public information specialists can advance from entry- to mid- to senior-level positions in their specialty. But in view of their strong communication and information skills, agencies may use these workers for both program specific work (that is as program staff for an assigned program) or at the agency level to deal with community and other public interactions. For example, health educators play a major role in organizing and coordinating community health planning efforts that lead to community health needs assessments, community health report cards, and ultimately to community health improvement initiatives. As community health improvement efforts have become a central role of local and state public health agencies, and as they continue to grow over the next decade, the need for health educators will continue to grow in comparison to other public health occupations. This greater emphasis on community planning and partnerships, as well as the need for more effective risk communication capabilities for bioterrorism and other threats, also increases the need and demand for public information specialists and coordinators.

Public health education, an increasing recognized and important occupational category within the public health workforce, has developed a credential for highly skilled health educators. Certified Health Education Specialists (CHES certified health educators) illustrate the movement toward credentialing as a means of increasing the professional stature of an occupation. Many public health workers currently providing health education services, however, do not qualify to sit for CHES exam because they have not completed a degree program in health education at the bachelor or master's level. For either group, however, ongoing continuing education initiatives will be important to strengthen the corps of workers providing health education services to the public.

## ADDITIONAL INFORMATION

There are many good sources of information on health education and public information as careers. Several sources are available for information on educational programs for health education as well as for continuing education and leadership development for practicing health educators seeking a professional credential.

Schools of public health are among the institutions offering graduate degrees in health administration. The Association of Schools of Public Health (http://www.asph.org) has identified a battery of behavioral science competencies appropriate for all students receiving the master's of public health (MPH) degree. These competencies provide a useful baseline for professional practice and summarize what an MPH graduate should be able to do (Table 7–4).

Additional sources of information on health education include the Web sites of several other organizations, including the American Association of

**Table 7–4** Social and Behavioral Science Competency Expectations for Graduates of MPH Degree Programs:

1. Describe the role of social and community factors in both the onset and solution of public health problems.

2. Identify the causes of social and behavioral factors that affect the health of individuals and populations.

3. Identify basic theories, concepts, and models from a range of social and behavioral disciplines that are used in public health research and practice.

4. Apply ethical principles to public health program planning, implementation, and evaluation.

5. Specify multiple targets and levels of intervention for social and behavioral science programs and/or policies.

6. Identify individual, organizational, and community concerns, assets, resources, and deficits for social and behavioral science interventions.

7. Use evidence-based approaches in the development and evaluation of social and behavioral science interventions.

8. Describe the merits of social and behavioral science interventions and policies.

9. Describe steps and procedures for the planning, implementing, and evaluating public health programs, policies, and interventions.

10. Identify critical stakeholders for the planning, implementation, and evaluation of public health programs, policies, and interventions.

*Source:* Association of Schools of Public Health (ASPH) MPH Core Competency Development Process, Version 1.2. Available at http://www.asph.org. Accessed August 2005.

Health Education (http://www.aahperd.org/aahe/template.cfm?template=main.html), the American College Health Association (http://www.acha.org), the American School Health Association (http://www.asha web.org), the Association of State and Territorial Directors of Health Promotion and Public Health Education (http://www.astdhpphe.org), the Center for the Advancement of Community-Based Public Health (http://www.cbph.org), the International Union for Health Promotion and Education (http://www.iuhpe.org), and the Coalition of National Health Education Organizations (http://www.hsc.usf.edu/CFH/cnheo/). The coalition, for example, has as its primary mission the mobilization of the resources of the health education profession in order to expand and improve health education, regardless of the setting.

The American Public Health Association Web site (http://www.apha.org) has several sections active in health education issues, including the public health education and health promotion section and the school health education section.

Another useful resource for health education and information is the *Healthy People 2010 Toolkit: A Field Guide to Health Planning* (http://www. health.gov/healthypeople/state/toolkit/). This toolkit contains practical guidance, technical tools, and resources for states, territories, tribes, and others involved in Healthy People planning. Additional sources of information include the *National Heart, Lung and Blood Institute Educational Materials Catalog* (http://www.nhlbi.nih.gov) and Web site of the Society of State Directors of Health and Physical Education and Recreation (http://www.thesociety.org).

Central to making health education a profession are the efforts of the Society of Public Health Educators (SOPHE) and the National Commission for Health Education Credentialing (http://www.nchec.org) with its competency-based credentialing program for professional health educators (certified health education specialist or CHES). CHES competencies are detailed in Table 7–5.

---

**Table 7–5** Certified Health Education Specialist Competency Expectations

---

Responsibility I

Assessing Individual and Community Needs for Health Education

A. Obtain health-related data about social and cultural environments, growth and development factors, needs, and interests.
   - Select valid sources of information about health needs and interests.
   - Utilize computerized sources of health-related information.
   - Employ or develop appropriate data-gathering instruments.
   - Apply survey techniques to acquire health data.

B. Distinguish between behaviors that foster and those that hinder well-being.
   - Investigate physical, social, emotional, and intellectual factors influencing health behaviors.
   - Identify behaviors that tend to promote or compromise health.
   - Recognize the role of learning and affective experience in shaping patterns of health behavior.

C. Infer needs for health education on the basis of obtained data.
   - Analyze needs assessment data.
   - Determine priority areas of need for health education.

Responsibility II

Planning Effective Health Education Programs

A. Recruit community organizations, resource people, and potential participants for support and assistance in program planning.

*continues*

---

**Table 7–5** *continued*

---

- Communicate need for the program to those who will be involved.
- Obtain commitments from personnel and decision makers who will be involved in the program.
- Seek ideas and opinions of those who will affect, or be affected by, the program.
- Incorporate feasible ideas and recommendations into the planning process.

B. Develop a logical scope and sequence plan for a health education program.
- Determine the range of health information requisite to a given program of instruction.
- Organize the subject areas composing the scope of a program in logical sequence.

C. Formulate appropriate and measurable program objectives.
- Infer educational objectives that facilitate achievement of specified competencies.
- Develop a framework of broadly stated, operational objectives relevant to the proposed health education program.

D. Design educational programs consistent with specified program objectives.
- Match proposed learning activities with those implicit in the stated objectives.
- Formulate a wide variety of the alternative educational methods.
- Select strategies best suited to implement educational objectives in a given setting.
- Plan a sequence of learning opportunities building upon, and reinforcing mastery of, preceding objectives.

Responsibility III

Implementing Health Education Programs

A. Exhibit competence in carrying out planned educational programs.
- Employ a wide range of educational methods and techniques.
- Apply individual or group process methods as appropriate to given learning situations.
- Utilize instructional equipment and other instructional media.
- Select methods that best facilitate the practice of program objectives.

B. Infer enabling objectives as needed to implement instructional programs in specified settings.
- Pretest learners to ascertain present abilities and knowledge relative to proposed program objectives.
- Develop subordinate measurable objectives as needed for instruction.

C. Select methods and media best suited to implement program plans for specific learners.
- Analyze learner characteristics, legal aspects, feasibility, and other considerations influencing choices among methods.
- Evaluate the efficacy of alternative methods and techniques capable of facilitating program objectives.

**Table 7–5** *continued*

- Determine the availability of information, personnel, time, and equipment needed to implement the program for a given audience.

D. Monitor educational programs, adjusting objectives and activities as necessary.

- Compare actual program activities with the stated objectives.
- Assess the relevance of existing program objectives to current needs.
- Revise program activities and objectives as necessitated by changes in learner needs.
- Appraise applicability of resources and materials relative to given educational objectives.

Responsibility IV

Evaluating Effectiveness of Health Education Programs

A. Develop plans to assess achievement of programs objectives.

- Determine standards of performance to be applied as criteria of effectiveness.
- Establish a realistic scope of evaluation efforts.
- Develop an inventory of existing valid and reliable tests and instruments.
- Select appropriate methods for evaluating program effectiveness.

B. Carry out evaluation plans.

- Facilitate administration of the tests and activities specified in the plan.
- Utilize data-collecting methods appropriate to the objectives.
- Analyze resulting evaluation data.

C. Interpret results of program evaluation.

- Apply criteria of effectiveness to obtained results of a program.
- Translate evaluation results into terms easily understood by others.
- Report effectiveness of educational programs in achieving proposed objectives.

D. Infer implication from findings for future program planning.

- Explore possible explanations for important evaluation findings.
- Recommend strategies for implementing results of evaluation.

Responsibility V

Coordinating Provision of Health Education Services

A. Develop a plan for coordinating health education services.

- Determine the extent of available health education services.
- Match health education services to proposed program activities.
- Identify gaps and overlaps in the provision of collaborative health services.

B. Facilitate cooperation between and among levels of program personnel.

- Promote cooperation and feedback among personnel related to the program.
- Apply various methods of conflict reduction as needed.
- Analyze the role of health educator as liaison between program staff and outside groups and organizations.

*continues*

---

**Table 7–5** *continued*

---

C. Formulate practical modes of collaboration among health agencies and organizations.

- Stimulate development of cooperation among personnel responsible for community health education programs.
- Suggest approaches for integrating health education within existing health programs.
- Develop plans for promoting collaborative efforts among health agencies and organizations with mutual interests.

D. Organize in-service training programs for teachers, volunteers, and other interested personnel.

- Plan an operational, competency-oriented training program.
- Utilize instructional resources that meet a variety of in-service training needs.
- Demonstrate a wide range of strategies for conducting in-service training programs.

Responsibility VI

Acting as a Resource Person in Health Education

A. Utilize computerized health information retrieval systems effectively.

- Match an information need with the appropriate retrieval system.
- Access principal online and other database health information resources.

B. Establish effective consultative relationships with those requesting assistance in solving health-related problems.

- Analyze parameters of effective consultative relationships.
- Describe special skills and abilities needed by health educators for consultation activities.
- Formulate a plan for providing consultation to other health professionals.
- Explain the process of marketing health education consultative services.

C. Interpret and respond to requests for health information.

- Analyze general processes for identifying the information needed to satisfy a request.
- Employ a wide range of approaches in referring requests to valid sources of health information.

D. Select effective educational resource materials for dissemination.

- Assemble educational material of value to the health of individuals and community groups.
- Evaluate the worth and applicability of resource materials for given audiences.
- Apply various processes in the acquisition of resource materials.
- Compare different methods for distributing educational materials.

Responsibility VII

Communicating Health and Health Education Needs, Concerns, and Resources

A. Interpret concepts, purposes, and theories of health education.

- Evaluate the state-of-the-art of health education.

**Table 7–5** *continued*

- Analyze the foundations of the discipline of health education.
- Describe major responsibilities of the health educator in the practice of health education.

B. Predict the impact of societal value systems on health education programs.

- Investigate social forces causing opposing viewpoints regarding health education needs and concerns.
- Employ a wide range of strategies for dealing with controversial health issues.

C. Select a variety of communication methods and techniques in providing health information.

- Utilize a wide range of techniques for communicating health and health education information.
- Demonstrate proficiency in communicating health information and health education needs.

D. Foster communication between health care providers and consumers.

- Interpret the significance and implications of health care providers' messages to consumers.
- Act as liaison between consumer groups and individuals and health care provider organizations.

*Source:* National Commission for Health Education Credentialing. Responsibilities and Competencies for CHES Credentialing. Available at http://www.nchec.org/aboutnchec/rc.htm. Accessed August 2005.

## CONCLUSION

In an age of communications and information technology, it is no wonder that public health educators and public information professionals play key roles in public health practice. Public health agencies are increasingly adding staff with these capabilities and utilizing existing staff across programs to address community-wide concerns and issues. Public health educators have led the way in establishing a credential that is based on relevant practice competencies and respected in practice settings. It is expected that opportunities will continue to grow for public health educators and public information specialists over the next decade.

## REFERENCES

1. Bureau of Labor Statistics, U.S. Department of Labor. May 2004 National, State, and Metropolitan Area Occupational Employment and Wage Estimates. Available at http://www.bls.gov/oes/current/oes_nat.htm. Accessed August 2005.

2. Health Resources and Services Administration (HRSA), Bureau of Health Professions, National Center for Health Workforce Information and Analysis and Center for Health Policy, Columbia School of Nursing. *The Public Health Workforce Enumeration 2000.* Washington, DC: HRSA; 2000. Available at http://www.phppo.cdc.gov/owpp/docs/library/2000/Public%20Health%20 Workforce%20Enumeration%202000.pdf. Accessed August 2005.

# CHAPTER 8

# Other Public Health Professional Occupations

This and the following chapter are organized somewhat differently than Chapters 3 through 7. This chapter highlights selected professional public health occupations within the public health workforce. These professional occupational categories and related technical occupational categories are addressed separately as the career links are not as clear for these occupations as for those addressed in earlier chapters.

Many standard occupational categories carry out professional roles or perform technical duties in support of professionals. Within the public health workforce these include nutritionists and dieticians, dietetic technicians, medical and public health social workers, mental health and substance abuse social workers, substance abuse and behavioral disorder counselors, medical and clinical laboratory technologists and technicians, physicians, veterinarians, pharmacists, dental health professionals, and administrative judges/hearing officers.

Nutritionists and dieticians work in a variety of settings for governmental public health agencies, voluntary organizations, and health care providers. Public health social workers often have positions in maternal and child health programs or in mental health services offered by public agencies. Mental health substance abuse social workers and substance abuse and behavioral disorder counselors work with psychologists and other mental health providers in programs that offer mental health services.

Not all public health agencies have laboratories, but those that provide public health and clinical laboratory services employ medical and clinical laboratory technologists and technicians. Those labs also employ public health laboratory scientists with special expertise in microbiology, chemistry, and physics.

Physicians were once the largest and most active professional occupational category in the public health workforce. Today, however, they represent only a small percentage of the public health workforce. Veterinarians play key roles in animal control and communicable disease control programs, and pharmacists are increasingly involved in clinical and emergency preparedness and response roles. Dental health professionals, including dentists and dental hygienists, coordinate oral health programs within public health agencies. Finally, administrative law judges/hearing officers are important personnel in the wide variety of administrative and regulatory processes of governmental public health agencies. Together, these varied professional categories demonstrate the multidisciplinary and interdisciplinary nature of modern public health practice.

This chapter focuses on the following public health professional and supporting technical occupations that make up key subsets of the overall public health workforce: (1) nutritionists and dieticians; (2) public health social, behavioral, and mental health workers; (3) public health laboratory workers; (4) public health physicians, veterinarians, and pharmacists; (5) public health dental workers; and (6) administrative judges/hearing officers. Data from several sources are used throughout this chapter, including the Bureau of Labor Statistics[1] and the *Public Health Workforce Enumeration 2000.*[2] Table 8–1 provides a public health practice profile for each of these occupational categories pointing out the prime public health purposes and essential public health services addressed by each category.

## NUTRITIONISTS AND DIETICIANS

Nutritionists, dieticians, and dietetic technicians primarily work toward preventing the spread of diseases and conditions related to diet and exercise (see Table 8–1). These categories monitor health status to identify community health problems; inform, educate, and empower people about health issues; and link people with needed personal health services. They may also be involved in research activities.

Nutritionists and dieticians may supervise the activities of a program or unit providing nutrition or food services, counsel individuals, or

**Table 8-1** Public Health Practice Profile for Selected Public Health Professional Occupations

| Selected Public Health Professional Occupations Make a Difference by: | | | | | |
|---|---|---|---|---|---|
| Nutr | Soc Beh MH | PH Lab | MD DVM Phar | Dent Wkrs | Adm Law Jdg |
| **Public Health Purposes** | | | | | |
| Preventing epidemics and the spread of disease — ✓ | | ✓ | ✓ | ✓ | ✓ |
| Protecting against environmental hazards | | ✓ | | | ✓ |
| Preventing injuries | | | | | |
| Promoting and encouraging healthy behaviors — ✓ | ✓ | | ✓ | ✓ | |
| Responding to disasters and assisting communities in recovery | ✓ | | | | |
| Assuring the quality and accessibility of health services — ✓ | ✓ | ✓ | ✓ | ✓ | ✓ |
| **Essential Public Health Services** | | | | | |
| Monitoring health status to identify community health problems — ✓ | | ✓ | ✓ | ✓ | |
| Diagnosing and investigating health problems and health hazards in the community | | ✓ | ✓ | | |
| Informing, educating, and empowering people about health issues — ✓ | ✓ | | | ✓ | |
| Mobilizing community partnerships to identify and solve health problems | ✓ | | | | |
| Developing policies and plans that support individual and community health efforts | ✓ | | | | ✓ |
| Enforcing laws and regulations that protect health and ensure safety | | ✓ | | | ✓ |
| Linking people with needed personal health services and assuring the provision of health care when otherwise unavailable — ✓ | ✓ | | ✓ | ✓ | |
| Assuring a competent public health and personal health care workforce | | | | | ✓ |
| Evaluating effectiveness, accessibility, and quality of personal and population-based health services — ✓ | ✓ | ✓ | ✓ | ✓ | ✓ |
| Researching new insights and innovative solutions to health problems — ✓ | | ✓ | ✓ | | ✓ |

conduct nutritional research. Nutritionists, dieticians, and dietetic technicians work in community-oriented programs such as the federally funded WIC program or state and locally funded maternal and child health programs, as well as in clinical settings, such as prenatal and well child clinics.

Bureau of Labor Statistics indicate that there are 47,000 nutritionists and dieticians in the United States and 25,000 dietetic technicians. Most nutritionists, dieticians, and dietetic technicians work for hospitals, long-term care facilities, and community care facilities for the elderly. Only 7300 nutritionists and dieticians and 1000 dietetic technicians work for federal, state, and local governmental agencies, primarily public health departments. The *Public Health Workforce Enumeration 2000* identified 6700 public health nutritionists in governmental public health agencies, largely based on information provided by the Association of State and Territorial Public Health Nutrition Directors.

The adjusted estimate of government-employed nutritionists (adjusted for underreporting of occupational categories in the year 2000 public health enumeration study) likely overestimates the number of government-employed nutritionists because the year 2000 public health enumeration included national data from a comprehensive independent enumeration of nutritionists compiled by the Association of State and Territorial Public Health Nutrition Directors. As a result, it is likely that the actual number of nutritionist positions in state and local public health agencies is close to the 6700 figure. Within state and local health agencies, most nutritionists work in WIC programs. WIC is short for Supplemental Foods Program for Women, Infants, and Children which is funded by the U.S. Department of Agriculture. Nutrition positions are also found in regulatory programs for hospitals, nursing homes, day care centers, and other facilities as well as Child and Adult Care Food Program (food stamps) and state Medicaid and school lunch programs.

Entry-level public health nutritionists plan and conduct nutritional programs that assist in the promotion of health and control of disease. Mid- and senior-level nutritionists may supervise activities of a program or unit of an agency providing quality food services, counsel individuals, or conduct nutritional research. Many nutritionists and dietetic technicians seek the registered dietician (RD) and registered dietetic technician (DTR) credential.

Entry-level professional public health nutritionists are responsible for participating in the implementation of nutrition programs and services. Work involves providing nutrition program services to local health units or health and human services professionals. General supervision is received from an administrative superior with professional supervision received from a higher-level nutritionist.

Essential and important duties of an entry-level public health nutritionist include:

- Carries out program policies and procedures in implementing nutritional components of general or specialized public health programs
- Coordinates nutrition program services with other nutrition or public health programs within an assigned area
- Confers with public health personnel on food and nutrition related to health programs or problems
- Participates in conducting studies and surveys of the relationships of dietary factors to health and disease, including compilation of data and interpretation of results
- Conducts formal training using educational materials and visual aids in the education of students and public health staff, and assists in the evaluation and recommendation for improvement of such materials
- Participates and works with higher-level nutritionists or consultants in in-service training of health personnel
- Prepares reports, records, and other data related to nutritional services
- Assists in monitoring local health units for compliance with federal or state regulations related to nutrition programs or grant projects

Key knowledge, skills, and abilities for entry-level public health nutritionists include:

- Working knowledge of the principles and practices of nutrition and food, particularly in relation to health and disease
- Knowledge of current developments in public health nutrition and their application to statewide and/or local nutrition programs
- Knowledge of social, cultural, and economic problems and their impact on public health nutrition
- Knowledge of the general organization and function of public health agencies

- Ability to effectively use educational materials for the nutrition education of individuals and groups
- Ability to gather, interpret, evaluate, and use statistical data
- Ability to present ideas clearly and concisely
- Ability to establish and maintain working relationships with professional and lay groups, other employees, and the general public

Minimum qualifications, in terms of experience and training, for entry-level public health nutrition positions may call for graduation from an accredited 4-year college or university with a bachelor degree, including or supplemented by at least 15 semester hours in foods and nutrition including at least one course in diet therapy and one course in community nutrition or nutrition in life cycle; or completion of an undergraduate curriculum accredited or approved by the American Dietetic Association. Registration or current eligibility for registration by the Commission on Dietetic Registration may be accepted in lieu of other specified qualifications. A registered dietician is identified as an *RD*.

Salaries for nutritionists and dieticians average $45,000 with the middle 50% earning between $36,000 and $54,000. In general, nutritionists working for state and local governmental agencies earn less than those working for hospitals and other health care providers. Mean salaries for nutritionists employed by state and local governmental agencies are $43,000 and $40,500 respectively (see Table 8–2). Starting salaries for entry-level nutritionists in a public health agency setting may be in the $26,000–36,000 range. The average salary for nutritionists employed by federal agencies, on the other hand, is nearly $60,000, well above the overall average for all nutritionists. Nutritionists working for federal health agencies work primarily as resources and consultants. Table 8–2 presents information on government employment and salaries for each of the public health professional occupations examined in this chapter.

## PUBLIC HEALTH SOCIAL, BEHAVIORAL, AND MENTAL HEALTH WORKERS

Public health social workers, mental health and substance abuse social workers, and substance abuse and behavioral disorder counselors promote and encourage healthy behaviors and often participate in responses to disasters and public health emergencies (see Table 8–1). They diagnose and

**Table 8–2** Number and Mean Salary for Selected Public Health Professional Occupations in Federal, State, and Local Governmental Agencies, May 2004

| Occupational Category | Federal Workers | Federal Worker Mean Salary | State Workers | State Worker Mean Salary | Local Workers | Local Worker Mean Salary | Total Federal, State, and Local Workers | Adjusted PH Enum. 2000 Workers |
|---|---|---|---|---|---|---|---|---|
| Nutritionists/dieticians | 1,360 | $59,340 | 2,480 | $43,020 | 3,490 | $40,560 | 7,330 | 10,330 |
| Public health social workers | NA | NA | 5,190 | $38,180 | 10,130 | $40,530 | 15,320 | 3,364 |
| Microbiologists | 2,200 | $79,570 | 1,250 | $44,890 | 510 | $55,520 | 3,960 | |
| Biochemists | 410 | $81,030 | 290 | $43,870 | 30 | $64,840 | 730 | |
| Laboratory specialists | 4,870 | $53,330 | 930 | $43,070 | 760 | $51,760 | 6,560 | 21,785 |
| Laboratory technicians | 2,310 | $35,220 | 1,150 | $31,840 | 1,290 | $31,390 | 4,750 | 8,182 |
| Public health physicians | 19,250 | $101,920 | 1,270 | $126,730 | 1,580 | $118,220 | 22,100 | 9,290 |
| Public health veterinarians | 1,070 | $78,210 | 520 | $62,190 | 140 | $71,690 | 1,730 | 3,150 |
| Public health pharmacists | 5,510 | $82,310 | 1,090 | $70,600 | 820 | $79,810 | 7,420 | 2,313 |
| Public health dentists | 1,240 | $84,090 | 270 | $53,260 | 60 | $55,840 | 1,570 | |
| Public health dental hygienists | 390 | $44,680 | 320 | $42,430 | 320 | $46,240 | 1,030 | 3,142 |
| Admin law judges/hearing officers | 4,160 | $104,750 | 7,670 | $60,910 | 3,000 | $63,160 | 14,830 | 929 |

*Source:* Data for federal, state, and local governmental agency workers from Bureau of Labor Statistics. May 2004 National, State, and Metropolitan Area Occupational Employment and Wage Estimates. Available at http://www.bls.gov. Accessed August 2005. See Chapter 2 for Adjusted Number of Public Health Workers from The Public Health Workforce Enumeration 2000.

investigate health problems, inform, educate, and empower people about issues, mobilize community partnerships, and link people with needed personal health services.

## Medical and Public Health Social Workers

Medical and public health social workers provide persons, families, or vulnerable populations with psychosocial support needed to cope with chronic, acute, or terminal illnesses, such as AIDS, cancer, or Alzheimer's disease. Public health social workers identify, plan, develop, implement, and evaluate social work interventions on the basis of social and interpersonal needs of total populations or populations at risk in order to improve the health of a community and promote and protect the health of individuals and families.

There are 104,000 medical and public health social workers in the United States. The majority work for hospitals, long-term care facilities, and nongovernmental home health care service agencies. Nearly 11,000 work for local governmental agencies, including local public health agencies. The *Public Health Workforce Enumeration 2000* identified 3400 medical and public health social work positions in governmental public health agencies.

Entry-level professional social workers may provide basic protective services with or, on behalf of, children, families, or aged, blind, or disabled clients in instances of abuse, neglect, or exploitation. Responsibilities may also include foster care, unmarried parent services, adoption, and services for character disorders and serious physical, mental, or emotional handicaps. Work is performed under close supervision as part of a training process to develop the worker's understanding and skill. Workers receive close supervision from a social service supervisor or higher-level social service worker within the framework of agency rules, regulations, and procedures.

Essential and important duties of an entry-level public health social worker include:

- Plans and conducts programs to combat social problems, prevent substance abuse, or improve community health and counseling services
- Collaborates with other professionals to evaluate patients' medical or physical condition and to assess client needs
- Serves as the primary case manager when families are served by more than one health agency resource

- Investigates child abuse or neglect cases and takes authorized protective action when necessary
- Refers patient, client, or family to community resources to assist in recovery from mental or physical illness and to provide access to services such as financial assistance, legal aid, housing, job placement, or education
- Counsels clients and patients in individual and group sessions to help them overcome dependencies, recover from illness, and adjust to life
- Organizes support groups or counsels family members to assist them in understanding, dealing with, and supporting the client or patient
- Advocates for clients or patients to resolve crises
- Identifies environmental impediments to client or patient progress through interviews and review of patient records
- Utilizes consultation data and social work experience to plan and coordinate client or patient care and rehabilitation, following through to ensure service efficacy
- Modifies treatment plans to comply with changes in clients' status
- Monitors, evaluates, and records client progress according to measurable goals described in treatment and care plan
- Supervises and directs other workers providing services to clients or patients
- Develops or advises on social policy and assist in community development
- Conducts social research to advance knowledge in the social work field

Relevant knowledge, skills, and abilities for entry-level public health social workers may include:

- Knowledge of human behavior and performance; individual differences in ability, personality, and interests; learning and motivation; psychological research methods; and the assessment and treatment of behavioral and affective disorders
- Knowledge of principles and processes for providing customer and personal services including assessment of customer needs, meeting quality standards for services, and evaluation of customer satisfaction
- Knowledge of principles, methods, and procedures for diagnosis, treatment, and rehabilitation of physical and mental dysfunctions, and for career counseling and guidance

- Knowledge of group behavior and dynamics, societal trends and influences, human migrations, ethnicity, cultures and their history and origins
- Knowledge of the principles and methods of interviewing
- Knowledge of the general provisions, objectives, and philosophy in social welfare program
- Knowledge of current social, economic, and community health problems
- Ability to plan and organize working time effectively
- Ability to work under a variety of situations and in all types of community environments
- Ability to provide protective services to clients following established rules and procedures
- Ability to work harmoniously with applicants, recipients, the general public, and other employees
- Ability to exercise good judgment in evaluating situations and in making decisions
- Ability to express ideas clearly, both orally and in writing, and to interpret laws and regulations

Minimum qualifications, in terms of experience and training, may call for graduation from an accredited 4-year college or university with major specialization (24 semester hours) in such areas as social work, family and child development, special education, psychology, sociology, gerontology, or related behavioral sciences. Professional employment in a public or private agency involving a substantial amount of time (over 50% of time) in the delivery of protective services to families, adults, children, or the aged may be substituted on a year-for-year basis for the required education.

The average salary for medical and public health social workers is $42,000 with the middle 50% earning between $32,000 and $50,000. Social workers employed by local governmental agencies have a lower average salary ($40,500) than those working for private organizations and schools.

## Behavioral and Mental Health Workers

Public health organizations increasingly employ a variety of behavioral and mental health workers, including mental health and substance abuse social workers, substance abuse and behavioral disorder counselors, and psychologists and other mental health providers.

Mental health and substance abuse social workers assess and treat individuals with mental, emotional, or substance abuse problems, including abuse of alcohol, tobacco, and/or other drugs. Duties may include individual and group therapy, crisis intervention, case management, client advocacy, prevention, and education. There are 109,000 mental health and substance abuse social workers in the United States, with 22,000 employed by state and local governmental agencies.

Mental health counselors counsel and advise individuals with an emphasis on prevention. They work with individuals and groups to promote optimal mental health and may help individuals deal with addictions and substance abuse; family, parenting, and marital problems; suicide; stress management; problems with self-esteem; and issues associated with aging and mental and emotional health. Of the 90,000 mental health counselors in the United States, 11,000 work for local government agencies and another 2000 work for state agencies.

Substance abuse and behavioral disorder counselors counsel and advise individuals with alcohol, drug, or other problems, such as gambling and eating disorders. They may counsel individuals, families, or groups or engage in prevention programs. Of the 69,000 substance abuse and behavioral disorder counselors, only 10,000 work for state and local governmental agencies (7000 work for local government agencies).

Only a small number (2400) of the government-employed behavioral and mental health personnel work in public health agencies. The average salary for mental health and substance abuse social workers is $36,000, with the middle 50% earning between $27,000 and $44,000. Mental health counselors have an average salary of $36,000 with the middle 50% earning between $26,000 and $44,000. Substance abuse and behavioral disorder counselors have a slightly lower average salary ($35,000), with the middle 50% earning between $26,000 and $41,000.

## PUBLIC HEALTH LABORATORY WORKERS

Public health laboratory workers prevent the spread of disease, protect against environmental hazards, and assure the quality of services (see Table 8–1). Lab workers diagnose and investigate health problems and disasters, evaluate the effectiveness and quality of services, and research new insights and innovative solutions to health problems.

Public health laboratories require a variety of professional and technical workers including public health scientists and laboratory technologists and technicians. Public health scientists are not one of the standard occupational categories tracked by the Bureau of Labor Statistics although there are several other standard occupational categories that work in this capacity (such as microbiologists and biochemists). Technologists and technicians working in medical and clinical labs, including public health labs, are among the occupations for which national data are compiled.

## Public Health Laboratory Scientists

Public health laboratory scientists are laboratory professionals who plan, design, and implement laboratory procedures to identify and quantify agents in the environment that may be hazardous to human health; biological agents believed to be involved in the etiology of diseases in animals or humans, such as bacteria, viruses, and parasites; or other physical, chemical, and biological hazards. Titles include microbiologist, chemist, toxicologist, physicist, and entomologist.

Public health laboratory scientists perform both professional and technical work in the public health laboratory. These include a variety of chemical, serological, viral, or bacteriological analyses of clinical or environmental specimens according to established procedures. Work involves performing complex tests under general supervision, assuring the accuracy of the tests through quality control procedures, notifying appropriate scientific and supervisory staff when a test system is not functioning and, in consultation with appropriate authorities, implementing and documenting appropriate remedial and corrective actions. Work may also involve communicating with health professionals in other agencies regarding routine questions concerning specimen requirements and tests offered. Work is performed under general supervision; however, the public health laboratory scientists are expected to exercise independent judgment within the framework of established procedures and policies.

Public health laboratory scientists include microbiologists, biochemists, and biophysicists. Microbiologists investigate the growth, structure, development, and other characteristics of microscopic organisms, such as bacteria, algae, or fungi. Biochemists and biophysicists study the chemical composition and physical principles of living cells and organisms, their electrical and mechanical energy, and related phenomena. They may conduct research to further understanding of the complex chemical combinations and reactions involved in metabolism, reproduction, growth, and heredity. Biochemists may also determine the effects of foods, drugs, serums, hormones, and other substances on tissues and vital processes of living organisms.

There are 14,000 microbiologists and 16,000 biochemists and biophysicists in the United States. Five thousand (5000) microbiologists work for federal, state, and local health agencies; federal agencies employ about half of these scientists. Fewer biochemists and biophysicists, an estimated 1000, work for governmental agencies. The *Public Health Workforce Enumeration 2000* identified 22,000 public health laboratory professionals working in governmental public health agencies.

Essential and important duties of a public health laboratory scientist include:

- Performs routine serologic tests for the presence of antibodies or antigens to various disease agents
- Performs a variety of bacteriological examinations for the presence of disease agents or contaminants in clinical or other specimens, such as feces, urine, sputum, spinal fluid, blood cultures, water specimens, dairy products, foods, and beverages
- Performs microscopic examinations of animal heads for rabies
- Performs microscopic examinations for tissue and intestinal protozoans, helminths, and nematodes
- Performs cultural and microscopic examinations for gonorrhea, and cultural, biochemical, and serological examinations for various species of bacteria
- Performs analytical chemical analysis on clinical and environmental samples using a variety of methodologies and instrumentation
- Evaluates methods and instruments for determination of blood alcohol content in breath, blood, urine or saliva; periodically performs quality assurance checks of field units; testifies in court as required
- Performs screening and confirmatory tests to detect inborn errors of metabolism and sickle cell disease
- Performs, records, and reviews quality control results to determine the validity, accuracy, or precision of tests performed and to ascertain the quality of reagents, chemicals, or media used for analysis

- Participates in sample accessioning and record keeping to ensure that all specimens are accounted for, appropriately handled, and properly and completely tested
- Records and reports results in the proper manner for the technical area of analysis; checks reports for accuracy; maintains confidentiality of reports
- Consults with public health personnel, physicians, other laboratorians, and health care professionals regarding the interpretation of results, collection of specimens, and the applicability of tests to particular circumstances

Knowledge, skills, and abilities relevant for public health laboratory scientists include:

- Knowledge of the principles and practices of microbiology or analytical chemistry
- Knowledge of accepted analytical techniques
- Knowledge of laboratory methods, materials, techniques, and safety procedures
- Knowledge of the principles, practices, and methods of a public health, medical, or other health-related analytical laboratory
- Knowledge of common laboratory equipment and apparatus, and where appropriate, some knowledge of the operation, maintenance, and repair of specific instruments, such as gas chromatographs, atomic absorption units, fluorescent microscopes, and spectrophotometer readers
- Working knowledge of statistics, the metric system, and mathematics for interpreting data and reporting results
- Ability to perceive colors and, where applicable, eyesight sufficiently strong to permit extended microscopic work
- Ability to perform assigned tasks exactly according to prescribed procedures, to accurately observe and interpret results, and to make reports
- Ability to communicate effectively
- Ability to establish and maintain working relationships with staff members, public health personnel, physicians, other laboratories, and the public
- Ability to effectively organize work

Minimum qualifications for public health laboratory scientists often call for two years of professional experience as a chemist, microbiologist, medical technologist, or associate public health laboratory scientist; and graduation from an accredited 4-year college or university with a bachelor degree with major specialization in a biological or chemical science, or medical technology. In some instances, possession of CLIA '88 certification will substitute for the educational requirements. Graduate education in the above areas may substitute on a year-for-year basis for the stated experience.

Microbiologists have an average salary of $62,000 with the middle 50% earning between $41,000 and $75,000. Mean salaries for microbiologists working for federal agencies are well above the mean salaries at state and local governmental agencies ($79,500 federal, $45,000 state, $55,500 local).

Biochemists and biophysicists have an average salary of $72,000 with the middle 50% earning between $50,000 and $89,000. Mean salaries for biochemists working for federal agencies are well above the mean salaries at state and local governmental agencies ($81,000 federal, $44,000 state, $65,000 local).

## Public Health Laboratory Technologist

Medical and clinical laboratory technologists perform complex medical laboratory tests for diagnosis, treatment, and prevention of disease. This involves technical work in the preparation of samples for analysis and the performance of routine medical and public health laboratory tests. Technologists may train and/or supervise other laboratory staff. Medical and clinical laboratory technicians perform routine medical laboratory tests for diagnosis, treatment, and prevention of disease and technicians. Lab technicians may work under the direction of a technologist.

Medical and clinical laboratory technologists number 152,000. The vast majority work for hospitals, nonhospital-based laboratories, physician offices, and universities. Federal health agencies employ 5000 lab technologists; state and local health agencies employ another 5000. There are 143,000 medical and clinical laboratory technicians employed by the same types of organizations as for lab technologists. The *Public Health Workforce Enumeration 2000* identified 8000 public health laboratory technicians working in governmental public health agencies.

Essential and important duties for a public health laboratory technologist include:

- Receives, counts, logs and labels samples submitted by field staff and individuals for testing

- Prepares samples for analysis by racking, centrifuging, filtering, weighing, and so on, and distributes prepared samples to appropriate testing areas
- Pipettes serum samples onto testing plates and adds antigen or reagents in accordance with standard laboratory procedures; stirs, rocks, shakes, and incubates mixture for specified time; reads test results in accordance with established parameters
- Draws blood and collects urine, stool, sputum, and other samples for analysis as ordered by physicians; performs routine analyses of specimens
- Maintains basic records consistent with assigned responsibilities
- Prepares sample specimen kits and shipping boxes for mailing
- Cleans and maintains sample containers, laboratory equipment, and work areas

Key knowledge, skills, and abilities for public health laboratory technologists include:

- Knowledge of basic science terminology, concepts, and principles
- Knowledge of laboratory procedures, techniques, and equipment
- Knowledge of blood-drawing techniques
- Ability to properly operate microscopes, centrifuges, autoclaves, sterilizers, or other laboratory equipment
- Ability to apply proper methods of handling and disposing of chemicals and infectious materials
- Ability to perform assigned tasks according to specific instructions and clearly prescribed procedures
- Ability to read, compare, identify, and record laboratory data accurately, such as names, numbers, sample descriptions, and so on
- Ability to perform basic mathematics and make accurate measurements
- Ability to make accurate observations and prepare accurate records of laboratory tests
- Ability to work with other employees, laboratory staff, health professionals, and the general public

Minimum qualifications for these positions may call for one year of experience in a medical or public health laboratory performing routine laboratory tests under the direction of a physician or qualified laboratory technician, and possession of a high school diploma or a GED certificate. College coursework with specialization in the chemical, physical, or biological sciences may substitute on a year-for-year basis for deficiencies in the required experience.

The average salary for laboratory technologists is $47,000 with the middle 50% earning between $39,000 and $55,000. Lab technicians have an average salary of $33,000 with the middle 50% earning between $25,000 and $38,000. Mean salaries for laboratory technicians are similar for technicians working for federal, state, and local governmental agencies ($35,000 federal, $32,000 state, $31,500 local).

## PUBLIC HEALTH PHYSICIANS, VETERINARIANS, AND PHARMACISTS

Public health physicians identify persons or groups at risk of illness or disability, and develop, implement, and evaluate programs or interventions designed to prevent, treat, or ameliorate such risks. Public health physicians may provide direct medical services within the context of such programs and includes physicians with MD and DO degrees working as either generalists or specialists. Only a small proportion of the total number of active physicians (800,000) in the United States work in public health settings, and only a small number of those public health physicians have training in public health or preventive medicine. For example, the number of physicians who are board certified in preventive medicine with a specialization in public health decreased from 2300 in 1980 to 1800 in 2000. Those with specializations in general preventive medicine increased from 800 to 1700, and those specializing in occupational medicine increased from 2400 to 3000 during that same period.

There are 22,000 physicians working for federal, state, and local governmental agencies; more than 19,000 work for federal agencies, however, mainly providing clinical care services. Only 3000 physicians work for state and local governmental agencies. The *Public Health Workforce Enumeration 2000* identified more than 9000 public health physicians working in federal, state, and local public health agencies. This total for public health physicians undercounts the actual number of physicians working in public health as many physicians function under other titles, including as agency administrators, epidemiologists, or occupational health specialists, are not counted as public health physicians. A reasonable estimate of the actual number of public health physicians is in the 10,000–12,000 range.

Public health veterinarians/animal control specialists identify and assess health risks to humans from animals; they plan, manage, and evaluate programs to reduce these risks. There are 1700 veterinarians working for governmental agencies, with more than half employed by federal agencies. The *Public Health Workforce Enumeration 2000* identified more than 3100 veterinarians and animal control specialists working in governmental public health agencies, indicating that professionals other than veterinarians coordinate and manage animal control programs at the local level.

Public health pharmacists combine pharmacy and public health skills to plan, organize, and perform drug-related activities with a specific public health focus or within a public health setting. Public health pharmacists may work in agency-run pharmacies, or serve as the liaison between private pharmacies and the public health agency in regards to standards, procedures, and education. They also dispense drugs prescribed by physicians and other health practitioners and provide information to patients about medications and their use. Pharmacists advise physicians and other health practitioners on the selection, dosage, interactions, and side effects of medications and are increasingly involved in Strategic National Stockpile planning and operations. The *Public Health Workforce Enumeration 2000* identified 2300 public health pharmacists working in federal, state, and local public health agencies. There are 7500 pharmacists working for federal, state, and local governmental agencies; more than 5500 work for federal agencies, however, mainly providing clinical pharmacy services. Only 2000 pharmacists work for state and local governmental agencies.

## PUBLIC HEALTH DENTAL WORKERS

Public health dental workers, a category limited to workers formally trained in dentistry or dental health, plan, develop, implement, and evaluate dental health programs to promote and maintain optimum oral health of the public. Public health dentists may provide comprehensive dental care; dental hygienists provide limited dental services under professional supervisions. There are 1600 dentists and 1000 dental hygienists working for governmental agencies in the United States. Many provide clinical rather than public health dental services, especially those working for federal agencies. The *Public Health Workforce Enumeration 2000* identified 3100 dental workers (both dentists and hygienists) in federal, state, and local public health agencies.

## ADMINISTRATIVE JUDGES AND HEARING OFFICERS

Administrative judges or hearing officers provide legal advice to public health agencies, provide legal representation of public health officials in courts and administrative law proceedings, and preside over administrative law hearings of various kinds. The *Public Health Workforce Enumeration 2000* identified 900 administrative judges/hearing officers working in federal, state, and local public health agencies. There are 15,000 hearing officers in the United States; nearly all work for federal, state, and local governmental agencies.

## ADDITIONAL INFORMATION

Many sources provide additional and more detailed information for the occupational categories addressed in Chapter 8.

The American Public Health Association (APHA, http://www.apha.org) has sections that focus on issues important to each of these occupational categories, including food and nutrition; social work; mental health; alcohol, tobacco, and other drugs; medical care; and oral health. APHA also has a laboratory special interest group, veterinary public health special interest group, and public health law forum.

The Association of State and Territorial Public Health Nutrition Directors (ASTPHND, http://www.astphnd.org/) provides information on and resources for public health nutrition professionals. For example, ASTPHND's Web site provides access to their recent survey of the public health nutrition workforce (http://www.astphnd.org/resource_files/1/1_resource_file1.pdf). Another resource for nutritionists is the American Dietetic Association (ADA, http://www.eatright.org/Public/), which has 65,000 members and works in concert with the Commission on Dietetic Registration (CDR, http://www.cdrnet.org/). More than 76,000 dietitians and dietetic technicians across the country and the world have taken CDR exams over the past several decades. CDR currently awards four separate and distinct credentials: Registered Dietitian (RD); Dietetic

Technician, Registered (DTR); Board Certified Specialist in Renal Nutrition (CSR); and Board Certified Specialist in Pediatric Nutrition (CSP). The commission's certification programs are fully accredited by the National Commission for Certifying Agencies (NCCA), the accrediting arm of the National Organization for Competency Assurance (NOCA).

Web sites of the National Association of Social Workers (http://www.socialworkers.org) and the Council on Social Work Education (http://www.cswe.org) provide information on accredited social work programs. The Association of Social Work Boards (http://www.aswb.org) is a good source of information on licensing requirements and testing procedures used for state licensing purposes.

Information on public health laboratory workers is available from the Association for Public Health Laboratories (http://www.aphl.org) and the National Center for Public Health Laboratory Leadership (http://www.aphl.org/national_center_for_phl_leadership/). The American College of Preventive Medicine (http://www.acpm.org) and American Medical Association (http://www.amaassn.org/) Web sites provide information on public health physicians.

## CONCLUSION

Professionals comprise the major share of the public health workforce although public health professionals are quite diverse in terms of their professional background and experience. Nutritionists are valuable resources for public health agencies and the communities they serve, although most nutritionist positions work within the massive federally funded WIC program. More local public health agencies than state public health agencies provide social, mental, and behavioral health services as these programs may be funded by and relate to state agencies other than the state health agency in many states. Public health laboratory expertise is essential for disease and threat detection, and one of the major impacts of increased federal spending for terrorism preparedness is resulting in upgraded lab capabilities for state and local public health agencies. Recruiting and retaining the many levels of laboratory professionals and technicians necessary for lab operations has emerged as an important priority for public health as well as national security concerns. Physicians once dominated the field of public health. Today they represent one of many important professions within the public health workforce, standing beside veterinarians, pharmacists, and dental health workers. The regulatory and administrative processes within governmental public health agencies now requires a level of legal expertise beyond that called for in the past. These many and varied professional categories provide public health with the multidisciplinary and interdisciplinary muscle needed to battle modern public health threats and issues.

## REFERENCES

1. Bureau of Labor Statistics, U.S. Department of Labor. May 2004 National, State, and Metropolitan Area Occupational Employment and Wage Estimates. Available at http://www.bls.gov/oes/current/oes_nat.htm. Accessed August 2005.
2. Health Resources and Services Administration (HRSA), Bureau of Health Professions, National Center for Health Workforce Information and Analysis and Center for Health Policy, Columbia School of Nursing. *The Public Health Workforce Enumeration 2000*. Washington, DC: HRSA; 2000. Available at http://www.phppo.cdc.gov/owpp/docs/library/2000/Public%20Health%20 Workforce%20Enumeration%202000.pdf. Accessed August 2005.

# CHAPTER 9

# Public Health Program Occupations

This and the previous chapter are organized somewhat differently than Chapters 3 through 7. This chapter highlights professional and technical public health occupations that are largely defined by the program in which they function. Each occupational category is addressed separately as the career links are not as clear for these occupations as for those addressed in earlier chapters.

The public health roles attributed to these various professional and technical occupation categories vary enormously. As the programs in which they work have a narrower focus than either their agency as a whole or a broad agency division such as environmental health or nursing, many of these occupations focus on only one or a few public health responsibilities and essential public health services.

Unlike many of the public health occupations described in previous chapters, some positions work in public health program units using titles that are not tracked by the Bureau of Labor Statistics as standard occupational categories. Some of these positions are generic titles such as program specialist or program coordinator. Others are very specific such as public health emergency response coordinators, a position that has increased in attention since 2001. As public health agencies increase their emphasis on policy development activities, policy analysts, health planners, and health economists are increasingly being hired by public agencies. The same can be said for health information specialists and data and computer analysts.

This chapter will focus on five public health occupations that compose key subsets of the overall public health workforce: (1) public health program specialists and coordinators; (2) public health emergency response coordinators; (3) public health policy analysts; (4) public health information specialists; (5) community outreach and other technical occupations. Data from several sources are used throughout this chapter, including the *Public Health Workforce Enumeration 2000*[1] and Bureau of Labor Statistics data.[2] Table 9–1 provides a public health practice profile for each of these occupational categories with information as to the prime public health purposes and essential public health services addressed by each category. Table 9–2 presents information on government employment and salaries for each category.

## PUBLIC HEALTH PROGRAM SPECIALISTS AND COORDINATORS

Public health program specialists plan, develop, implement, and evaluate programs or interventions designed to identify persons at risk of specified health problems, and to prevent, treat, or ameliorate such problems. This includes public health workers reported as public health program specialists without specific designation of a program, as well as those reported as specialists working in a specific program (such as maternal and child health, AIDS awareness, immunization, or retail food inspection programs). Public health program specialists have a wide range of educational preparation, including many individuals who have preparation in a specific occupational category or profession (such as dental health, environmental health, nutrition, or nursing). The *Public Health Workforce Enumeration 2000* identified 12,000 public health program specialists.

A large number of public health program specialists work in licensing and regulatory programs performing various types of inspections. Many different titles are used, such as licensure, inspection, and regulatory specialist. These positions audit, inspect, and survey programs, institutions, equipment, products, and personnel, using approved standards for design or performance. This title includes workers who perform regular inspections of a specified class of sites or facilities, such as restaurants, nursing homes, and hospitals whose personnel and materials present constant and predictable threats to the public, without specification of educational preparation. This classification also includes a number of individuals with preparation in environmental health, nursing, and other health fields. The *Public Health Workforce Enumeration 2000* identified 21,000

**Table 9–1** Public Health Practice Profile for Selected Public Health Program Occupations

Selected Public Health Program Occupations Make a Difference by:

| | PH Prog Spec | ERC | PH Pol An | Hlth Info | Out Wkrs |
|---|---|---|---|---|---|
| **Public Health Purposes** | | | | | |
| Preventing epidemics and the spread of disease | | ✓ | ✓ | ✓ | ✓ |
| Protecting against environmental hazards | ✓ | | ✓ | | |
| Preventing injuries | ✓ | ✓ | | ✓ | |
| Promoting and encouraging healthy behaviors | ✓ | | | | ✓ |
| Responding to disasters and assisting communities in recovery | | ✓ | | | |
| Assuring the quality and accessibility of health services | | | ✓ | ✓ | |
| **Essential Public Health Services** | | | | | |
| Monitoring health status to identify community health problems | ✓ | | | ✓ | |
| Diagnosing and investigating health problems and health hazards in the community | ✓ | ✓ | | | |
| Informing, educating, and empowering people about health issues | | | ✓ | ✓ | ✓ |
| Mobilizing community partnerships to identify and solve health problems | | ✓ | ✓ | | ✓ |
| Developing policies and plans that support individual and community health efforts | ✓ | ✓ | ✓ | ✓ | |
| Enforcing laws and regulations that protect health and ensure safety | ✓ | | | | |
| Linking people with needed personal health services and assuring the provision of health care when otherwise unavailable | | ✓ | | | ✓ |
| Assuring a competent public health and personal health care workforce | | | | | |
| Evaluating effectiveness, accessibility, and quality of personal and population-based health services | ✓ | ✓ | ✓ | ✓ | |
| Researching new insights and innovative solutions to health problems | | | ✓ | ✓ | |

**Table 9-2** Number and Mean Salary for Selected Public Health Program Occupations in Federal, State, and Local Governmental Agencies, May 2004

| Occupational Category | Federal, State, and Local Worker Estimated Mean Salary | Adjusted PH Enum. 2000 Workers |
|---|---|---|
| Public Health Specialists | $45,000 | 33,401 |
| Emergency Response Coordinators | $45,500 | NA |
| Public Health Policy Analysts | NA | 5,687 |
| Public Health Information Specialists | $44,000 | 7,078 |
| Community Outreach Workers | $31,000 | 902 |
| Other Technical Occupations | NA | (est) 13,500 |
| Other Paraprofessional Occupations | NA | 26,129 |

See Chapter 2 for Adjusted Number of Public Health Workers from *Public Health Workforce Enumeration 2000.*

licensure/inspection/regulatory specialists working in federal, state, and local public health agencies.

Public health specialists carry responsibility for planning, performing, or supervising technical and professional work involving public health and consumer protection services. This includes performing inspections, surveys, and investigations to identify and eliminate conditions hazardous to life and health, providing consultative services and assistance in assigned areas of responsibility, ensuring corrective actions are taken to eliminate public health or other hazards, and ensuring compliance with applicable statutes and regulations.

The functions within this job family vary by level and from program to program, but may include the following:

- Develops, implements, and manages projects and initiatives for an assigned program or unit
- Develops and implements activities to ensure effective operations and compliance with established standards and/or contracted goals and objectives
- Serves as a team leader on specific projects
- Coordinates program activities which may include: fiscal monitoring; grant writing; monitoring of funded programs or agencies to ensure compliance; report preparation and writing; and assisting with developing and distributing communications, brochures, and educational materials

- Coordinates/oversees activities that may include: health education; training; development and oversight of requests for proposals and grants; and developing and distributing communications, brochures, and educational materials
- Collaborates and meets with management staff to determine program requirements, standards, and goals
- Evaluates projects or initiatives to determine effectiveness and to recommend changes and improvements
- Supervise employees; trains and evaluates staff; reviews the work of subordinates for completeness, accuracy, and content
- Assists in overseeing specialized research and evaluation projects
- Delivers services according to established program protocols
- Conducts inspections, surveys, and investigations of food establishments, lodging facilities, barber shops, public bathing places, schools, day care centers, nursing homes, hospitals, and other regulated facilities to identify public health hazards or environmental conditions that are detrimental to life and health
- Monitors state food supplies and products, provides training and technical assistance, and ensures compliance with applicable laws, rules and regulations; assists in the implementation of Hazard Analysis Critical Control Point (HACCP) systems in food establishments and in verifying implementation
- Responds to complaints concerning foodborne illnesses, adulterated foods, food tampering, recalls, insect or rodent infestation, or other issues related to food establishments or the sale of food and food products
- Reviews and acts on various epidemiological reports and complaints, including animal bites, rabies, and disease outbreaks; conducts environmental assessments and other surveys related to lodging, public bathing, and barber services; performs inspections for lead contamination and other public health hazards or nuisances
- Provides emergency response services for complaints concerning foodborne illnesses, fires in food establishments, accidents involving the transportation of food, incidents concerning food or water contamination, and power outages or natural disasters involving food products; conducts inspections or investigations on an as-needed basis including on weekends and at night

- Directs the embargo and disposal of food products found unfit for human consumption; conducts evaluations to determine imminent hazards to life or health that warrant the closure of a facility
- Prepares records, reports, and correspondence concerning regulatory actions as needed; conducts follow-up inspections and surveys to ensure corrective actions have been taken and that public health hazards are eliminated; testifies at hearings and court proceedings concerning regulatory actions as required

The public health specialist series within a personnel system may include three or more levels that are distinguished by the level of complexity of specific job assignments, the extent of responsibility assigned for specific tasks, the level of expertise required for completion of the assigned work, and the responsibility assigned for providing leadership to others.

For public health program specialists working in an inspection or regulatory program, for example, the entry level of the series involves assigned duties and responsibilities in a training status to build skills in conducting inspections and investigations, performing basic professional analysis, and interpreting state and federal laws. Entry-level public health specialists perform tasks involving the evaluation of inspection or survey data and the preparation of technical records and reports, and assist in making recommendations concerning remedial actions to correct public health hazards and provide for consumer protection.

Knowledge, skills, and abilities required at the entry level include knowledge of the causes, impact, and prevention of public health problems in regulated establishments; of food microbiology as it applies to preventing foodborne illness; of basic epidemiology and chemistry; of mathematical concepts including basic statistical analysis; of food processing techniques such as modified atmospheric packaging; and of rules and regulations governing food establishments, public bathing places, nursing homes, schools, day care facilities, or other licensed establishments. Abilities required include the ability to conduct inspections and investigations of regulated facilities; to identify the causes of foodborne illnesses and related health hazards; to analyze and evaluate environmental and sanitary conditions; to organize work and work independently; to communicate effectively, both orally and in writing; and to use computers to organize data and generate reports.

Experience and education requirements at this level consist of a bachelor degree with at least 30 semester hours in a biological, medical, or physical science; food science or technology; and in chemistry, nutrition, engineering, epidemiology, or closely related scientific field.

Midlevel public health specialist positions involve more advanced assigned duties for inspections, surveys, and investigations related to public health services, consumer protection, and the enforcement of applicable state and federal laws in the assigned area of responsibility. Midlevel public health specialists evaluate inspection and survey data, prepare technical records and reports, make recommendations concerning required remedial actions, and provide technical assistance and training as needed to correct public health or consumer protection problems. Some responsibility may also be assigned for providing limited guidance and training to entry-level employees in performing various consumer protection program duties. In addition, midlevel public health specialist positions may involve a clear specialization in a consumer protection or public health discipline and recognition as an expert in the specialty along with a high degree of technical and administrative freedom to plan, develop, organize, and conduct all phases of the work necessary for completion within broad program guidelines.

Knowledge, skills, and abilities required at this midlevel include those identified in the entry level plus the ability to make recommendations concerning the implementation of HAACP systems and verify implementation; to conduct preoperational inspections to determine compliance with approved plans; to assist in planning and presenting education and training programs; to plan and conduct field investigations; to ensure that corrective action has been completed to eliminate health hazards; to analyze and interpret engineering plans and specifications; and to assist in developing HACCP plans for the regulated food industry.

Experience and education requirements at this level consist of those identified for entry-level positions plus two years of professional public health or consumer protection or a master's degree in a listed field and successful completion of training in conducting food establishment inspections plus two additional years of qualifying experience.

Salary scales vary greatly from agency to agency although entry-level positions may be in the $25,000–30,000 range with midlevel positions in the $35,000–45,000 range. Higher-level public health specialist positions that oversee several program areas or units can expect salaries equivalent to other midlevel managers in these organizations. Job growth for public health specialists is expected to be about average for all positions in the health field.

## PUBLIC HEALTH EMERGENCY RESPONSE COORDINATORS

Public health emergency response coordinators perform planning functions for a local public health agency ensuring compliance with federal and state planning guidelines and regulations. These positions coordinate response plans with the state health department as well as other federal, state, and local government entities; perform all hazard, bioterrorism, and emergency planning; and coordinate plans with various response agencies, volunteer organizations, businesses, and private industries.

Massive federal bioterrorism preparedness funding for state and local public health agencies stimulated a rapid increase in the number of emergency response positions in the United States, making this title one of the fastest growing within the public health workforce. There was no information on public health emergency response coordinators available in the *Public Health Workforce Enumeration 2000.*

Important and essential duties for a public health emergency response coordinator include:

- Performs administrative, technical, and planning duties to integrate bioterrorism and emergency response plans with response activities for other emergency management programs
- Develops and maintains the local public health agency's emergency operations plan (EOP)
- Reviews and maintains bioterrorism response appendices to meet CDC planning guidance and local standard operating guidelines
- Assists with coordination, integration, and implementation of emergency response plans and procedures from various jurisdictions, governmental entities, private industries, utility companies, and so on
- Reviews specialized studies and reports, formulates comments and summarizes content, and provides emergency planning recommendations

- Coordinates with the local jurisdiction's emergency management agency and the state health department in continual development and review of effective emergency preparedness and response activities
- Identifies unique planning considerations for bioterrorism threats
- Assists the public health community in developing jurisdictional emergency plans by attending meetings and facilitating discussions, reviewing concepts and procedures, and coordinating emergency response efforts of various agency units
- Acts as a resource for the public health community and the local public health agency in documenting their standard operating guidelines and operational checklists
- Coordinates overall emergency planning activities
- Conducts regular review of local, state, federal, and private industry emergency response plans, employing standard emergency management concepts and strategic methodologies
- Works in conjunction with the executive director, environmental health supervisor, risk communicator, epidemiologist, and public information officer to promote awareness of local public health agency emergency response plans and procedures
- Provides requisite planning activity reports, budget submissions, and other required documentation for federal and state emergency response funding sources
- Assists with the development of operational drills and exercise scenarios designed to train, test, and evaluate emergency response concepts or standard operating guidelines
- Adjusts emergency plans, procedures, or protocols to reflect changes and improve efficiency as appropriate
- Demonstrates continuous effort to improve operations, decrease turnaround times, streamline work processes, and work cooperatively and jointly to provide quality seamless customer service

Relevant knowledge, skills, and abilities for public health emergency response coordinators include:

- Skill in organization and planning techniques
- Skill in public relations and public speaking
- Skill in computer and communication equipment operation
- Knowledge of basic budget development and fiscal management
- Knowledge of public health and epidemiology

- Ability to establish and maintain effective working relationships with other government and public health officials, employees, agencies, volunteers, and the public
- Ability to communicate effectively, verbally and in writing
- Ability to learn the principles, practices, and techniques involved in emergency management
- Knowledge of principles and practices of governmental and public health agency structures and resources

Special requirements for public health emergency response coordinator positions may include the ability to travel and to be on call 24 hours a day, seven days a week. Emergency response coordinators may be required to complete training courses as recommended and made available through federal or state public health and emergency management agencies. In some instances, emergency response coordinators may be required to complete the Certified Emergency Manager (CEM) program through the National Coordinating Council on Emergency Management within some specified period of time.

Working conditions for this position include most work being performed in an office, library, computer room, or other environmentally controlled room. Emergency response activities may require work in a full-body protective suit with respirator protection from potential biological, chemical, or nuclear material hazards.

Minimum qualifications call for the equivalent of a master's degree in public health, biological sciences, community health, emergency management, planning, hazard assessment, business or public administration, or other related field; and two years of emergency management, community planning, or other related work experience. Selected applicants are subject to, and must pass, a full background check. In addition, emergency response coordinators generally are required to possess a valid state driver's license. Other organizations may require five years of responsible experience in public administration, research and finance, including three years of emergency management experience and a master's degree in public or business administration, government management, industrial engineering, or a related field. Other combinations of experience and education that meet the minimum requirements may be substituted.

Bureau of Labor Statistics data identify 920 emergency management specialists working for state governmental agencies and 5080 working for local governmentaal agencies in 2004. The mean salary for these positions was $45,500.

## PUBLIC HEALTH POLICY ANALYSTS

Public policy is one of the tools used by public health to promote conditions in which individuals and communities can be healthy. Public health policy analysts analyze needs and plans for the development of public health and other programs, facilities and resources, and/or analyze and evaluate the implications of alternative policies relating to public health and health care for a defined population. Public health analysts determine the questions that such policies will raise, answer those questions, and help shape policies that make our society a better place to live.

Public health policy analysts function under many different titles, including health planners, researchers, and health economists. Health economists conduct research, prepare reports, or formulate plans to aid in the solution of economic problems arising from the production and distribution of goods and services related to public health and health care. Health economists may collect and process economic and statistical data using econometric and sampling techniques.

Public health policy analysts must be able to dissect a problem, analyze and interpret data, and evaluate and create alternative courses of action. They provide information to government officials and the public about which policies will be most effective in meeting society's public health goals.

Public health policy analysts work in national, state, and local governments, nonprofit agencies, "think tanks," consulting firms, community action groups, and direct service providers. International health and development organizations also employ public health policy analysts. The *Public Health Workforce Enumeration 2000* identified nearly 6000 public health policy analysts, planners, researchers, and economists. Because of the wide variation in titles used for this function, it is likely that there are actually many more public health analyst positions in the public health workforce.

Important and essential duties of a public health policy analyst include:

- Conducts site visits to assess the operations and costs of state, federal, and local health care programs

- Conducts literature reviews
- Performs quantitative analyses with large databases to determine program outcomes or conduct policy simulations
- Writes chapters of analytic reports and proposals for new projects
- Tracks financial progress of projects using computerized spreadsheets, prepares reports for monthly project reviews, and assists with budget revisions and contract proposals

Key knowledge, skills, and abilities for public health policy analyst positions include:

- Knowledge of current policy issues in one or more of the following areas: managed care, public health infrastructure, state health policy, health care reimbursement issues, mental health/substance abuse, maternal and child health, disability, long-term care, or other relevant areas
- Knowledge of health care policy issues related to employer-based coverage, managed care, Medicaid, Medicare, and the uninsured
- Knowledge of how to use data to affect policy and systemic changes
- Ability to establish collaborative working relationships with diverse interest groups and stakeholders
- Excellent writing and verbal skills, particularly in presenting complex information in a clear, comprehensible format

Minimum qualifications for public health policy analyst positions vary greatly, but generally require a master's degree in public policy, public health, economics, statistics, or a related field, or equivalent experience in a clinical field, and extensive knowledge of quantitative and qualitative research methods. In some instances, a bachelor degree and a minimum of five years experience, preferably in health care advocacy or policy analysis, may be acceptable. Invariably, work experience with state or federal government, a foundation, a policy research organization, or a health care program is desirable.

Salaries for public health analysts vary considerably based on education, experience, and specific duties within an organization. With little information available on employment trends for these positions, it is difficult to assess future job prospects, although the number of such positions does not appear to be declining.

## PUBLIC HEALTH INFORMATION SPECIALISTS AND ANALYSTS

Health information systems and data analysts plan, direct, or coordinate activities in areas such as electronic data processing, information systems, systems analysis, and computer programming. They often work with computer specialists who manage the specialized technical aspects of computer operation, applications, operating systems, and hardware. Common titles include computing consultant, applications programmer, computer service technician, data entry technician, data processing specialist, network technician, information technology specialist, and vital records support specialist. Not included are titles that operate computers as part of administrative or professional tasks.

Important and essential duties of a health information specialist include:

- Plans and coordinate the collection, analysis, and dissemination of complex disease and other health data and information
- Performs health risk and community needs appraisals
- Monitors and evaluates programs for effectiveness and quality
- Collaborates with other agencies, organizations, and stakeholders in the identification and monitoring of community health needs
- Exercises independent judgment in analyzing problems, issues and situations; develops and implements recommendations
- Plans and conducts meetings
- Presents information and represents the agency at public and other meetings
- Complies with legal standards and requirements
- Collects, researches, verifies, enters, updates, analyzes, summarizes, and presents complex disease and other health information and data
- Records information and data accurately following procedures; prepares complete reports on time with supporting conclusions and recommendations, such as the health status report
- Communicates changes and progress and completes projects on time and within budget
- Formulates recommendations anticipating possible ramifications and appropriately communicates significance of findings

Health information specialist positions require a bachelor degree in public health or a related field and five years of progressively responsible experience in public health evaluation or a related health field. A master's degree in public health is preferred. These positions require knowledge of core public health functions; epidemiological principles and practices including symptoms, causes, means of transmission and methods of control of communicable, chronic, and complex disease; principles of disease investigation, control, and prevention; and emergency response principles and practices. These positions also require familiarity with the operation of computers and a variety of office software including word processing, spreadsheet, database, geographical information systems (GIS), mapping, statistical, and other applications related to the area of assignment.

The *Public Health Workforce Enumeration 2000* identified 900 health information specialists and 6000 computer specialists working for governmental public health agencies. Salaries for health information specialists are often in the $40,000–50,000 range. Health information specialist jobs are projected to be among the fastest growing in the health sector.

## COMMUNITY OUTREACH WORKERS AND OTHER TECHNICAL OCCUPATIONS

Community outreach workers assist public health professionals in community contacts, referrals, or program development. This category includes individuals with on-the-job training in specific program areas but who generally lack postsecondary education or credentials. Community outreach workers provide health advising, information and referrals, carry out client orientation and intakes, and advocate for clients and communities. They work under dozens of different titles, such as community health advisor, health worker, public health aide, community health outreach worker, community health aide, immunization outreach worker, Early Periodic Screening, Diagnosis, and Treatment (EPSDT) outreach workers, maternal and infant advocate, and school health aide.

Other technician titles are also widely used by public health agencies. This includes safety, research, hearing and vision, and health promotion technicians, as well as emergency service personnel. The Public Health Workforce Enumeration 2006 identified 900 outreach workers, and between 10,000 and 15,000 other technicians.

The starting salary for a community outreach worker at some metropolitan health agencies is in the $28,000–34,000 range. Several institutions offer certificate programs for community outreach workers that are accepted as a minimum qualification for the civil service health worker positions. CHWs who work for community-based organizations generally make somewhat less. Minimum qualifications may require an associate's degree with 18 credits in health science/education, or and associate degree and one year experience in a health or human service agency providing referral assistance to the public. In some instances a high school diploma or GED and three years of experience, may be sufficient.

## ADDITIONAL INFORMATION

Many sources provide additional and more detailed information for the occupational categories addressed in Chapter 9. For example, the Federal Emergency Management Agency (FEMA) is a rich source of information for public health emergency response coordinators, and the Community Health Planning and Policy Development section of the American Public Health Association's Web site (APHA, http://www.apha.org) provides useful information for public health policy analysts.

Similarly, the American Health Information Management Association (AHIMA, http://www.ahima.org) is the premier association of health information management professionals with 50,000 members committed to advancing the health information management profession. AHIMA focuses on advocacy, education, certification, and lifelong learning and works through the Commission on Accreditation for Health Informatics and Information Management Education (CAHIM) to accredit degree-granting programs in health informatics and information management. CAHIM establishes quality standards for the educational preparation of future health information management professionals.

Useful information and resources for community outreach workers are available through the American Public Health Association (APHA, http://www.apha.org) and its Community Health Workers Special Interest Group. Another source for information on innovative training and certification programs for community outreach is Community Health Works (http://www.communityhealthworks.org/chwcertificate/).

## CONCLUSION

Public health organizations use many different titles for public health program staff. Indeed, most public health workers function within a defined program or program-related unit such as environmental health, maternal and child health, WIC (Supplemental Food Program for Women, Infants and Children), or immunization program. Program specialists work on all aspects of program planning, implementation, and evaluation in concert with professionals, technicians, and administrative support personnel. Because the programs in which they work often have specific goals and objectives, program specialists are at risk of operating in an isolated environment. This contributes to the critique that programs operate as silos within an agency, often unrelated to the operation of the many other silos housed within that same agency. Because of their generalist skills, program specialists may move from one program to another as a means of career and salary advancement. Their crosscutting, core, generalist public health practice skills are generally acquired through work experiences rather than academic preparation. The size and impact of this corps of public health program specialists argues that development and enhancement of these crosscutting competencies should be a central strategy of public health workforce development efforts.

## REFERENCES

1.  Health Resources and Services Administration (HRSA), Bureau of Health Professions, National Center for Health Workforce Information and Analysis and Center for Health Policy, Columbia School of Nursing. *The Public Health Workforce Enumeration 2000.* Washington, DC: HRSA; 2000. Available at http://www.phppo.cdc.gov/owpp/docs/library/2000/Public%20Health%20 Workforce%20Enumeration%202000.pdf. Accessed August 2005.
2.  Bureau of Labor Statistics, U.S. Department of Labor. May 2004 National, State, and Metropolitan Area Occupational Employment and Wage Estimates. Available at http://www.bls.gov/oes/current/oes_nat.htm. Accessed August 2005.

# CHAPTER 10

# Looking to the Future

For too long too little attention has been directed to the public health workforce and its needs. Despite ample warnings in the 1988 IOM report,[1] there were few efforts between 1980 when HRSA produced crude estimates of the size and composition for the U.S. Congress[2] and 2000 when Kristine Gebbie and colleagues completed their landmark enumeration report on the public health workforce at the turn of the century for HRSA.[3] Two decades of inattention provide eloquent testimony to the low priority given to the public health system's most important asset—its workforce.

Beginning in the year 2002, funding for workforce preparedness and training increased dramatically. This influx of funding also brought increased expectations for positive change and greater accountability for results. As a result, the public health system is now under the microscope with federal, state, and local governments needing to show that the vital signs of the public health infrastructure, including its workforce, are improving. But decades of inattention left little information to serve as a basis for comparison.

A central challenge for public health workforce development efforts over the next decade is to provide more and better information about key dimensions of the public health workforce in terms of its size, distribution, composition, and competency, as well as its impact on public health goals and community health. This book, like the *Public Health Workforce Enumeration 2000*, seeks to advance this important agenda. This final chapter addresses several critical questions important to current and future public health workers:

- Will the public health workforce increase or decrease in size over the next 10 years? What trends in the overall economy, the health sector, or the public sector will impact public health jobs and career opportunities over this period?

- Where will job opportunities be most abundant, and which occupational categories are likely to grow most rapidly and be in greatest demand?
- What core competencies and skills will require the greatest attention, and what training and education opportunities are available to prepare workers for jobs and careers in public health?

The sections that follow examine each of these questions and associated challenges.

## PUBLIC HEALTH WORKFORCE GROWTH

Will the public health workforce increase or decrease in size over the next 10 years? There should be little controversy over this question, but there is. One reason for controversy derives from the lack of accurate information on the size of the public health workforce between 1980 and 2000. Another relates to the many complex forces within public health and the broader economy that influence the number of public health workers needed.

In hindsight, it is clear that the frequently cited figure that the workforce numbered 500,000 in 1980 lacked precision in terms of what was included and how it was generated. This is unfortunate because the 500,000 figure from 1980 is frequently cited as documentation that the public health workforce must be shrinking since only 450,000 public health workers were enumerated in 2000. As noted in Chapter 1, the HRSA 1980 estimate actually indicated that only 250,000 of the 500,000 public health workers were in the primary public health workforce consisting of federal, state, and local public health agency workers and selected others who devoted most of their work efforts on public health activities.[2] Within this 250,000 figure, there were faculty and researchers at academic institutions; occupational health physicians and nurses working for various private companies; health educators teaching in schools; and administrators working in hospitals, nursing homes and other medical care settings. The actual number of public health professionals working for federal, state, and local public health agencies in 1980, after adjusting for these inclusions, was closer to 140,000. The total for the comparable categories from the *Public Health Workforce Enumeration 2000* was 260,000, a figure that indicates the public health workforce is growing rather than shrinking. Data from the employment census of governmental agencies supports this conclusion showing there has been a steady increase in full-time equivalent workers of governmental health agencies over the past decade (See Table 10–1, as well as Table 1–3 and Figure 1–1 in Chapter 1).[4]

These findings indicate that the public health workforce has been increasing since 1980 and throughout the 1990s and into the early years of the current decade. This is consistent with the documented expansion of the health sector within the overall economy, which continues to grow at a more rapid rate than the rest of the economy. If public health activities continue to maintain their small share of total health spending, funding for public health activities and public health workers will grow commensurately. It is conceivable that public health activities could even increase their share of overall health spending, fostering even more rapid growth of employment opportunities.

There is evidence, however, that the growth of the public health workforce may be slowing or even reversing. The number of full-time equivalent

**Table 10–1** Average Annual Change in the Number of Public Health Workers, Selected Sources and Years, 1980–2004

| Time Period | Average Annual Change (+/−) |
| --- | --- |
| 1980*–2000** | + 6000 |
| 1994–1999*** | + 5400 |
| 2000–2003*** | + 8700 |
| 2003–2004*** | − 3000 |

*Sources:*
* Health Resources and Services Administration (HRSA), U.S. Department of Health and Human Services. *Public Health Personnel in the United States, 1980: Second Report to Congress.* Washington, DC: U.S. Public Health Service (PHS); 1982.
** Health Resources and Services Administration (HRSA), Bureau of Health Professions, National Center for Health Workforce Information and Analysis and Center for Health Policy, Columbia School of Nursing. *The Public Health Workforce Enumeration 2000.* Washington, DC: HRSA; 2000. Available at http://www.phppo.cdc.gov/owpp/docs/library/2000/Public%20Health%20Workforce%20Enumeration%202000.pdf. Accessed August 2005.
*** U.S. Bureau of the Census. Federal, State, and Local Governments, Public Employment and Payroll Data. Available at http://www.census.gov/govs/www/apes.html. Accessed August 2005.

workers for federal, state, and local health agencies climbed steadily through 2001 reaching its peak of nearly 556,000 in 2003 before declining by about 3,000 in 2004 (see Table 1–3 in Chapter 1). Interestingly, federal health agency workers actually increased by 3000 while state and local workers fell by more than 6000. Bioterrorism funding for federal health agencies largely explains the increase in the number of federal health workers in 2004. But the number of FTE state and local public health workers fell by 6000 even while federal bioterrorism funding for state and local public health agencies was being used to support more than 6000 positions (about 2000 in state agencies and 4000 in local agencies). It appears that state and local governments moved existing staff onto the federal bioterrorism grants in response to fiscal pressures on state and local government budgets. Rather than a net increase of 6000 new positions, there was a net reduction of 6000 positions indicating that funding sources other than the federal bioterrorism grants were supporting 12,000 fewer positions.

This scenario illustrates how federal funding to states and localities for bioterrorism preparedness serves as a temptation to replace or supplant state and local support for public health with federal money. The funding of epidemiologists further illustrates this phenomenon. In 2004 federal bioterrorism funds paid the salaries of 460 epidemiologists; among 390 epidemiologists working on bioterrorism and emergency response activities, 62% were funded by the federal government. Infectious disease epidemiologists did not increase between 2001 and 2004, but in 2004 nearly 20% were paid through federal bioterrorism funds.[5] This scenario may also be true for several other public health occupational categories, such as laboratory workers and emergency response coordinators. It underscores the important role of the underlying financial health of state and local governments in determining the size of the public health workforce.

Two additional modern forces affect public health workforce size. These are the expansion of information technology and the resulting increase in worker productivity. Public health practice, by its very nature, is information dependent and information driven. Enhanced information technology tools and increased individual worker productivity mean fewer workers are needed to support the work of administrators, professionals, and technical staff. This trend would tend to increase the proportion of professionals within the public health workforce; however, these trends also mean fewer professionals are needed to perform the same volume of work. The net effect is therefore difficult to predict in terms of the number and types of workers needed.

The influence of these trends will be affected by events and forces within the overall economy, the health system, and the public sector in general. Public health workers and public health agencies are key components of the public health system, but it is important to consider the larger context in which they operate. This larger environment is in constant flux, undergoing changes that impact the public health system and its components. For example, information and communication technologies advance continuously. These developments enable public health agencies and workers to carry out their duties in a more efficient and effective manner. The work of public health is especially information dependent. The speed at which information is accessed and communicated significantly affects how well public health achieves its mission and objectives. Advances in information and communications technology improve public health practice and public health outcomes. There is every reason to believe that these advances will continue at least at levels achieved in recent decades. The net effect is to make public health workers more effective and productive. The challenge is to assure that public health workers have access to the education and training resources that assure this happens.

Trends within the health sector will also continue to affect public health workers. Health is highly valued both as a personal and societal goal. The economic value placed on health exceeds $1.5 trillion annually, or more than $5000 per person for every man, woman, and child in the United States. There is no indication that health will assume a lower priority within the American social value system. In recent years, for example, expenditures for health purposes have grown faster than the rate for the overall economy. In effect, health is becoming an even greater priority. Among the two general strategies to achieve health—preventive and therapeutic approaches—the balance may be slowly shifting toward more prevention. There is still a notable imbalance with a 25 to 1 ratio. But this shift is likely to continue. Taken together with an increased priority on health itself, public health activities including those carried out by public health agencies and workers should continue to increase in size, importance, and value to society.

The value placed on public health activities can be measured in economic terms, such as funding levels for programs, services, and the workers who implement public health programs and services. To sustain or even enhance public health funding, national leadership is necessary. Federal health agencies such as CDC and HRSA within DHHS are especially important in the area of public health workforce development. In addition to national leadership, state and local governments must remain committed to and invested in public health objectives. But states and local governments face difficult economic circumstances and tough choices across the United States and are looking to cut back services that are either low priority or which have other funding sources. If state and local governments supplant their own funding with the new federal funds, the overall effort will be less than it should be.

Beyond funding, administrative and bureaucratic obstacles challenge public health workforce development efforts in the public sector. State and local agencies are often the source of some of the most significant recruitment and retention problems facing the public health workforce. These include slow hiring by governmental agencies, civil service systems, hiring freezes, budget crises affecting state and local government, and the lack of career ladders, competitive salary structures, and other forms of recognition that value workers for their skill and performance.

Despite the uncertainties inherent in these influences, past trends and current forces suggest that professional and administrative jobs and careers in public health are likely to grow over the next decade. Unfortunately, it will be difficult to measure the progress that has been made without deployment of a standard taxonomy for public health occupations and more comprehensive enumeration strategies and tools that provide better information on the key dimensions of the public health workforce, including its size and distribution in official agencies and private and voluntary organizations.

## PUBLIC HEALTH WORKFORCE DISTRIBUTION AND COMPOSITION

In addition to the size of the public health workforce, its distribution and composition are important to current and future public health workers. Key questions include: where will public health job opportunities be most abundant? Which occupational categories are likely to grow most rapidly and be in greatest demand?

Job opportunities generally track with population density and demographic shifts. Within the health sector, job opportunities cluster around metropolitan areas. Public health positions also follow this pattern. There are more positions and therefore more opportunities in metropolitan areas than there are in rural areas. General demographic trends indicate a continuing shift of population from the Northeast and Midwest regions of the United States to the South, Southwest, and West Coast. It is likely that health sector jobs and public health positions will also follow this pattern.

The ratio of positions to population, however, can be higher in rural areas (and states that have higher proportions of their population living in nonmetropolitan areas). This occurs because there is a basic core staffing that must be present regardless of the size of the population and because rural and remote communities often lack other public health resources and assets. For example, local public health agencies in small as well as large communities will have an agency administrator, director of nursing, and environmental director. Public health agencies serving larger communities may have more total workers, but the ratio of workers to population is often lower due to the effect of core (or overhead) staffing. In addition, nongovernmental resources are often lacking in rural communities. Governmental agencies may constitute a larger proportion of a rural community's overall resources than for urban or suburban communities. A higher public health worker to population ratio in rural areas raises issues of efficiency in terms of scarce resources, including public health professionals, and can be used as an argument for consolidation of several small local public health agencies into one large agency.

Table 10–2 provides a snapshot describing the distribution and composition of the public health workforce from a different perspective by aggregating the public health practice profiles from Chapters 3 through 9. This composite profile illustrates the breadth of roles in addressing public health's broad purposes and essential services as well as the contribution of the various public health occupational categories and titles.

This composite highlights the importance of preventing the spread of disease and assuring the quality of health services as public health purposes. The majority of public health occupations place significant emphasis on these purposes. Only a few public health occupations and titles focus on emergency response as a primary duty. Virtually all, however, have roles in responding to public health emergencies as a secondary-level responsibility.

Among the 10 essential public health services, nearly all public health occupations and titles are actively involved in evaluating the effectiveness, accessibility, and quality of personal and population-based health services.

**Table 10–2** Composite Public Health Practice Profile for Public Health Occupations and Titles Addressed in Chapters 3–9

| | PH Adm | Env Hlth | PH Nurs | Epi | PH Ed | Nutr | Soc Beh MH | PH Lab | MD DVM Phar | Dent Wkrs | Adm Law Jdg | PH Prog Spec | ERC | PH Pol An | Hlth Info | Out Wkrs |
|---|---|---|---|---|---|---|---|---|---|---|---|---|---|---|---|---|
| **Public Health Purposes** | | | | | | | | | | | | | | | | |
| Preventing epidemics and the spread of disease | ✓ | ✓ | ✓ | ✓ | ✓ | | ✓ | ✓ | ✓ | ✓ | ✓ | | ✓ | ✓ | ✓ | |
| Protecting against environmental hazards | | ✓ | | ✓ | | | | ✓ | | | ✓ | ✓ | ✓ | ✓ | | |
| Preventing injuries | | ✓ | | ✓ | ✓ | | | | | | ✓ | ✓ | | | ✓ | |
| Promoting and encouraging healthy behaviors | | | ✓ | | ✓ | ✓ | ✓ | | ✓ | ✓ | | ✓ | | | ✓ | |
| Responding to disasters and assisting communities in recovery | ✓ | | | | | | | ✓ | | | | | ✓ | | | |
| Assuring the quality and accessibility of health services | ✓ | | ✓ | | | ✓ | ✓ | ✓ | ✓ | ✓ | ✓ | | ✓ | ✓ | | |
| **Essential Public Health Services** | | | | | | | | | | | | | | | | |
| Monitoring health status to identify community health problems | | ✓ | | ✓ | | ✓ | | ✓✓ | ✓ | | ✓ | | | ✓ | | |
| Diagnosing and investigating health problems and health hazards in the community | | ✓ | ✓ | ✓ | | | ✓ | ✓ | | | ✓ | ✓ | | | | |
| Informing, educating, and empowering people about health issues | | ✓ | ✓ | | ✓ | ✓ | ✓ | | ✓ | | | | ✓ | ✓ | ✓ | |
| Mobilizing community partnerships to identify and solve health problems | ✓ | | | | ✓ | | ✓ | | | | | ✓ | ✓ | | ✓ | |

Developing policies and plans that support individual and community health efforts ✓ ✓ ✓ ✓ ✓ ✓ ✓

Enforcing laws and regulations that protect health and ensure safety ✓ ✓ ✓ ✓ ✓

Linking people with needed personal health services and assuring the provision of health care when otherwise unavailable ✓ ✓ ✓ ✓ ✓ ✓ ✓

Assuring a competent public health and personal health care workforce ✓ ✓ ✓

Evaluating effectiveness, accessibility, and quality of personal and population-based health services ✓ ✓ ✓ ✓ ✓ ✓ ✓ ✓ ✓ ✓ ✓ ✓ ✓

Researching new insights and innovative solutions to health problems ✓ ✓ ✓ ✓ ✓ ✓ ✓ ✓

---

*Notes:* PH Admin—Public Health Administrator; Env Hlth—Environmental Health Practitioner; PH Nurs—Public Health Nurse; PH Ed—Public Health Educator; Nutr—Nutritionist; Soc Beh MH—Public Health Social, Behavioral, and Mental Health Workers; PH Lab—Public Health Laboratory Worker; MD DVM Phar—Public Health Physicians, Veterinarians, and Pharmacists; Dent Wkrs—Dental Health Workers; Adm Law Jdg—Administrative Law Judge; PH Prog Spec—Public Health Program Specialist; ERC—Emergency Response Coordinator; PH Pol An—Public Health Policy Analyst; Hlth Info—Health Information Specialist; and Out Wkrs—Outreach Workers.

Eight other essential public health services are widely distributed across the various occupational categories and titles. Only a few public health occupations focus extensively on assuring a competent workforce.

As noted in Chapter 2, some health sector occupations will grow more rapidly than others, even while the health sector grows more rapidly than the rest of the economy.[6] Among the many public health occupations, several appear to be growing rapidly and several others appear to be in danger of their supply not keeping pace with anticipated demand.

It is not surprising that public health nurses and environmental health practitioners are repeatedly identified as the positions in greatest demand. Indeed, these occupational categories are the largest in the public health workforce, and it is only natural that these categories undergo greater turnover than others. For registered nurses, there is substantial evidence of a current national shortage. For environmental health practitioners, this is not so clear.

The aftermath of terrorist events of 2001, including the series of anthrax spore attacks through the postal system, spotlighted the need for two professional positions: the first, emergency response coordinators, is new to the list of public health occupations; the second—epidemiologists—is one of the oldest public health professional occupations. State and local public health agencies are rapidly hiring emergency response coordinators. These people come to these new positions with a wide range of academic and experiential qualifications. Epidemiologists, on the other hand, have more restrictive qualifications in terms of academic preparation such as master's and doctoral degrees. Concerns over the past few decades that epidemiologists were in short supply and great demand are now heightened as agencies seek to quickly hire these specialists. The number of epidemiologists coming out of graduate programs does not appear to be keeping pace with the need despite an increase in interest as measured by the number of applications for epidemiology training programs.

Prior to 2001, health educators and community health planners were steadily growing professional categories in the public health workforce. Expansion of health education and promotion services, and an increase in community health planning and community health improvement activities, account for this trend. It is not clear whether this trend will continue in view of the current emphasis on bioterrorism and public health emergency preparedness.

# PUBLIC HEALTH WORKFORCE SKILLS AND COMPETENCIES

Beyond workforce size, distribution, and composition, are issues related to the core competencies and skills that will be most important in public health practice and how these skills are best acquired. Establishing and promoting competencies for public health workers is tricky business. For one thing, public health workers come from a variety of professional backgrounds, many of which have their own core competencies. For example, public health nursing has a set of core competencies (see Chapter 5), and health educators use a sophisticated competency framework for purposes of certification (see Chapter 7). The same can be said for public health physicians, administrators, epidemiologists, and several other public health professional occupations. Identifying a common core for these various professional categories generally leads to a framework with very general and nonspecific competencies that are difficult to relate to a specific situation or problem. The Council on Linkages between Academia and Public Health Practice spent more than a decade grappling with this problem before arriving at a set of core competencies for public health professionals in 2001 (See Appendix A).

The national public health organizations endorsed and adopted these core competencies, which track to the essential public health services framework (see Table 10–3 for an example), as the basis for assessing and enhancing the skills of public health workers. Core public health practice competencies serve as a useful benchmark for competency frameworks developed to serve state or local public health systems or to guide the development of more focused skills, such as in public health law, informatics, genomics, and emergency preparedness. Emergency response competencies for all public health workers are available in Appendix B.

There are several important and practical uses for competency frameworks. Core competencies can serve as models whenever an agency's job descriptions are developed, updated, or revised. As competency-oriented job descriptions become more widely used, core competencies can guide orientation and training activities for new employees. Core competencies are also useful in employee self-assessment activities as well as in personnel evaluation activities when supervisors review the past performance of employees and set performance expectations for the next cycle. The use of competencies within personnel and human resources systems is growing

---

**Table 10–3** Core Public Health Competencies Related to Essential Public Health Service #2: "Diagnose and Investigate Health Problems and Health Hazards in the Community"

---

Analytic/Assessment Skills

- Defines a problem
- Determines appropriate uses and limitations of both quantitative and qualitative data
- Selects and defines variables relevant to defined public health problems
- Identifies relevant and appropriate data and information sources
- Evaluates the integrity and comparability of data and identifies gaps in data sources
- Applies ethical principles to the collection, maintenance, use, and dissemination of data and information
- Partners with communities to attach meaning to collected quantitative and qualitative data
- Makes relevant inferences from quantitative and qualitative data
- Obtains and interprets information regarding risks and benefits to the community
- Recognizes how the data illuminate ethical, political, scientific, economic, and overall public health issues

Policy Development/Program Planning Skills

- Collects, summarizes, and interprets information relevant to an issue
- States policy options and writes clear and concise policy statements
- Articulates the health, fiscal, administrative, legal, social, and political implications of each policy option
- States the feasibility and expected outcomes of each policy option
- Decides on the appropriate course of action
- Develops mechanisms to monitor and evaluate programs for their effectiveness and quality

Communication Skills

- Communicates effectively both in writing and orally, or in other ways; solicits input from individuals and organizations
- Leads and participates in groups to address specific issues
- Uses the media, advanced technologies, and community networks to communicate information
- Effectively presents accurate demographic, statistical, programmatic, and scientific information for professional and lay audiences
- Listens to others in an unbiased manner, respects points of view of others, and promotes the expression of diverse opinions and perspectives (attitude)

Cultural Competency Skills

- Utilizes appropriate methods for interacting sensitively, effectively, and professionally with persons from diverse cultural, socioeconomic, educational, racial, ethnic, and professional backgrounds, and persons of all ages and lifestyle preferences
- Understands the dynamic forces contributing to cultural diversity (attitude)

Community Dimensions of Practice Skills
- Accomplishes effective community engagements
- Identifies community assets and available resources
- Develops, implements, and evaluates a community public health assessment

Basic Public Health Sciences Skills
- Defines, assesses, and understands the health status of populations, determinants of health and illness, factors contributing to health promotion and disease prevention, and factors influencing the use of health services
- Identifies and applies basic research methods used in public health
- Applies the basic public health sciences including behavioral and social sciences, biostatistics, epidemiology, environmental public health, and prevention of chronic and infectious diseases and injuries

Financial Planning and Management Skills
- Develops and presents a budget
- Manages programs within budget constraints
- Applies budget processes
- Develops strategies for determining budget priorities
- Monitors program performance
- Prepares proposals for funding from external sources
- Applies basic human relations skills to the management of organizations, motivation of personnel, and resolution of conflicts
- Manages information systems for collection, retrieval, and use of data for decision making

Leadership and Systems Thinking Skills
- Creates a culture of ethical standards within organizations and communities
- Identifies internal and external issues that may impact delivery of essential public health services (i.e., strategic planning)

---

*Source:* Council on Linkage between Academia and Practice. Competency list by essential public health service. Available at http://www.train.org/Competencies/essential.aspx#2. Accessed August 2005.

slowly within the public sector, although widespread implementation could take decades.

The identification of core competencies for public health practice and for emergency preparedness and response demonstrate the support for competency-based training among practice organizations. A companion effort to identify a panel of core competencies for graduates of master's of public health (MPH) programs in schools of public health is under development under the auspices of the Association of Schools of Public Health (ASPH). This panel of competencies addresses discipline-specific competencies for behavioral sciences, health administration, epidemiology, biostatistics, environmental health, and public health biology as well as crosscutting competencies in the areas of communication, informatics, cultural proficiency, ecological determinants of health, leadership, policy development, professionalism, program development and evaluation, and systems thinking (see Appendix C).

Despite this progress, formidable challenges lie ahead.[7,8] These include the establishment of mechanisms to support workforce planning and training in all states and local jurisdictions, and refinement and validation of public health practice competencies associated with each of the various disciplines that compose the workforce. Enhanced competencies are necessary to improve basic, advanced, and continuing education curricula for public health workers. Also needed are strategies to certify competencies among practitioners. In addition, large scale assessments of current levels of workforce preparedness as measured by core competencies are lacking. For education and training of the public health workforce to be taken seriously, both academic and practice interests must view public health workforce development as an important priority.

Education and training opportunities for public health workers are widely available in 2005 and likely to expand even further over the next decade. The first school of public health was established in 1916 at the Johns Hopkins School of Hygiene and Public Health with the support of the Rockefeller Foundation. In 1969, there were only 12 schools of public health, but that number grew to 37 by mid-2005, with a half dozen new schools in the pipeline. The number of accredited programs offering the MPH and equivalent degrees is also increasing (see Appendix D for a catalog of accredited schools and programs). Many unaccredited programs also exist.

Before 1970, students in public health training were primarily physicians or other disciplines with professional degrees. In recent decades, however, more than two thirds of the students enter public health training in order to obtain their primary postgraduate degrees. Public health training evolved from a second degree for medical professionals to a primary health discipline. Schools of public health that initially emphasized the study of hygiene and sanitation have expanded their curricula to address five core disciplines: biostatistics, epidemiology, health services administration, health education/behavioral science, and environmental science.

The number of individuals earning graduate degrees in public health doubled between 1975 and 2005, from 3000 to more than 6000.[9]

Surprisingly, this increase has not had a significant impact on the number and proportion of professionals trained in public health in the primary public health workforce. In the 1970s about one half of MPH graduates took jobs with governmental public health agencies, the primary public health workforce. Currently, only about one in five MPH graduates take jobs with governmental public health agencies.

Despite this impressive growth of public health schools and programs, most public health workers continue to receive their professional preparation elsewhere. This is not surprising in view of the number of training programs for key occupational categories in the public health workforce. There are more than 1500 basic RN training programs at the bachelor, associate, or diploma level; well in excess of 1000 LPN training programs; more than 150 programs in health administration; and several hundred programs offering training in environmental health sciences.

In sum, educational resources contribute to a national network of nearly 40 accredited schools of public health, another 90 graduate training programs in public health, and as many as 500 other graduate-level education programs in areas related to public health, such as health administration, public health nursing, and environmental engineering. Sources for additional information on discipline-specific education and training are provided in Chapters 3 through 9.

Training activities that focus on public health workers rather than students are also extensive. HRSA has long been the primary federal health agency supporting development of the various health professions, although the public health workforce has never been a priority for that agency. Because many public health workers come from other health disciplines, however, HRSA support for training other health professionals also benefits the public health workforce. Throughout the 1990s, HRSA training activities for public health focused increasingly on strengthening links between schools of public health (SPH) and public health agencies. Early in the 1990s, HRSA initiated support for the Council on Linkages between Academia and Practice, which has grown to include representation from many prominent public health academic and practice organizations. Since 1999, HRSA has funded Public Health Training Centers, which are multistate training collaborations involving SPHs and health agencies, with 14 such centers (with approximately $5 million in annual funding) operating in late 2003. Beginning in 2002, HRSA also funded states and several large cities to support hospital bioterrorism planning and provided funds for curriculum development and training for health care professionals and for community-wide planning related to bioterrorism and other public health emergencies.

During the 1990s, the Centers for Disease Control and Prevention (CDC) became increasingly engaged in supporting capacity development and improving state-based public health systems through the establishment of national and regional leadership development projects in the early 1990s. CDC also provided direct financial assistance to state public health systems for emergency preparedness later in that decade. CDC encouraged states and large cities to utilize this funding to improve the capacity of their public health infrastructures in order to respond to a wide range of both emergency and routine threats, including bioterrorism preparedness. CDC increasingly emphasized and supported public health workforce development as the cornerstone of infrastructure improvement. Between October 2000 and October 2002, through its cooperative agreement with the Association of Schools of Public Health, CDC awarded substantial grants (approximately $1 million per center per year) to more than two dozen academic Centers for Public Health Preparedness.

Since 1998 funding for public health workforce development through SPHs has increased dramatically, from under $1 million (primarily from HRSA) in 1997 to more than $30 million (mainly from CDC) in 2005. Approximately another $70–80 million for public health training is available in the bioterrorism grants awarded to states and several large cities, an estimated 10% of those grants. A total of more than $100 million is being programmed specifically for public health workforce development in 2005 in addition to resources that prepare other health professionals to participate in responses to public health emergencies.[7]

The extent of organized workforce development activities within state and local health departments and other public health organizations is unkown. Nonetheless, virtually all public health organizations provide some form of orientation, training, and support of continuing education for their workers. Costs for these activities are often buried in agency budgets as human resources, administrative support, and employee travel expenditures encompassing both direct and indirect, or opportunity costs for time spent away from performing official duties. Aggregating these costs would likely represent a significant pool of resources.

Efforts to forge links between academic and training partners and public health practice agencies at all levels of government are advancing, although unevenly from state to state. Comprehensive approaches that serve the entire public health workforce with an extensive menu of options for workers at varying stages of career development are lacking. More limited approaches that increase the number of workers who can acquire formal public health training through degree programs or that provide advanced skills to specific categories of workers within the public health workforce are useful but not sufficient. These efforts serve a relatively small portion of the overall public health workforce. More comprehensive and systems based approaches are needed.

## PUBLIC HEALTH WORKFORCE DEVELOPMENT

Education and training are key components of public health workforce strategies but, by themselves, they are not sufficient. Comprehensive public health workforce development efforts assess and promote competencies in addition to enhancing them. Efforts to promote the acquisition of public health competencies focus on several fronts, but necessarily emphasize the workplace and the organizations that employ workers. Critical skills and core competencies are promoted in the workplace through job descriptions and performance appraisals that are organized around those skills and competencies. Managers and supervisors work with their employees to manage the professional development of workers and build skills that are necessary for career advancement. These administrative and personnel policies and practice create a culture that values competent performance and the acquisition of new skills.

A complementary approach to promote competencies relies on external bodies to validate and recognize skill levels through credentialing programs. Previous chapters identify many different forms of credentials for various categories of public health workers. For example, nutritionists may earn the RD (registered dietician) credential, health educators may become CHES (Certified Health Education Specialists), physicians may achieve board certification in preventive medicine and public health, and many different credentials are available to environmental health practitioners. With discipline specific credentials available to so many different public health worker occupational categories, it should come as no surprise that there are now efforts to develop credentials specific to public health.

The intent of any credential is to distinguish someone who is eligible for some status from others who are not. Identifying individuals who have demonstrated practice-relevant competencies at a specified level (from frontline workers to senior professionals, specialists, and leaders) provides an incentive for individuals to enhance their skills. Health professions have taken various approaches to credentialing that include licensing (for physicians and nurses), certification (for health-education specialists), and registration (for dieticians and sanitarians). These examples suggest that credentialing is already widely used for public health workers; examples include board-certified preventive-medicine physicians, certified community-health nurses and health-education specialists, and certified, registered environmental health practitioners. There is still a need for credentials for those who would not fit into these specialty-specific credentials, such as public-health physicians not certified in preventive medicine, or health educators who are not certified health-education specialists. Because many, indeed most, workers will not be able to meet the specific requirements for specialty credentialing, such as the 3-year residency for physicians or completion of a health education degree at the undergraduate or graduate level for certified health educators, a midlevel public health-specific credential could be attractive to many public health disciplines. Fledgling competency-based credentialing programs for public health managers and for public health emergency response coordinators exist in one state using an independent certification board.[10] The Association of Schools of Public Health is planning for a credential for graduates of MPH degree programs based on a national test. These and other models focus more on public health practice competencies rather than on a worker's core discipline, making them fertile ground for turf battles with professional organizations. Considerable input from these professional organizations and from professionals in practice will be needed, however, for any framework to be valued and widely used. A three-prong credentialing strategy emerged from the National Public Health Workforce Development Conference in early 2003 calling for recognition of public health competency at a basic or Public Health 101 level and at a leadership level as well as expansion of existing credentialing activities for public health disciplines to cover those not now included.[11]

For workers to value credentials and the competencies upon which they are based, employers and health agencies must find value in them as well, and base decisions about hiring, promotion, salaries, and the like on an individual worker's demonstration of those competencies. Improving workers' ability to perform their functions competently relies on both worker training and work management strategies.[7] As performance standards for public health organizations and public health systems gain headway through initiatives such as the National Public Health Performance Standards Program and NACCHO's Mobilizing for Action through Planning and Partnerships (MAPP) process, competency-based performance standards for workers will increasingly be viewed as key ingredients of organizational and system performance.

An innovative NACCHO program, Public Health Ready, holds great promise for promoting public health workforce preparedness. Public Health Ready recognizes public health agencies that meet standards for worker competency, agency preparedness plans, and regular exercises of those plans.[12] Workers can demonstrate preparedness competencies during those drills and simulations, furthering the ability of the agency to verify and document the preparedness levels of the organization and its staff. As this approach is deployed beyond several dozen pilot sites certified in 2004 and 2005, it could serve to focus public health workforce development efforts through its emphasis on the work, workers, and work organizations that constitute the governmental public health enterprise.

Although several forms of incentives are slowly advancing, one key element of a system of incentives remains lacking: There is no common currency in the form of a public health continuing-education unit (CEU) that assures quality and consistency of training activities nationally. Neither CDC, nor any of the national public health organizations, has sought to serve in this capacity. A common currency that has credibility in the practice sector and is linked with organized workforce development strategies and funding from recent bioterrorism preparedness legislation would provide a considerable incentive for competency-based approaches to public health workforce development. Nonetheless, the obstacles and inertia that have accrued over several decades remain formidable challenges for the public health system.

## CONCLUSION

Concerns over the future of the public health workforce are mounting. Sources point to the aging of the public health workforce, current shortages of public health nurses and epidemiologists, and the imminent retirement of many public health professionals. Legislative proposals in

Congress would authorize more than $200 million for scholarships and loan repayment programs to push more public health professionals through the pipeline and into positions in state and local agencies.[13–15]

Responses to these concerns, however, reflect a view that public health workforce development strategies must produce more public health workers. Strategies that focus on the pipeline are useful, but they will never be sufficient to assure an effective public health workforce over the long term. Strategies that focus on the workforce itself are also needed.[7]

The public health workforce is growing and will continue to grow for years to come. Many public health occupational categories will see a steady increase; others will grow even more rapidly. As a population-based enterprise, public health jobs should mirror demographic changes in terms of both location of job opportunities and the diversity and cultural proficiency of workers. Core public health practice competencies will increasingly influence education and training programs and find their way into the human resource activities and personnel systems of governmental public health agencies. Worker recognition initiatives based on relevant competencies, such as credentialing and certification programs, will also grow in order to address the need for both heightened accountability and expanded career pathways. The recent influx of resources to support public health workforce development will continue only if measurable progress and impact can be demonstrated. Without those resources, however, the progress of public health workforce development efforts could stall. In the end, the most important asset of the public health system remains its workforce.

## REFERENCES

1. Institute of Medicine, National Academy of Sciences. *The Future of Public Health*. Washington, DC: National Academy Press; 1988.
2. Health Resources and Services Administration (HRSA), U.S. Department of Health and Human Services. *Public Health Personnel in the United States, 1980: Second Report to Congress*. Washington, DC: U.S. Public Health Service (PHS); 1982.
3. Health Resources and Services Administration (HRSA), Bureau of Health Professions, National Center for Health Workforce Information and Analysis and Center for Health Policy, Columbia School of Nursing. *The Public Health Workforce Enumeration 2000*. Washington, DC: HRSA; 2000. Available at

http://www.phppo.cdc.gov/owpp/docs/library/2000/Public%20Health%20
Workforce%20Enumeration%202000.pdf. Accessed August 2005.

4. U.S. Bureau of the Census. Federal, State, and Local Governments, Public
   Employment and Payroll Data. Available at http://www.census.gov/govs/
   www/apes.html. Accessed August 2005.

5. Council of State and Territorial Epidemiologists (CSTE). *2004 National
   Assessment of Epidemiologic Capacity: Findings and Recommendations.* Washington, DC: CSTE; 2004. Available at http://www.cste.org/Assessment/ECA/
   pdffiles/ECAfinal05.pdf. Accessed August 2005.

6. Bureau of Labor Statistics, U.S. Department of Labor. *Occupational Outlook
   Handbook, 2004–2005 Edition.* Available at http://www.bls.gov/oco/. Accessed
   August 2005.

7. Turnock BJ. Public health workforce preparedness roadmap. *J Public Health
   Manage Pract.* 2003;9:471–480.

8. Tilson H, Gebbie KM. The public health workforce. *Ann Rev Pub Health.*
   2004;25:341–356. Available at http://arjournals.annualreviews.org/doi/full/
   10.1146/annurev.publhealth.25.102802.124357. Accessed August 2005.

9. U.S. Department of Health and Human Services (DHHS). *Health United States
   2004.* Washington, DC: National Center for Health Statistics; 2004.

10. Turnock BJ. Competency-based credentialing of public health administrators in
    Illinois. *J Public Health Manage Pract.* 2001;7:74–82.

11. Cioffi JP, Lichtveld MY, Thielen L, Miner K. Credentialing the public health
    workforce: an idea whose time has come. *J Public Health Manage Pract.* 2003;
    6:451–458.

12. National Association of County and City Health Officials. Project Public
    Health Ready. Available at http://www.naccho.org/topics/emergency/pphr.cfm.
    Accessed August 2005.

13. Association of State and Territorial Health Officials, Council of State
    Governments, and National Association of State Personnel Executives. State
    Public Health Employee Worker Shortage Report: A Civil Service Recruitment
    and Retention Crisis. Available at http://www.astho.org/pubs/Workforce-
    Survey-Report-2.pdf. Accessed August 2005.

14. Health Resources and Services Administration, National Center for Health
    Workforce Analysis. Public Health Workforce Study. Available at http://www.
    bhpr.hrsa.gov/healthworkforce/reports/publichealth/. Accessed August 2005.

15. Health Resources and Services Administration, Bureau of Health Professions.
    The Key Ingredient of the National Prevention Agenda: Workforce Develop-
    ment. Available at ftp://ftp.hrsa.gov/bhpr/nationalcenter/hp2010.pdf. Accessed
    August 2005.

# Appendices

- Appendix A—Council on Linkages Between Academia and Practice Core Competencies with Skill Levels
- Appendix B—Core Public Health Worker Competencies for Emergency Preparedness and Response
- Appendix C—Association of Schools of Public Health (ASPH) MPH Core Competency Development Project Version 1.2
- Appendix D—Accredited Schools of Public Health and Public Health Programs
- Appendix E—Public Health Training, Continuing Education, and Employment Resources for Public Health Workers

# Council on Linkages Between Academia and Practice Core Competencies with Skill Levels

## Domain #1: Analytic Assessment Skills

| Specific Competencies | Frontline Staff | Senior-Level Staff | Supervisory and Management Staff |
|---|---|---|---|
| Defines a problem | Knowledgeable to proficient | Proficient | Proficient |
| Determines appropriate uses and limitations of both quantitative and qualitative data | Aware to knowledgeable | Proficient | Proficient |
| Selects and defines variables relevant to defined public health problems | Aware to knowledgeable | Proficient | Proficient |
| Identifies relevant and appropriate data and information sources | Knowledgeable | Proficient | Proficient |
| Evaluates the integrity and comparability of data and identifies gaps in data sources | Aware | Proficient | Proficient |
| Applies ethical principles to the collection, maintenance, use, and dissemination of data and information | Knowledgeable to Proficient | Proficient | Proficient |
| Partners with communities to attach meaning to collected quantitative and qualitative data | Aware to knowledgeable | Proficient | Proficient |
| Makes relevant inferences from quantitative and qualitative data | Aware to knowledgeable | Proficient | Proficient |
| Obtains and interprets information regarding risks and benefits to the community | Aware to knowledgeable | Proficient | Proficient |
| Applies data collection processes, information technology applications, and computer systems storage/retrieval strategies | Aware to knowledgeable | Knowledgeable to proficient | Knowledgeable to proficient |
| Recognizes how the data illuminates ethical, political, scientific, economic, and overall public health issues | Aware | Knowledgeable to proficient | Proficient |

## Domain #2: Policy Development/Program Planning Skills

| Specific Competencies | Frontline Staff | Senior-Level Staff | Supervisory and Management Staff |
|---|---|---|---|
| Collects, summarizes, and interprets information relevant to an issue | Knowledgeable | Proficient | Proficient |
| States policy options and writes clear and concise policy statements | Aware | Knowledgeable to proficient | Proficient |
| Identifies, interprets, and implements public health laws, regulations, and policies related to specific programs | Aware | Knowledgeable to proficient | Proficient |
| Articulates the health, fiscal, administrative, legal, social, and political implications of each policy option | Aware | Knowledgeable | Proficient |
| States the feasibility and expected outcomes of each policy option | Aware | Knowledgeable | Proficient |
| Utilizes current techniques in decision analysis and health planning | Aware | Knowledgeable to proficient | Proficient |
| Decides on the appropriate course of action | Aware | Knowledgeable to proficient | Proficient |
| Develops a plan to implement policy, including goals, outcome and process objectives, and implementation steps | Aware | Knowledgeable to proficient | Proficient |
| Translates policy into organizational plans, structures, and programs | Aware | Knowledgeable to proficient | Proficient |
| Prepares and implements emergency response plans | Aware to knowledgeable | Knowledgeable to proficient | Proficient |
| Develops mechanisms to monitor and evaluate programs for their effectiveness and quality | Aware to knowledgeable | Proficient | Proficient |

## Domain #3: Communication Skills

| Specific Competencies | Frontline Staff | Senior-Level Staff | Supervisory and Management Staff |
|---|---|---|---|
| Communicates effectively both in writing and orally, or in other ways | Proficient | Proficient | Proficient |
| Solicits input from individuals and organizations | Knowledgeable to proficient | Proficient | Proficient |
| Advocates for public health programs and resources | Knowledgeable | Proficient | Proficient |
| Leads and participates in groups to address specific issues | Knowledgeable | Proficient | Proficient |
| Uses the media, advanced technologies, and community networks to communicate information | Aware to knowledgeable | Proficient | Proficient |
| Effectively presents accurate demographic, statistical, programmatic, and scientific information for professional and lay audiences | Knowledgeable | Proficient | Proficient |
| **Attitudes** | | | |
| Listens to others in an unbiased manner, respects points of view of others, and promotes the expression of diverse opinions and perspectives | Proficient | Proficient | Proficient |

## Domain #4: Cultural Competency Skills

| Specific Competencies | Frontline Staff | Senior-Level Staff | Supervisory and Management Staff |
|---|---|---|---|
| Utilizes appropriate methods for interacting sensitively, effectively, and professionally with persons from diverse cultural, socioeconomic, educational, racial, ethnic, and professional backgrounds, and persons of all ages and lifestyle preferences | Proficient | Proficient | Proficient |
| Identifies the role of cultural, social, and behavioral factors in determining the delivery of public health services | Knowledgeable | Proficient | Proficient |
| Develops and adapts approaches to problems that take into account cultural differences | Proficient | Proficient | Proficient |
| **Attitudes** | | | |
| Understands the dynamic forces contributing to cultural diversity | Knowledgeable | Knowledgeable to proficient | Proficient |
| Understands the importance of a diverse public health workforce | Knowledgeable | Proficient | Proficient |

## Domain #5: Community Dimensions of Practice Skills

| Specific Competencies | Frontline Staff | Senior-Level Staff | Supervisory and Management Staff |
|---|---|---|---|
| Establishes and maintains linkages with key stakeholders | Knowledgeable | Proficient | Proficient |
| Utilizes leadership, team building, negotiation, and conflict resolution skills to build community partnerships | Aware to proficient | Proficient | Proficient |
| Collaborates with community partners to promote the health of the population | Knowledgeable to proficient | Proficient | Proficient |
| Identifies how public and private organizations operate within a community | Knowledgeable | Proficient | Proficient |
| Accomplishes effective community engagements | Aware to knowledgeable | Proficient | Proficient |
| Identifies community assets and available resources | Knowledgeable to proficient | Proficient | Proficient |
| Develops, implements, and evaluates a community public health assessment | Knowledgeable | Proficient | Proficient |
| Describes the role of government in the delivery of community health services | Knowledgeable | Proficient | Proficient |

## Domain #6: Basic Public Health Sciences Skills

| Specific Competencies | Frontline Staff | Senior-Level Staff | Supervisory and Management Staff |
|---|---|---|---|
| Identifies the individual's and organization's responsibilities within the context of the Essential Public Health Services and core functions | Knowledgeable | Proficient | Proficient |
| Defines, assesses, and understands the health status of populations, determinants of health and illness, factors contributing to health promotion and disease prevention, and factors influencing the use of health services | Knowledgeable | Proficient | Proficient |
| Understands the historical development, structure, and interaction of public health and health care systems | Aware | Knowledgeable | Proficient |
| Identifies and applies basic research methods used in public health | Aware | Proficient | Proficient |
| Applies the basic public health sciences including behavioral and social sciences, biostatistics, epidemiology, environmental public health, and prevention of chronic and infectious diseases and injuries | Knowledgeable | Proficient | Proficient |
| Identifies and retrieves current relevant scientific evidence | Knowledgeable | Proficient | Proficient |
| Identifies the limitations of research and the importance of observations and interrelationships | Knowledgeable | Proficient | Proficient |

**Attitudes**

| | | | |
|---|---|---|---|
| Develops a lifelong commitment to rigorous critical thinking | Knowledgeable to proficient | Proficient | Proficient |

## Domain #7: Financial Planning and Management Skills

| Specific Competencies | Frontline Staff | Senior-Level Staff | Supervisory and Management Staff |
|---|---|---|---|
| Develops and presents a budget | Aware | Knowledgeable | Proficient |
| Manages programs within budget constraints | Aware | Knowledgeable to proficient | Proficient |
| Applies budget processes | Aware | Knowledgeable | Proficient |
| Develops strategies for determining budget priorities | Aware | Knowledgeable | Proficient |
| Monitors program performance | Aware to knowledgeable | Proficient | Proficient |
| Prepares proposals for funding from external sources | Aware | Proficient | Proficient |
| Applies basic human relations skills to the management of organizations, motivation of personnel, and resolution of conflicts | Aware to knowledgeable | Proficient | Proficient |
| Manages information systems for collection, retrieval, and use of data for decision making | Aware | Knowledgeable to proficient | Proficient |
| Negotiates and develops contracts and other documents for the provision of population-based services | Aware | Knowledgeable | Proficient |
| Conducts cost-effectiveness, cost-benefit, and cost utility analyses | Aware | Knowledgeable | Proficient |

## Domain #8: Leadership and Systems Thinking Skills

| Specific Competencies | Frontline Staff | Senior-Level Staff | Supervisory and Management Staff |
|---|---|---|---|
| Creates a culture of ethical standards within organizations and communities | Knowledgeable to proficient | Proficient | Proficient |
| Helps create key values and shared vision and uses these principles to guide action | Aware to knowledgeable | Knowledgeable to proficient | Proficient |
| Identifies internal and external issues that may impact delivery of essential public health services (i.e., strategic planning) | Aware | Knowledgeable to proficient | Proficient |
| Facilitates collaboration with internal and external groups to ensure participation of key stakeholders | Aware | Knowledgeable to proficient | Proficient |
| Promotes team and organizational learning | Knowledgeable | Knowledgeable to proficient | Proficient |
| Contributes to development, implementation, and monitoring of organizational performance standards | Aware to knowledgeable | Knowledgeable to proficient | Proficient |
| Uses the legal and political system to effect change | Aware | Knowledgeable | Proficient |
| Applies the theory of organizational structures to professional practice | Aware | Knowledgeable | Proficient |

*Source:* Council on Linkages between Academia and Practice. Available at http://www.train.org/Competencies/corecomp.pdf. Accessed August 2005.

# Core Public Health Worker Competencies for Emergency Preparedness and Response

For the public health system to meet performance standards in emergency preparedness all public health workers must be competent to:

1. Describe the public heath role in emergency response in a range of emergencies that might arise. (e.g., "This department provides surveillance, investigation, and public information in disease outbreaks and collaborates with other agencies in biological, environmental, and weather emergencies.")
2. Describe the chain of command in emergency response.
3. Identify and locate the agency emergency response plan (or the pertinent portion of the plan).
4. Describe his or her functional role(s) in emergency response and demonstrate his or her role(s) in regular drills.
5. Demonstrate correct use of all communication equipment used for emergency communication (phone, fax, radio, etc.).
6. Describe communication role(s) in emergency response:
   - Within agency
   - Media
   - General public
   - Personal (family, neighbors)

7. Identify limits to own knowledge/skill/authority, and identify key system resources for referring matters that exceed these limits.
8. Apply creative problem solving and flexible thinking to unusual challenges within his or her functional responsibilities and evaluate effectiveness of all actions taken.
9. Recognize deviations from the norm that might indicate an emergency and describe appropriate reaction (e.g., communicate clearly within the chain of command).

## Additional Competencies for Public Health Leaders and Administrators

The following competencies will be combined with those of the Professional (see below) for leader/administrators who also have medical, nursing, or other professional duties:

1. Describe the chain of command and management system (incident command system or similar protocol) for emergency response in the jurisdiction.
2. Communicate public health information/roles/capacities/legal authority accurately to all emergency response partners, such as other public health agencies, other health agencies, and other government agencies during planning, drills and actual emergencies (e.g., includes contributing to effective community-wide response through leadership, team building, negotiation, and conflict resolution).
3. Maintain regular communication with emergency response partners (includes maintaining a current directory of partners and identifying appropriate methods for contact in emergencies).
4. Assure that the agency (or agency unit) has a written, updated plan for major categories of emergencies that respects the culture of the community.
5. Assure that the agency (or agency unit) regularly practices all parts of emergency response.
6. Evaluate every emergency response drill/emergency response to identify needed internal/external improvements.
7. Assure that knowledge/skill gaps identified through emergency response planning, drills and evaluation are filled.

The following competencies will be combined with those of the Leader/Administrator for professionals who also have management duties:

1. Demonstrate readiness to apply professional skills to a range of emergency situations during regular drills (e.g., access, use and interpretation of surveillance data; access to and use of lab resources; access to and use of science-based investigation protocols and risk assessment; selection and use of appropriate personal protective equipment).
2. Maintain regular communication with partner professionals in other agencies involved in emergency response (e.g., includes contributing to effective community-wide response through leadership, team building, negotiation, and conflict resolution).
3. Participate in continuing education to maintain up-to-date knowledge in areas relevant to emergency response (e.g., emerging infectious diseases, hazardous materials, diagnostic tests, etc.).

## Additional Competencies for Public Health Technical and Support Staff

1. Demonstrate the use of equipment (including personal protective equipment) and skills associated with his or her functional role in emergency response during regular drills.
2. Describe at least one resource for backup/support in key areas of responsibility.

# Association of Schools of Public Health (ASPH) MPH Core Competency Development Project Version 1.2

Upon graduation a student with an MPH should be able to:

## Biostatistics

1. Describe the roles biostatistics serves in the discipline of public health.
2. Distinguish among the different measurement scales and the implications for selection of statistical methods to be used based on these distinctions.
3. Apply descriptive techniques commonly used to summarize public health data.
4. Use basic concepts of probability, random variation, and commonly used statistical probability distributions.
5. Apply common statistical methods for inference.
6. Describe preferred methodological alternatives to commonly used statistical methods when assumptions are not met.
7. Apply descriptive and inferential methodologies according to the type of study design for answering a particular research question.

8. Interpret results of statistical analyses found in public health studies.
9. Develop written and oral presentations based on statistical analyses for both public health professionals and educated lay audiences.
10. Use vital statistics and other public health records in the description of population health characteristics and in public health research and evaluation.

## Environmental Health

1. Specify approaches for assessing, preventing, and controlling environmental hazards that pose risks to human health and safety.
2. Describe the direct and indirect human, ecological, and safety effects of major environmental and occupational agents.
3. Specify current environmental risk assessment methods.
4. Describe genetic, physiologic, and psychosocial factors that affect susceptibility to adverse health outcomes following exposure to environmental hazards.
5. Discuss various risk management and risk communication approaches in relation to issues of environmental justice and equity.
6. Explain the general mechanisms of toxicity in eliciting a toxic response to various environmental exposures.
7. Develop a testable model of environmental injury.
8. Describe federal and state regulatory programs, guidelines, and authorities that control environmental health issues.

## Epidemiology

1. Recognize the importance of epidemiology for informing scientific, ethical, economic, and political discussion of health issues.
2. Describe a public health problem in terms of magnitude, person, time, and place.
3. Utilize the basic terminology and definitions of epidemiology.
4. Identify key sources of data for epidemiologic purposes.
5. Calculate basic epidemiology measures.
6. Evaluate the strengths and limitations of epidemiologic reports.
7. Draw appropriate inferences from epidemiologic data.
8. Communicate epidemiologic information to lay and professional audiences.
9. Comprehend basic ethical and legal principles pertaining to the collection, maintenance, use, and dissemination of epidemiologic data.

10. Recognize the principles and limitations of public health screening programs.

## Health Policy and Management

1. Identify the main components and issues of the organization, financing, and delivery of health services and public health systems in the United States.
2. Discuss the policy process for improving the health status of populations.
3. Describe the legal and ethical bases for public health and health services.
4. Apply quality and performance improvement concepts to address organizational performance issues.
5. Demonstrate leadership skills for building partnerships.
6. Apply "systems thinking" for resolving organizational problems.
7. Apply principles of strategic planning and marketing to public health.
8. Apply the principles of program planning, development, budgeting, management, and evaluation in organizational and community initiatives.
9. Communicate health policy and management issues using appropriate channels and technologies.
10. Explain methods of ensuring community health safety and preparedness.

## Behavioral and Social Sciences

1. Describe the role of social and community factors in both the onset and solution of public health problems.
2. Identify the causes of social and behavioral factors that affect health of individuals and populations.
3. Identify basic theories, concepts, and models from a range of social and behavioral disciplines that are used in public health research and practice.
4. Apply ethical principles to public health program planning, implementation and evaluation.
5. Specify multiple targets and levels of intervention for social and behavioral science programs and/or policies.

6. Identify individual, organizational, and community concerns, assets, resources, and deficits for social and behavioral science interventions.
7. Use evidence-based approaches in the development and evaluation of social and behavioral science interventions.
8. Describe the merits of social and behavioral science interventions and policies.
9. Describe steps and procedures for the planning, implementation, and evaluation of public health programs, policies, and interventions.
10. Identify critical stakeholders for the planning, implementation, and evaluation of public health programs, policies, and interventions.

## Communication

1. Develop cogent and persuasive written materials regarding public health topics.
2. Deliver oral presentations using recognized criteria for effective information dissemination.
3. Demonstrate accurate comprehension and interpretation when listening to others.
4. Adapt language and delivery modalities to specific audiences.
5. Use media, advanced technologies, and community networks to disseminate information about public health issues.
6. Provide information on public health topics to both lay and professional audiences.
7. Facilitate collective information sharing, discussion, and problem solving.

## Diversity and Cultural Proficiency

1. Demonstrate sensitivity to varied cultural, ethnic, and socioeconomic backgrounds of individuals and groups, including: education, health literacy, race, gender, age, profession, political preferences, health conditions, religion/spirituality, place of origin, sexual orientation, and gender identity.
2. Recognize the importance of a diverse public health workforce.
3. Identify the diverse cultural values and traditions in a community.
4. Demonstrate tolerance with differences in perspectives, norms, and values of others.

5. Identify the impact of cultural values on attitudes and expectations of others.
6. Acknowledge the influence of diversity and culture in program planning and implementation.
7. Recognize the varied levels of health access among individuals and within communities.
8. Interact productively with diverse coworkers, partners, and other stakeholders.

## Leadership

1. Encourage continual quality improvement for self and work environment.
2. Recognize the importance of maintaining positive relationships with stakeholders.
3. Adopt best practices from other disciplines, fields, or organizations.
4. Solicit ideas and opinions to learn from others in forming decisions.
5. Provide examples of visions, missions, and core values for an organization.
6. Encourage commitment to teamwork.
7. Demonstrate basic negotiation and conflict management skills.

## Professionalism and Ethics

1. Appreciate the need for lifelong learning in the field of public health.
2. Apply ethical principles in both personal and professional interactions.
3. Encourage the incorporation of core values in work activities.
4. Develop professional networks in support of one's discipline or the field of public health.
5. Consider the effect of public health decisions on social justice and equity.
6. Apply evidence-based concepts in public health decision making.

## Program Planning and Assessment

1. Prepare a program budget.
2. Outline steps and procedures for planning programs, policies, and interventions.

3. Identify individual, organizational, and community concerns, needs, assets, and resources for public health interventions and programs.
4. Monitor program performance and intervention fidelity.
5. Prepare proposals for funding from internal or external sources.

## Systems Thinking

1. Identify connections among the public health disciplines and other health and health-related areas.
2. Describe how different system levels influence each other and affect health problems.
3. Outline the 10 essential public health services and their application to the major disciplines of public health.
4. Identify current issues in the legislation and regulation of the U.S. health care system.
5. Describe the legal and political processes in developing health promotion and disease prevention at the national, state, or local levels.
6. Map the organizational relationships in the delivery of health care in a community, including networks for addressing continuity of care.
7. Explain the roles of the public and private sector in meeting health needs and priorities.
8. Describe how globalization influences population health.

## Public Health Biology

1. Explain the role of biology in the ecological model of population-based health.
2. Integrate general biological and molecular concepts into public health.
3. Explain the biological and molecular basis of public health.
4. Articulate how biological, chemical, and physical agents affect human health.
5. Apply biological principles to development and implementation of disease prevention, control, or management programs.
6. Describe how behavior alters human biology.
7. Specify the role of the immune system in population health.
8. Explain how genetics and genomics affect disease processes and public health policy and practice.

9. Identify the ethical, social, and legal issues implied by public health biology.
10. Apply evidence-based biological and molecular concepts to inform public health laws, policies, and regulations.

*Source:* Association of Schools of Public Health (ASPH) MPH Core Competency Development Project Version 1.2. Available at http://www.asph.org. Accessed August 2005.

# Accredited Schools of Public Health and Public Health Programs

## *Accredited Schools of Public Health*

**University of Alabama at Birmingham School of Public Health**
1530 Third Ave., South
RPHB 140
Birmingham, AL 35294-0022
(205) 975-7742
http://www.uab.edu/PublicHealth/

**University of Arizona**
Mel and Enid Zuckerman Arizona College of Public Health
1501 N. Campbell Ave.
PO Box 245163
Tucson, AZ 85724-5163
(520) 626-7083
http://www.publichealth.arizona.edu/

**University of Arkansas for Medical Sciences College of Public Health**
4301 W. Markham, #820
Little Rock, AR 72205-7199
(501) 526-6600
http://www.uams.edu/coph

**Boston University School of Public Health**
715 Albany St.
Boston, MA 02118
(617) 638-4640
http://www.bumc.bu.edu/SPH

**University of California, Berkeley School of Public Health**
19 Earl Warren Hall
Berkeley, CA 94720
(510) 642-2082
http://http://ist-socrates.berkeley.edu/~sph/

**University of California, Los Angeles School of Public Health**
Center for the Health Sciences
Box 951772
Los Angeles, CA 90095
(310) 825-6381
http://www.ph.ucla.edu

**Columbia University Mailman School of Public Health**
722 West 168th St., 14th Floor
New York, NY 10032
(212) 305-3929
http://mailman.hs.columbia.edu

**Drexel University School of Public Health**
Mail Stop 660
245 N. 15th St.
Philadelphia, PA 19102-1192
(215) 762-3940
http://www.drexel.edu/pubhealth/default.html

**Emory University Rollins School of Public Health**
1518 Clifton Rd., NE
Atlanta, GA 30322
(404) 727-8720
http://www.sph.emory.edu

**George Washington University School of Public Health and Health Services**
2300 Eye St., N.W.,
Washington, DC 20037
(202) 994-5179
http://www.gwumc.edu/sphhs

**Harvard University School of Public Health**
677 Huntington Ave.
Boston, MA 02115
(617) 432-1025
http://www.hsph.harvard.edu

**University of Illinois at Chicago School of Public Health**
1603 West Taylor St., MC: 923
Chicago, IL 60612-4394
(312) 996-6620
http://www.uic.edu/sph/

**University of Iowa College of Public Health**
200 Hawkins Dr., E220H1 GH
Iowa City, IA 52242
(319) 384-5452
http://www.public-health.uiowa.edu

**Johns Hopkins University Bloomberg School of Public Health**
615 North Wolfe St.
Baltimore, MD 21205-2179
(410) 955-3540
http://www.jhsph.edu

**University of Kentucky College of Public Health**
121 Washington St.
Lexington, KY 40536
(859) 257-5678
http://www.mc.uky.edu/publichealth/

**Loma Linda University School of Public Health**
Loma Linda, CA 92350
(909) 558-4578
http://www.llu.edu/llu/sph/

**University of Massachusetts Amherst School of Public Health and Health Sciences**
715 North Pleasant St.
108 Arnold House
Amherst, MA 01003
(413) 545-1303
http://www.umass.edu/sphhs

University of Medicine and
Dentistry of New Jersey
Rutgers, The State University of
New Jersey
New Jersey Institute of Technology
School of Public Health
683 Hoes Lane West
PO Box 9
Piscataway, NJ 08854
(732) 235-9700
http://sph.umdnj.edu/

University of Michigan School of
Public Health
109 South Observatory St.
Ann Arbor, MI 48109-2029
(734) 763-5454
http://www.sph.umich.edu/

University of Minnesota School of
Public Health
Mayo Mail Code 197
420 Delaware St., SE
Minneapolis, MN 55455-0381
(612) 624-6669
http://www.sph.umn.edu

University at Albany, State
University of New York School of
Public Health
One University Pl.
Rensselaer, NY 12144-3456
(518) 402-0283
http://www.albany.edu/sph/

New York Medical College School
of Public Health
Valhalla, NY 10595
(914) 594-4531
http://www.nymc.edu/sph/

University of North Carolina,
Chapel Hill School of Public
Health
170 Rosenau Hall
CB #7400
Chapel Hill, NC 27599-7400
(919) 966-3215
http://www.sph.unc.edu/

University of North Texas Health
Science Center School of Public
Health
3500 Camp Bowie Blvd.
Fort Worth, TX 76107-2699
(817) 735-2323
http://www.hsc.unt.edu/education/sph/

Ohio State University School of
Public Health
College of Medicine and Public
Health
M-116 Starling Loving Hall
320 W. 10th Ave.
Columbus, OH 43210-1240
(614) 293-3913
http://www.sph.osu.edu

University of Oklahoma College of
Public Health
PO Box 26901
801 NE 13th St.
Oklahoma City, OK 73104-5072
(405) 271-2232
http://w3.ouhsc.edu/coph/

University of Pittsburgh Graduate
School of Public Health
A-624 Crabtree Hall
130 DeSoto St.
Pittsburgh, PA 15261
(412) 624-3001
http://www.publichealth.pitt.edu

**University of Puerto Rico Graduate School of Public Health**
Medical Sciences Campus
PO Box 365067
San Juan, Puerto Rico 00936
(787) 764-5975
http://www.rcm.upr.edu/

**Saint Louis University School of Public Health**
3545 Lafayette Ave., Suite 300
St. Louis, MO 63104-1314
(314) 977-8100
http://publichealth.slu.edu

**San Diego State University Graduate School of Public Health**
San Diego, CA 92182-4162
(619) 594-1255
http://publichealth.sdsu.edu/

**University of South Carolina Arnold School of Public Health**
800 Sumter St.
109 Health Sciences Building (#76)
Columbia, SC 29208
(803) 777-5032
http://www.sph.sc.edu/

**University of South Florida College of Public Health**
13201 Bruce B. Downs Blvd.
  (MDC-56)
Tampa, FL 33612-3805
(813) 974-6603
http://www.hsc.usf.edu/publichealth/

**Texas A & M University System Health Science Center**
School of Rural Public Health
1266 TAMU
College Station, TX 77843-1266
(979) 845-2387
http://tamushsc.tamu.edu/SRPH

**University of Texas School of Public Health at Houston**
PO Box 20186
Houston, TX 77225
(713) 500-9050
http://www.sph.uth.tmc.edu/

**Tulane University Health Sciences Center School of Public Health and Tropical Medicine**
1440 Canal St., Suite 2430
New Orleans, LA 70112-2715
(504) 988-5397
http://www.sph.tulane.edu

**University of Washington School of Public Health and Community Medicine**
Box 357230
Seattle, WA 98195
(206) 543-1144
http://sphcm.washington.edu

**Yale University Department of Epidemiology and Public Health**
School of Medicine
PO Box 208034
60 College St.
New Haven, CT 06520-8034
(203) 785-2867
http://info.med.yale.edu/eph/

## Graduate Programs in Community Health Education

**Armstrong Atlantic State University**
MPH Program in Community Health
  Education
Department of Health Sciences
11935 Abercorn St.
Savannah, GA 31419-1997
(912) 921-5480
http://www.armstrong.edu/
  Administration/grad_catalog/
  cat/hp/science/mph.htm

**California State University,
  Long Beach**
MPH and MS Programs in
  Community Health Education
College of Health & Human Services
1250 Bellflower Blvd.
Long Beach, CA 90840
(562) 985-4057
http://www.csulb.edu/depts/hs/htdocs/

**California State University,
  Northridge**
MPH Program in Community Health
  Education
College of Health & Human
  Development
18111 Nordhoff St.
Northridge, CA 91330
(818) 677-2997
http://www.csun.edu/~hchsc006

**East Stroudsburg University**
MPH Program in Community Health
  Education
Health Department
East Stroudsburg, PA 18301
(570) 422-3702
http://www.esu.edu/mph

**Idaho State University**
MPH Program in Community Health
  Education
Kasiska College of Health Professions
Department of Health & Nutrition
  Sciences
Campus Box 8109
Pocatello, ID 83209-8109
(208) 282-2729
http://www.isu.edu/departments/chp

**Indiana University at Bloomington**
MPH Program in Community Health
  Education
Department of Applied Health
  Science
School of Health, Physical Education
  and Recreation
1025 E. 7th Street
HPER 116
Bloomington, IN 47405-4801
(812) 855-0068
http://www.indiana.edu/~aphealth

**University of Maryland, College Park**
MPH Program in Community Health
  Education
Department of Public and
  Community Health
Valley Drive, Suite 2387
College Park, MD 20742-2611
(301) 405-2464
http://www.hhp.umd.edu/dpch/

**New Mexico State University**
MPH Program in Community Health
  Education
College of Health and Social Services
PO Box 30001, Department 3HLS
Las Cruces, NM 88003-8001
(505) 646-4300
http://www.nmsu.edu/~hlthdpt/

**New York University**
Community Public Health Program
Department of Nutrition, Food
    Studies and Public Health
Steinhardt School of Education
35 W. 4th St., Suite 1200
New York, NY 10012
(212) 998-5780
http://www.education.nyu.edu/

**University of North Carolina,**
    **Greensboro**
MPH Program in Community Health
    Education
Department of Public Health
    Education
Health and Human Performance
    Building, Suite 437
Greensboro, NC 27402-6170
(336) 334-5532
http://www.uncg.edu/phe

**University of Northern Colorado**
MPH Program in Community Health
    Education
Department of Community Health &
    Nutrition
College of Health & Human Sciences
Greeley, CO 80639
(970) 351-2755
http://www.unco.edu/HHS/chn/chn.
    htm

**San Francisco State University**
MPH Program in Community Health
    Education
Department of Health Education
1600 Holloway Ave. - HSS 326
San Francisco, CA 94132-4161
(415) 338-1413
http://www.sfsu.edu/~hed/

**San Jose State University**
MPH Program in Community Health
    Education
Department of Health Science
School of Applied Sciences and Arts
San Jose, CA 95192
(408) 924-2970
http://www.sjsu.edu/hs/

**Southern Connecticut State**
    **University**
MPH Program in Community Health
    Education
Department of Public Health
144 Farnham Ave.
New Haven, CT 06515-1355
(203) 392-6954
http://www.southernct.edu/
    departments/ publichealth

**Temple University**
MPH Program in Community Health
    Education
Department of Public Health
304 Vivacqua Hall
PO Box 2843
Philadelphia, PA 19122
(215) 204-8726
http://www.temple.edu/publichealth

**University of Wisconsin—**
    **La Crosse**
MPH Program in Community Health
    Education
Department of Health Education and
    Health Promotion
203 Mitchell Hall
La Crosse, WI 54601
(608) 785-8163
http://www.uwlax.edu/eeshr/HEHP/

## Accredited Graduate Programs in Community Health/Preventive Medicine

**Bowling Green State University**
**Medical College of Ohio**
**University of Toledo**
Northwest Ohio Consortium MPH
  Program
c/o Medical College of Ohio
Department of Public Health
3014 Arlington Ave.
Toledo, OH 43614
(419) 383-5356
http://www.nocphmph.org

**Brooklyn College—City University**
**of New York**
Department of Health and Nutrition
  Sciences
2900 Bedford Ave.
Brooklyn, NY 11210
(718) 951-5026
http://academic.brooklyn.cuny.edu/
  hns/health_sciences/graduate/mph/
  index.htm

**Brown University**
MPH Program
Department of Community Health
Box G-A4
Providence, RI 02912
(401) 863-2059
http://bms.brown.edu/pubhealth/
  mph/

**California State University, Fresno**
MPH Program
College of Health and Human
  Services
2345 E. San Ramon Ave.
Fresno, CA 93740-0030
(559) 278-4014
http://www.csufresno.edu/mph

**University of Colorado at Denver**
**and Health Sciences Center**
MSPH Program
Department of Preventive Medicine
  & Biometrics
4200 E. Ninth Ave., Mail Stop B-119,
  Room 1832C
Denver, CO 80262
(303) 315-8350
http://www.uchsc.edu/pmb/pmb

**University of Connecticut**
Graduate Program in Public Health
Department of Community Medicine
  and Health Care
School of Medicine
263 Farmington Ave.
Farmington, CT 06030-6325
(860) 679-1510
http://grad.uchc.edu/

**Dartmouth Medical School**
MPH Program
Center for Evaluative Clinical
  Sciences
Department of Educational Programs
Hinman Box 7252, MML Building
Hanover, NH 03755-3871
(603) 650-1782
http://www.dartmouth.edu/~cecs/grad
  programs/degree_programs.html

**Des Moines University—**
**Osteopathic Medical Center**
Public Health Program
3200 Grand Ave.
Des Moines, IA 50312
(515) 271-1720
http://www.dmu.edu/dhm/mph/
  index.htm

**East Tennessee State University**
MPH Program
Department of Public Health
PO Box 70674
Johnson City, TN 37614-0674
(423) 439-4332
http://www.etsu.edu/cpah/pubheal/

**Eastern Virginia Medical School**
Old Dominion University
Graduate Program of Public Health
Eastern Virginia Medical School
PO Box 1980
Norfolk, VA 23501-1980
(757) 446-6120
http://www.evms.edu/hlthprof/mph/
index. html

**Florida A & M University**
MPH Program
Institute of Public Health
Science Research Center, Room 207D
Tallahassee, Florida 32307
(850) 599-3254
http://pharmacy.famu.edu/Institute
PublicHealth.asp

**Florida International University**
Graduate Program in Public Health
Robert R. Stempel School of Public
  Health
11200 SW 8th St., VH 216
Miami, FL 33199
(305) 348-7158
http://ssph.fiu.edu

**University of Hawaii**
MPH Program
John A. Burns School of Medicine
Department of Public Health Sciences
  and Epidemiology
1960 East West Rd.
Honolulu, HI 96822
(808) 956-5739
http://www.hawaii.edu/publichealth/

**Hunter College, City University of
  New York**
MPH Program in Urban Public
  Health
School of Health Sciences
CUNY, 425 E. 25th St.
New York, NY 10010
(212) 481-5111
http://www.hunter.cuny.edu/health/
uph

**Indiana University—Indianapolis**
MPH Program
School of Medicine
Department of Public Health
1050 Wishard Blvd., 4th Floor,
  Room 4167
Indianapolis, IN 46202-2872
(317) 278-0337
http://www.pbhealth.iupui.edu

**University of Kansas School of
  Medicine**
KU-MPH Program
Departments of Preventive Medicine
  and Public Health
1010 N. Kansas
Wichita, KS 67214-3199
(316) 293-2627
http://www.kumc.edu/mph

**Louisiana State University Health
  Sciences Center**
MPH Program
Department of Public Health and
  Preventive Medicine
1600 Canal St., 8th Floor
New Orleans, LA 70112
(504) 599-1396
http://publichealth.lsuhsc.edu

**University of Miami**
MPH Program
Leonard M. Miller School of
  Medicine
Department of Epidemiology and
  Public Health
PO Box 016069 (R669)
Miami, FL 33101
(305) 243-6759
http://www.epidemiology.med.miami.
  edu/

**Morehouse School of Medicine**
MPH Program
Department of Community Health
  and Preventive Medicine
720 Westview Dr., SW
Atlanta, GA 30310-1495
(404) 752-1831
http://www.msm.edu

**Morgan State University**
Public Health Program
School of Graduate Studies
1700 East Cold Spring Lane
Jenkins Building 343
Baltimore, MD 21251
(443) 885-3238
http://php.morgan.edu

**University of Nebraska Medical
  Center**
University of Nebraska at Omaha
MPH Program
Collaborating Center for Public
  Health and Community Service
115 South 49th Ave.
Omaha, NE 68132
(402) 561-7566
http://www.unmc.edu/mph/

**University of New Mexico**
MPH Program
School of Medicine
1 University of New Mexico, MSC 09
  5060
Albuquerque, NM 87131
(505) 272-4173
http://hsc.unm.edu/som/fcm/MPH/

**University of Akron**
**Cleveland State University**
**Kent State University**
**Northeastern Ohio Universities
  College of Medicine**
**Ohio University**
**Youngstown State University**
Consortium of Eastern Ohio Master
  of Public Health
Division of Community Health
  Sciences
4209 State Route 44
PO Box 95
Rootstown, OH 44272-0095
(330) 325-6179
http://www.neoucom.edu/MPH/

**Northern Illinois University**
MPH Program
Public Health and Health Education
  Programs
School of Allied Health Professions
DeKalb, IL 60115-2854
(815) 753-1384
http://www.ahp.niu.edu/ph

**Northwestern University**
MPH Program
Feinberg School of Medicine
Department of Preventive Medicine
680 N. Lake Shore Dr., Suite 1102
Chicago, IL 60611
(312) 503-0027
http://www.publichealth.
  northwestern.edu/

**Nova Southeastern University**
MPH Program
College of Osteopathic Medicine
3200 South University Dr.
Fort Lauderdale, FL 33328
(954) 262-1613
http://www.nova.edu/ph

**Portland State University**
**Oregon Health and Science**
  **University**
**Oregon State University**
**Oregon MPH Program**
**Portland State University**
PO Box 751
Portland, OR 97201-0751
(503) 725-5106
http://www.oregonmph.org

**University of Rochester**
MPH Program
School of Medicine and Dentistry
Dept. of Community and Preventive
  Medicine
601 Elmwood Ave.
Box 644
Rochester, NY 14642
(585) 275-7882
http://www.urmc.rochester.edu/cpm/
  education/index.html

**University of Southern California**
MPH Program
Keck School of Medicine
Department of Preventive Medicine
1000 South Fremont Ave., Unit 8,
  Room 5133
Alhambra, CA 91803
(626) 457-6678
http://www.usc.edu/medicine/mph

**University of Southern Mississippi**
MPH Program
Center for Community Health
College of Health & Human Sciences
Box 5122
Hattiesburg, MS 39406-5122
(601) 266-5437
http://www.usm.edu/chs

**University of Tennessee**
MPH Program
Department of Education, Health,
  and Exercise Sciences
1914 Andy Holt Ave.
Knoxville, TN 37996-2710
(865) 974-6674
http://hes.utk.edu/grad/public_health.
  html

**University of Texas Medical Branch**
  **at Galveston**
Graduate Program in Public Health
Department of Preventive Medicine
  and Community Health
301 University Blvd.
1.116 Ewing Hall
Galveston, TX 77555-1150
(409) 772-1128
http://www.utmb.edu/pmch/mph/
  default. htm

**Tufts University School of Medicine**
Graduate Programs in Public Health
Department of Public Health and
  Family Medicine
136 Harrison Ave.
Boston, MA 02111
(617) 636-6584
http://www.tufts.edu/med/gpph/
  index.html

**Uniformed Services University of the Health Sciences**
MPH, MTM&H, MSPH Programs
Department of Preventive Medicine
and Biometrics
School of Medicine
4301 Jones Bridge Rd.
Bethesda, MD 20814-4799
(301) 295-3050
http://cim.usuhs.mil/geo/
preventivemedicine.htm

**University of Utah**
MPH and MSPH Programs
Department of Family and Preventive
Medicine
Public Health Programs
375 Chipeta Way, Suite A
Salt Lake City, UT 84108
(801) 587-3315
http://www.med.utah.edu/dfpm/mph.
htm

**Virginia Commonwealth University**
MPH Program
Department of Epidemiology and
Community Health
PO Box 980212
Richmond, VA 23298-0212
(804) 828-9785
http://www.commed.vcu.edu/

**West Chester University**
MPH Program
Department of Health
West Chester, PA 19383
(610) 436-2931
http://health-sciences.wcupa.edu/
health/mph. htm

**West Virginia University**
MPH Program
Department of Community Medicine
PO Box 9190
Morgantown, WV 26506-9190
(304) 293-2502
http://www.hsc.wvu.edu/som/cmed/

**Western Kentucky University**
MPH Program
Department of Public Health
1 Big Red Way
Bowling Green, KY 42101
(270) 745-4797
http://www.wku.edu/Dept/Academic/
chhs/publichealth/

**Wichita State University**
MPH Program
Department of Public Health Sciences
1845 N. Fairmount
Box 152
Wichita, KS 67260-0152
(316) 978-3060
http://www.wichita.edu/PHS

**Medical College of Wisconsin**
MPH Programs
Division of Public Health
8701 Watertown Plank Rd.
Milwaukee, WI 53226
(414) 456-4510
http://instruct.mcw.edu/prevmed/

# Public Health Training, Continuing Education, and Employment Resources for Public Health Workers

**Public Health Training Centers**
http://bhpr.hrsa.gov/publichealth/
phtc.htm

**Centers for Public Health Preparedness**
http://www.asph.org/acphp/index.cfm

**Trainingfinder.org**
http://www.train.org/DesktopShell.
aspx

**Public Health Employment Connection**
http://cfusion.sph.emory.edu/PHEC/
phec.cfm

**Public Health Jobs.net**
http://www.publichealthjobs.net/

**Public Health Jobs.com**
http://www.publichealthjobs.com/

**American Public Health Association Public Health Career Mart**
http://www.apha.org/career/

**Public Health Jobs Worldwide**
http://www.jobspublichealth.com/

**Explore Health Careers Web site**
(Josiah Macy Jr. Foundation and
Association of Academic Health
Centers)
http://www.explorehealthcareers.org/

# INDEX

## A

Accrediting Commission on Education for Health Services Administration (ACHESA), 67, 74

Administrative law judges/hearing officers, 170, 187

Administrative public health occupations, 31–32

Administrative support public health occupations, 32–33

Administrators. *See* Public health administrators

Agencies. *See* Public health organizations/agencies

Agency for Health Care Research and Quality (AHRQ), 45

Agency for Toxic Substances and Disease Registry (ATSDR), 45

American Academy of Environmental Engineers, 102

American Association of Health Education, 161–162

American Board of Industrial Hygiene (ABIH), 96, 102

American College of Healthcare Executives, 67, 74

American College of Preventive Medicine, 188

American Dietetic Association (ADA), 187

American Medical Association, 188

American Nurses Association (ANA)

Congress on Nursing Practice and Economics, 121

credentialing by, 120

*Standards of Public Health Nursing Practice*, 121–123

American Nursing Credentialing Center (ANCC), 120

American Public Health Association (APHA)

community health planning and policy development section, 205

epidemiology section, 143

health administration section, 75

on health education issues, 162

information provided by, 187

public health mission of, 21–22

public health nursing section, 105–106, 120, 121

Web site for, 102

Anthrax spore attacks, 216

Association for Public Health Laboratories, 188

Association of Community Health Nurse Educators (ACHNE), 121

Association of Schools of Public Health (ASPH)

behavioral science competencies identified by, 161

epidemiology and disease control competencies, 143

health administration competencies, 75, 102, 219

information on accredited schools of public health, 120

MPH Core Competency Development Project Version 1.2, 245–251

Association of Social Work Boards, 188

Association of State and Territorial Directors of Nursing (ASTDN), 121

Association of State and Territorial Health Officials (ASTHO), 46

Association of State and Territorial Public Health Nutrition Directors (ASTPHND), 172, 187

Association of University Programs in Health Administration (AUPHA), 74

**B**

Behavior and mental health workers, 178–179

Behavioral disorder counselors, 179

Biochemists, 180–181

Biophysicists, 180, 181

Biostatisticians

  essential duties of, 134–135

  function of, 125–126

  minimum qualifications for, 139–140, 144

  practice profile of, 127

  salary for, 142

Bioterrorism preparedness funding, 125, 210

Board Certified Specialist in Pediatric Nutrition (CSP), 188

Board Certified Specialist in Renal Nutrition (CSR), 188

Board of Certified Safety Professionals (BCSP), 101

Board of Safety Professionals (CSP), 96

Bureau of Labor Statistics (BLS)

  on emergency management specialists, 200–201

  on nutritionists and dieticians, 172

  on public health administrators, 58

  standard occupational categories, 27, 33, 34

**C**

Centers for Disease Control and Prevention (CDC)

  budget for, 45

  Epidemiologic Intelligence Service, 143

  function of, 43, 222

Centers for Medicare and Medicaid Services (CMS), 45

Certification. *See* Credentialing/certification

Certified Emergency Manager (CEM), 200

Certified environmental health technician (CEHT), 101

Certified food safety professional (CFSP), 101

Certified health education specialists (CHES)

  core competencies for, 163–167

  credentialing for, 161, 163

Certified industrial hygienist (CIH), 96, 102

Certified safety professional (CSP), 96, 101

Chadwick, Edwin, 3, 4

Cities, 50

Commission on Accreditation of Healthcare Management Education, 74

Commission on Dietetic Registration (CDR), 187

Communicable disease investigators. *See also* Infection control/disease investigators

  essential duties of, 129–131

  minimum qualifications for, 135–137

Community health nurses, 120

Community Health Works, 205

Community outreach professionals, 204–205

Congress on Nursing Practice and Economics (American Nurses Association), 121

Core competencies, 75, 102, 161, 162, 219. *See also specific public health occupations*

Core functions, 11

Council of State and Territorial Epidemiologists (CSTE), 127, 143

Council on Certification of Health, Environmental, and Safety Technologist (OHST), 102

Council on Linkages between Academia and Public Health Practice, 217–219, 231–239

Council on Social Work Education, 188

Counties, 50

Credentialing/certification
environmental/occupational, 6, 9, 74, 100–102
function of, 223–225
National Environmental Health Association, 100–102
nursing, 120
overview of, 23–24

# D

*Definition of Public Health Nursing* (American Public Health Association), 121

Dental health professionals, 170, 186–187

Department of Health and Human Services (DHHS), 42, 45

Department of Homeland Security
emergency preparedness and response activities, 42
health-related responsibilities of, 45

Department of Labor (U.S.), 33

Dieticians
essential duties of, 170, 172–173
function of, 169
minimum qualifications for, 174
for nutritionists, 174
statistics regarding, 172

Disease investigators. *See* Communicable disease investigators; Infection control/disease investigators

Doctor of public health (DrPH), 66

# E

Education. *See* Public health education; Training

Emergency prepardness and response, 241–243

Environmental engineering technicians
practice profile of, 79
salary for, 97–98

Environmental engineers, 97
essential duties of, 82–83
minimum qualifications for, 90–91
practice profile of, 79
salary for, 97

Environmental health, 77–78

Environmental/occupational health workers. *See also specific environmental/occupational health workers*
career prospects for, 99–100
essential duties of, 81–90
information resources for, 100–102
minimum qualifications for, 90–96
occupational classifications for, 78–81
practice profile of, 81, 82
salary for, 97–99
typical day for, 78
workplace considerations for, 96–97

Environmental Protection Agency (EPA), 45

Environmental science and protection technicians, 80. *See also* Environmental/occupational health workers

Environmental specialists, 97–98
entry-level, 84–85, 92
essential duties of, 84–88
midlevel, 85–87, 92–93
minimum requirements for, 92–95
practice profile of, 79–80
senior-level, 87–88, 94–95

Epidemiologic Intelligence Service (EIS) (Centers for Disease Control and Prevention), 143

Epidemiologists
bioterrorism funding and, 210
entry-level, 131–132, 137–139
essential duties of, 131–134
minimum qualifications for, 137–139, 144

occupational classification of, 126–127
practice profile of, 128–129
salary for, 141–142
senior-level, 132–134, 139
typical day for, 126
Epidemiology/disease control professionals.
  *See also specific occupations*
  career prospects for, 142
  essential duties of, 129–135
  information resources for, 143
  minimum qualifications for, 135–140,
    144
  occupational classification for, 125–127
  overview of, 125, 143–144
  practice profile of, 128–129
  salary for, 141–142
  workplace considerations for, 140–141

**F**

Federal Emergency Management Association
  (FEMA), 205
Federal environmental statutes, 47–48
Federal public health agencies
  public health responsibilities of, 45, 47,
    211–212
  types of, 42–45
Food and Drug Administration (FDA), 44
*The Future of Public Health* (Institute of
  Medicine), 8–10

**G**

Gebbie, Kristine, 207

**H**

Hazard Analysis Critical Control Point
  (HAACC) systems, 195, 197
Health care expenditures, 14
Health officers
  essential duties of, 64–66
  knowledge, skills, and abilities of,
    70–71

Health Resources and Services
  Administration (HRSA)
  budget for, 45
  on education and training, 22, 221–222
  function of, 43
  *Public Health Workforce Enumeration
    2000*, 34
  on workforce size, 16, 18
Health services managers
  experiences and education of, 68–69
  function of, 61–62
  minimum qualifications for, 67–68
*Healthy People 2010 Toolkit: A Field Guide to
  Health Planning*, 163

**I**

Indian Health Service (IHS), 43
Infection control/disease investigators
  essential duties of, 129–131
  function of, 126
  practice profile of, 127
Institute of Medicine (IOM), 8–10

**J**

Jenner, Edward, 3
Johns Hopkins School of Hygiene and
  Public Health, 220

**L**

Laboratories, 169–170
Legislation, 47–48
Licensed practical/vocational nurses
  (LPNs/LVNs)
  essential duties of, 112–113
  explanation of, 107
  minimum qualifications for, 116–117
  salary for, 118, 119
Local public health agencies (LPHAs)
  expenditures of, 51
  funding for, 52
  historical background of, 49

public health positions in, 20, 21
relations between state and, 49–50
services provided by, 52–54
Local public health agency directors
essential duties of, 62–64
experience and education for, 70
minimum qualifications for, 69–70

## M

Masters of Public Health (MPH), 11
core competencies for graduates with, 75,
102, 161, 162, 219
Medicaid program, 45
Medical and public health social workers
core competencies for, 177–178
essential duties of, 176–177
minimum qualifications for, 178
role of, 174, 175
salary for, 178
Medicare program, 45
Mental health workers, 178–179
Microbiologists, 180, 181
Mobilizing for Action through Planning and
Partnerships (MAPP) (National
Association of County and City
Health Officials), 225
MPH Core Competency Development
Project Version 1.2 (Association of
Schools of Public Health (ASPH),
245–251

## N

National Association of County and City
Health Officials (NACCHO), 21,
51, 225
National Association of Social Workers
(NASW), 188
National Center for Public Health
Laboratory, 188
National Commission for Certifying
Agencies (NCCA), 188

National Commission for Health Education
Credentialing, 163
National Coordinating Council on
Emergency Management, 200
National Environmental Health Association
(NEHA), 100–102
*National Heart, Lung and Blood Institute
Educational Materials Catalog,*
163
National Institutes of Health (NIH)
budget for, 45
function of, 43–44
National Organization for Competency
Assurance (NOCA), 188
National Public Health Leadership Institute,
75
National Public Health Performance
Standards Program, 225
National Vaccination Board (England), 4
Nongovernmental organizations, 54
Nursing. *See* Public health nurses
Nutritionists
essential duties of, 170, 172–173
minimum qualifications for, 173–174
salary for, 174
statistics regarding, 172
work settings for, 169

## O

Occupational health and safety specialists
essential duties of, 88–90
minimum requirements for, 95–96
practice profile of, 80
salary for, 99
Occupational health and safety technicians,
80
Occupational health professionals, 77–78
Office of Personnel Management (U.S.),
30
Office of Public Health Emergency
Preparedness and Response
(Department of Health and
Human Services), 42

Onsite wastewater system installers, 100
Organizations. *See* Public health
organizations/agencies

# P
Pharmacists, 186
PhD degree, 66
Physicians
function of, 170
public health, 185–186
Practical nurses. *See* Licensed
practical/vocational nurses
(LPNs/LVNs)
Professional public health occupations, 31
Public health
definitions of, 7–11
historical background of, 2–7
overview of, 1–2
sanitary movement and, 4, 7, 77
Public health administrators
career prospects for, 73–74
essential duties of, 60–66
information resources for, 74–76
minimum qualifications for, 66–71
occupational classification for, 57–59
practice profile of, 59–60
salary for, 72, 73
typical day for, 58
workplace considerations for, 71–73
Public health education. *See also specific
public health occupations*
accredited graduate programs in
community health/preventative
medicine, 259–263
accredited schools of, 253–256
graduate programs in community health
education, 257–259
statistics regarding, 22–23
Public health educators
career prospects for, 160–161
entry-level, 149–151, 155–156
essential duties of, 149–154

minimum qualifications for, 154–157
occupational classification for, 147–149
overview of, 147
practice profile of, 149
salary for, 159–160
senior-level, 151–152, 156–157
workplace considerations for, 159
Public health emergency response
coordinators
essential duties of, 198–199
function of, 198
minimum qualifications for, 199–200
Public Health Foundation, 46
*Public Health in America*, 48–49
Public health information
specialists/analysts, 203–204
Public health laboratory scientists
core competencies for, 182
essential duties of, 181–182
function of, 180
minimum qualifications for, 182–183
salary for, 183
types of, 180–181
Public health laboratory technologists,
183–185
Public health laboratory workers
laboratory technologists as, 183–185
overview of, 179–180
scientists as, 180–183
Public Health Leadership Society, 75
Public health nurses
career prospects for, 119–120
entry-level, 109–111, 114–115
essential duties of, 108–113
information resources for, 120–121, 123
minimum qualifications for, 113–117
occupational classification for, 107
overview of, 105–106, 123
practice profile of, 107–109
salary for, 118, 119
senior-level, 111–112, 115–116
typical day for, 106
workplace considerations for, 117–118

Public health occupations. *See also specific occupations*
administrative, 31–32
administrative support, 32–33
classifications of, 30–36
essential duties in, 38
information resources on, 41–42, 265
list of, 28–29
minimum qualifications for, 38–39
opportunities in, 40–41
overview of, 27–30, 169–170
practice profiles for, 39–40, 214–215
professional, 31
salary for, 39–40, 175
technical, 32
workplace considerations in, 39
Public health organizations/agencies
federal, 42–45
local, 49–54
nongovernmental, 54
state, 46–49
Public health pharmacists, 186
Public health policy analysts, 201–202
Public health practice
aspects of, 13–14
core competencies for emergency
preparedness and response,
241–243
profile of, 36–38
Public Health Practitioner Certification
Board, 74
Public health professionals. *See also specific public health professionals*
composition of, 19–21
development of, 223–225
distribution and composition of,
212–216
education and training of, 22–24
full-time, 14–18
future outlook for, 225–226
growth in, 208–212
information resources for, 265
mission for, 21–22

overview of, 11–13, 188–189,
207–208
practice profile for, 171
size and distribution of, 13–19
skills and competencies for, 217–223
Public health program
specialists/coordinators
core competencies for, 196
functions of, 194–196
minimum requirements for, 197
overview of, 192, 194
practice profile for, 193
salary for, 194, 197–198
Public Health Service (PHS) (Department
of Health and Human Services),
42, 45
Public health services, 11, 82
Public health social workers. *See* Medical
and public health social workers
*Public Health Workforce Enumeration 2000*
(Health Resources and Services
Administration), 34, 58, 59
on environmental/occupational workers,
79–81
on epidemiologists/disease control
professionals, 127
on nutritionists, 172
on outreach workers, 204
on public health dental professionals,
187
on public health emergency response
coordinators, 198
on public health information specialists,
204
on public health laboratory professionals,
181
on public health nursing, 107, 119
on public health pharmacists, 186
on public health physicians, 185
on public health policy analysts, 201
on public health program specialists, 192,
194
on public health veterinarians, 186

Public information specialists/coordinators
career prospects for, 160–161
essential duties of, 152–154
information resources for, 161–163
minimum qualifications for, 157–159
salary for, 160

**Q**
Quad Council of Public Health Nursing
Organizations, 121
*Quad Council PHN Competencies*, 121

**R**
Registered dietetic technician (DTR), 172,
188
Registered dietician (RD), 172, 187
Registered environmental health specialist/
registered sanitarian (REHS/RS),
100–101
Registered environmental technician (RET),
101
Registered hazardous substances professional
(RHSP), 101
Registered hazardous substances specialist
(RHSS), 101
Registered nurses (RNs), 107. *See also* Public
health nurses
qualifications for, 113–114
salary for, 118, 119
*Report of the Sanitary Commission of
Massachusetts* (Shattuck), 4
*Report on an Inquiry into the Sanitary
Conditions of the Laboring
Population of Great Britain*
(Chadwick), 4
Rockefeller Foundation, 220
Rockefeller Sanitary Commission, 49

**S**
Salary
for environmental/occupational health
workers, 97–99

for epidemiology/disease control
professionals, 141–142
for nutritionists, 174
for public health administrators, 72, 73
for public health educators, 159–160
for public health laboratory scientists,
183
for public health nurses, 118, 119
for public health occupations, 39–40,
177
Sanitary movement, 4, 7, 77
Satcher, David, 9
ScD degree, 66
Shattuck, Lemuel, 4
Snow, John, 3–4, 77, 125
Social workers
medical and public health, 174–178
mental health and substance abuse,
179
Society of Public Health Educators
(SOPHE), 163
Society of State Directors of Health and
Physical Education and
Recreation, 163
Standard occupational categories (SOCs)
(Bureau of Labor Statistics), 27,
33, 34
*Standards of Public Health Nursing Practice*
(American Nurses Association),
121–123
State health agencies
function of, 46–49
relations between local and, 49–50
Substance Abuse and Mental Health Services
Administration (SAMHSA), 44
Substance abuse counselors, 179
Supplemental Food Program for Women,
Infants, and Children (WIC), 46,
172

**T**
Taxes, 50
Technical public health occupations, 32

Training, 22–23. *See also* Public health
  education
Turnock, B. J., 9

## U

United States
  health workers in, 15
  public health mission in, 12
University of North Carolina, 75, 76

## V

Veterinarians, 170, 186
Vickers, Geoffrey, 10–11

## W

WIC programs. *See* Supplemental Food
  Program for Women, Infants, and
  Children (WIC)
Winslow, C.E.A., 10
Workforce. *See* Public health professionals
Workplace considerations
  for environmental/occupational health
    workers, 96–97
  for epidemiologists/disease control
    professionals, 140–141
  for public health administrators, 71–73
  for public health educators, 159
  for public health nurses, 117–118